prisoner
#1056

prisoner #1056

HOW I SURVIVED WAR
AND FOUND PEACE.

ROY RATNAVEL

VIKING

VIKING

an imprint of Penguin Canada, a division of Penguin Random House Canada Limited

Canada • USA • UK • Ireland • Australia • New Zealand • India • South Africa • China

First published 2023
Copyright © 2023 by Roy Ratnavel

All images courtesy of the author unless otherwise stated.

www.penguinrandomhouse.ca

LIBRARY AND ARCHIVES CANADA CATALOGUING IN PUBLICATION

Title: Prisoner #1056 : how I survived war and found peace / Roy Ratnavel.
Other titles: Prisoner number 1056 | Prisoner number one thousand fifty six
Names: Ratnavel, Roy, 1969– author.
Identifiers: Canadiana (print) 20220220158 | Canadiana (ebook) 20220220166 | ISBN 9780735245723 (hardcover) | ISBN 9780735245730 (EPUB)
Subjects: LCSH: Ratnavel, Roy, 1969– | LCSH: Refugees—Sri Lanka—Biography. | LCSH: Refugees—Canada—Biography. | LCSH: Tamil (Indic people)—Canada—Biography. | LCSH: Financial executives—Canada—Biography. | LCSH: Businessmen—Canada—Biography.
Classification: LCC DS489.86.R38 A3 2023 | DDC 954.9303/2092—dc23

Book design by Dylan Browne
Cover design by Dylan Browne
Cover images: (grunge frame) © LoudRedCreative, (stone texture) © Jackyenjoyphotography, both Getty Images

Printed in Canada

10 9 8 7 6 5 4 3 2 1

Penguin
Random House
VIKING CANADA

This book is dedicated to freedom and democracy.
My appreciation for both is boundless.

"Death is not extinguishing the light;
it is only putting out the lamp because the dawn has come."
—*Rabindranath Tagore*

CONTENTS

ACKNOWLEDGEMENTS

I wrote this book as an act of gratitude to my father, whom I observed intently as a young boy. He instilled in me a love of the English language. By observing and listening to him, I learned how humanity functions. Learning English from him helped me put this knowledge into words.

I would not have been able to write this book without the invaluable insights I received from my publisher Penguin Random House Canada, editor Nick Garrison, and my mentor Bill Holland, who provided unrelenting support. As well, I would like to acknowledge my literary agent Michael Levine at Westwood Creative Artists for his tireless efforts to promote this project widely. Special thanks to Jonathan Kay; it was out of our periodic discussions over the last decade of our friendship that some of the ideas explored in this book were developed.

I am also deeply indebted and thankful to my dear friend Bahi Kandavel for donating countless hours of his personal time and providing me with very honest feedback at every stage of this project; without him, it would not have been possible to complete this work. He made me realize how rewarding and enjoyable the process of creating a book can be.

Finally, I'm grateful to my wife, Sue, and son, Aaron, for never once complaining when I spent many hundreds of hours working on this book. They never once said, "You're wasting your time! Come and spend time with us instead." This book would not have been possible without them. Throughout this book project, I have been thankful for their love and understanding and for all the encouragement they have given me. Especially to my wife for always putting up with my craziness and for being endlessly tolerant and supportive.

|

THE PRISONER

There are some places that will surprise you. There are places that melt away your assumptions and your prejudices, places where your cynicism seems irrelevant. They lead you to believe that maybe there is hope in the world. Point Pedro was one of those places. At least that's how I remember it. The consensual chaos of daily commerce, the aromas of unforgettably delicious food. Tough, immensely proud people who put a lot of value in education and a strong family.

My Am'mā (*mom*), Aṇṇā (*elder brother*), and I lived in Point Pedro, my family's ancestral town. Sri Lanka—located in the Indian Ocean just eighteen nautical miles from the southern tip of India—is a country shaped like a teardrop, and Point Pedro is on the northern tip. Its tall white lighthouse looks over the Bay of Bengal, towering there as a guardian of the land and a friend to those navigating the unfriendly waves. Along the eastern side of the teardrop, sand dunes as tall as one hundred feet form a beach twenty miles long and three miles wide.

Point Pedro was named by the Portuguese when they colonized Sri Lanka in 1505—*Ponta das Pedras* meaning the *Rocky Cape*. The name of the town in Tamil is Paruthithuṟai, which means *Cotton Harbour*. Cotton was grown around Point Pedro in the fertile yellow soil. The harbour exported cotton to South India's textile industry for centuries. Only a few kilometres apart, South India and Northern Sri Lanka have

1

had a commercial trade relationship that was further strengthened through a shared language and culture since the dawn of the Iron Age.

At sunrise, fishing boats would return from the unpredictable Indian Ocean to the narrow beaches of the northern shore with their daily catch, adding to the commercial chaos. Women's fatigued and concerned eyes would gleam with relief at the sight of their men on the horizon, returning safely from the rough sea. They had survived another night.

Point Pedro is my hometown. I wasn't born there, however. I was born in the south of the country, in the capital city of Colombo. That was where my Appā (*dad*) worked, at The Ceylon Government Railway as an administrator, when I was born in 1969.

But storm clouds of ethnic resentment had hung over Sri Lanka from the moment the British left in 1948. As the colonial administration wound down, strife between two linguistic groups—minority Tamils, who are predominantly Hindus, and majority Sinhalese, mostly Buddhists—began to ferment. Whether intentionally or not, the British poisoned the well of their former colony on the way out the door when they transferred power to the Sinhalese majority. February 4, 1948, marked the end of one form of injustice and the beginning of another. The relations between the two groups could only be volatile from that moment on. The country was on an irreversible and ugly path. For Tamils, it marked the beginning of the end—of not only freedom but also hope of a better future.

A plaque at the northernmost tip of the island bears the Sri Lankan flag and the motto "Unity in Diversity Is the Strength of Sri Lanka." But the residents of Point Pedro did not quite see things that way. The city is in the Vaṭamarāṭchi region, which literally means *rule of the Northerners* in Tamil. It was the birthplace of the Tamil resistance movement.

Soon after the British left behind Sri Lanka's treasures—rich tea crops nestled amidst majestic mountains, picturesque and pristine beaches, precious stones such as sapphires and garnets—Sri Lanka's first prime minister enacted discriminatory laws against Tamils that, over time, turned the young promising nation into a hell on earth for Tamils. Sri Lanka passed the Sinhala Only Act, which replaced English with Sinhala as the only official language of the country. Tamils saw this as a deliberate attempt to discourage them from working in the Sri Lankan government and other public services. Instead of sunshine in independent Ceylon—as it was formerly known—darkness set on divided Sri Lanka.

This darkness would last for many decades, consume countless lives, and leave scars that would define a generation. I was part of a generation who found ourselves on the wrong side of Sri Lanka's racial order.

While living in Colombo, my Appā became very concerned for the safety of both of his sons due to the escalating racial tensions as Tamils were singled out on the streets as a despised minority. That is how our family ended up back in Point Pedro among other Tamils, where we would be safer, free from the threat of violence.

My Appā stayed in Colombo. He had to make a living. From then on, I saw him only a few times a year. My Am'mā stayed home and took care of us. She liked cooking and made mouth-watering traditional Tamil curries. Her Point Pedro fish curry was to *die* for. I remember her as an elegant, stylish young lady in those days. She liked nice clothes, jewellery, and handbags to accentuate her beautiful sarees and neatly combed hair. She was the epitome of style and exquisite taste. She enjoyed making new clothes for family and friends, like most Tamil ladies of her generation. That's what moms did back then.

I had a fun-filled, laughter-loaded life during those days, pulling pranks and just being a teenager. Of course, I also had to go to school. My brother and I studied at Hartley College, an all-boys school founded in 1838 by British Methodist missionaries. The school, one of the oldest in Sri Lanka, was named after Wesleyan priest and missionary Reverend

Marshall Hartley. The college credo is "Fiat Lux" (*Let there be light*)—and these words aren't merely inscribed on a plaque but form the enviable DNA of this long-standing and impeccable institution, which continues to produce many an intellectual. My father, uncles, and cousins all studied here; I was continuing the family legacy.

Most of us biked to school along the oceanfront with the salty wind in our hair, while some of my classmates bused in daily from a distance and a few stayed in the hostel. We played cricket at lunchtime after scarfing down what our mothers had packed us for the day. Sometimes we would sample each other's food and buy warm fish buns at the canteen on credit. There were enough of us among four classes in each grade to form a few cricket teams. Our tournament went on for months as we could only play for about forty-five minutes per day. Our dark complexion got darker from the unforgiving sun while the tips of our black hair began to tinge. We sang boisterous songs from the movies, which would take a romantic tone if the Methodist schoolgirls were in the vicinity. Then we would hurry back to the class to beat the dreaded late bell and avoid the cane of the headmaster. We sat on wooden benches, head to toe in sweat, and listened to teachers pontificate in the open-air classroom to the rhythmic humming of the Point Pedro Ocean in the background. And yes, we studied hard to avoid the wrath of our parents. Doing well at school was mandatory.

Looking back, it is difficult not to imagine that we all knew this couldn't last. Sri Lanka had set its course toward calamity, and though we hoped for one more day of peace, dread hung over even the sunny days of youth.

And then the storm clouds burst.

Thugs came during the day and in the night, by the hundreds, looking for vengeance. In the first hours of July 24, 1983, the first innocent blood was spilled. Sri Lanka would bleed for decades.

Until that moment, the hatred and violence had been delegated to the army. On July 23, the Tamil Tigers conducted a deadly ambush in the northern town of Thirunelvēli in the Jaffna District, killing thirteen Sri Lankan Army soldiers from the notorious fifteen-man army patrol known as Four Four Bravo. The patrol was being targeted to avenge the rape of three Tamil schoolgirls and the death of Charles Lucas Anthony, commonly known by the *nom de guerre* Seelan, a leading member of the Liberation Tigers of Tamil Eelam (LTTE), an insurgent group formed in 1976. Before this armed insurrection, Tamils tried on numerous occasions to gain their rights through democratic means— but to no avail.

Though there were two other riots against Tamils in 1958 and 1977, the astonishing brutality of the 1983 riots was the tipping point. This act of vengeance by LTTE lit the fuse of communal tension. The result was the Black July riots, which lasted for seven days. If the Sri Lankan ethnic conflict can be said to have had a beginning, this was it.

July 24, 1983, was like 9/11 for Sri Lanka's Tamils. Day after day, Tamils were targeted on the capital streets of Colombo as they went about their business inside buses on the way to work. Sinhalese mobs identified Tamils, stripped them naked, kicked and beat them before setting them ablaze or hacking them into pieces with machetes. Some families were burned to death inside their cars. Mobs raped Tamil women, looted and burned Tamil homes and businesses. Even while Tamils were sleeping in their own homes—it didn't matter. Tamil homes were identified with ruthless efficiency with the help of voter lists distributed by the Sri Lankan government. Doors and windows were smashed in, hinges bursting as the mob howled on one side and its victims cried out in terror on the other. Women and children were not spared by the thugs drunk on anti-Tamil bloodlust.

When the riot was over, almost three thousand Tamils lay dead. Even the peaceful Buddhist monks in their saffron-coloured robes did not stand apart from the violence. For those nightmarish days, the Buddha's teachings of liberating sentient beings from suffering were set aside, forgotten, or simply ignored. Those Tamils who took shelter behind walls were burned alive. To this day, not a single perpetrator has been brought to justice.

The president of Sri Lanka, J.R. Jayewardene, seemed to fret that perhaps he hadn't gone far enough. He told Ian Ward of London's *Daily Telegraph*, "I am not worried about the opinion of the Jaffna [Tamil] people; now we cannot think of them, not about their lives or their opinion . . . really if I starve the Tamils out, the Sinhala people will be happy."

His words made it impossible for Tamils to think of themselves as Sri Lankans any more. The war began to intensify in the north. The idyllic period of my childhood was over. When it was all over, more than one million Tamils went into exile.

On nights of heavy bombardment, my brother and I would lie on the floor of our ancestral home, making a game of determining whether the shrieking overhead was a bomb or a shell from the naval guns bombarding the city. At a very young age, children learn to recognize the different sounds of war, not just the bombs and shells, but the thud and whistle of anti aircraft fire; the back and forth of the machine guns as the army approached and the Tamil fighters responded; the crack of the incendiaries as they landed; the shockwaves from high explosive bombs, preceded by a seismic wave that we could feel as we lay on the ground. And when the firing stopped, the haunting screams of poor souls filling the silence.

When I was about fifteen, I saw a crowd gathered in the aftermath of a bombing raid to help those who had been caught in the open. I ran toward the frantic group. As I got there, I saw a lady moaning under a pile of rubble. Her right eyeball was hanging from its socket. I pulled her out to carry her away. But she was too light. She was missing most of her body below her waist. She said something, but I could not make it out. I asked, "Do you want me to inform your family?" She nodded. A moment later she died.

By then the cries around me were growing weaker as the victims died one by one. The lady I pulled out of the rubble was staring at me with her one good eye. Sometimes I can still see that eye when I close my eyes at night.

These horrors slowly became a normal occurrence for us. Planes would casually peer through the clouds and cause chaos for an hour or two and then vanish, leaving behind a trail of death, despair, and destruction. Sometimes I saw kids crying, pressing themselves against a parent's lifeless body. I couldn't find the words to express how I felt about the annihilation of so much that seemed good and decent to me. A child that age does not have the vocabulary for these horrors.

On another occasion, I was with my older cousin who was good with electronics. I had gone to speak to him very early in the morning before school to see if he would help me with a project I was working on. I wanted to create a make-believe scene of an aerial bombing raid—the roar, the sparks, the whole works. He enthusiastically agreed to help, and I decided to head home to have breakfast. Then I heard the familiar thunder of a Mirage 2000 bomber—the Sri Lankan Air Force's French-made killing machine. The sound of a Mirage ripping the air is unmistakable. And then I heard a huge blast. I felt it. I turned my bicycle around in a panic. As the planes howled above me, I saw a cloud of smoke and dust. Someone was in pain. I knew immediately it was my cousin, Navanīthaṇ. He was hit.

My good friend Suthā arrived at the scene too. I begged him to go get help—a car and a driver, as there was no ambulance. He came back after what felt like an eternity. My cousin was bleeding badly. We were loading him into the back of the car when we heard the chatter of attack helicopters. These are more dangerous than bombers as they fly low, search, and destroy any moving object. But the driver was brave and crafty. He would pull under big sacred fig trees, Arasa Maram in Tamil (meaning *king of trees*), to hide under their dense green foliage. Once the helicopter was out of sight, then he would continue.

Finally, we ended up at Mānthikai hospital—the only hospital that was close by. My cousin was still bleeding badly and was in shock. When the orderlies came with the stretchers, one of them grabbed me and put me on a stretcher. He thought I was also hit and bleeding. I had so much of my cousin's blood on me, it looked like I was bleeding.

After my cousin was admitted and stable, I set out to go home. As I walked onto my lane, I saw people gathered around the entrance of my home. People were crying. My heart started beating like a scared rabbit's. I thought something had happened to Am'mā during the air raid. As I got closer, my aunt started cheering. I was really confused. Then my Am'mā came running out of the house and hugged me as I approached the gate and then slapped me silly. It turned out that someone saw my cousin and me chatting, and no one saw us afterwards. Everyone was convinced that we were both dead. Am'mā was relieved but so upset that I took such risk and made her worry so much. It's funny how relief and anger and love are so tightly braided together in war.

My Am'mā had to feed me for few weeks after that incident because every time I attempted to eat, all I could smell was burning flesh and blood on my hand.

Tragedy did not strike every day, but every night I worried I would not see the next day. Every night, I would feel relief when I heard return fire come from the Tamil side and the intensity of enemy fire begin to fade away. Eventually, I would sleep through it all.

At school, teachers would sometime ask us to stand and observe a moment of silence for our schoolmates who had been killed. I remember the fates of two boys in our class. Rōṣhaṉ's house was blown to smith-ereens by the Sri Lankan Navy's nightly shelling. His body was never found. Skanthakumār was dragged out of his house, kicking and scream-ing, by a gang of drunken soldiers and was shot like an animal right in front of his parents. He was their only son. I am incapable of recalling all my schoolmates who were killed in this manner. But I do recall that such incidents created many more Tamil Tigers than they destroyed. Many boys dropped out of school and joined the armed resistance.

This went on for years. Then in May 1987, the Sri Lankan armed forces launched an offensive called Operation Liberation to recapture part of the territory in the Jaffna Peninsula from the Tamil Tigers. That included Point Pedro. By then, my brother had moved out of the house—and out of the country. My Appā happened to be home. I was so happy to see him as that opportunity rarely presented itself.

Whenever he visited Point Pedro on vacation, my Appā and I would be on our bicycles. I shadowed him everywhere he went, with puppy-like devotion as I idolized him. I loved biking around with him. Every street sign was faded by years of neglect and roads were pockmarked by shrapnel from exploded shells. But the heart of the town was untouched. We would pedal along the road that curved along the shore, with its shops and stalls as vibrant as they had been in peacetime. It must have been good for him to get away from Colombo. For me, these were moments to cherish.

I loved biking with him. But I never liked the fish market, with its crowds and noise and the shouts of the fishmongers luring in customers. Some of them did not cajole the customers with soft words and humble gestures. Other seafood vendors pitched their product in mounting crescendos, trying to outdo the next seller in the stall. The colourful ladies would not hesitate to cut you up with their verbal machete of Tamil cuss words.

The deal was men fished, and women sold their catch. They bantered with each other, haggled, and drove a hard bargain with their customers to negotiate the best price for their men's fish. Shoppers—some short, some tall, some heavy, some thin, some old, and some young—bargained with vendors, trying to get the best items for the best prices. Now and then, some lady would sing a Tamil hit song at the top of her lungs proudly, even when not carrying the tune well. I can still smell and hear the fish market.

But what may look and sound like chaos up close reveals itself as order when you step back. This was how buyers and sellers set their prices. Some permanent stalls were structured well with great displays of seafood, while some hawkers just spread their items on the ground. This was how it had always been done—some shoppers broiling under the midday sun; others sheltering under the tin roof; others standing on the street by the ocean and looking to the clear sky that seemed to stretch to eternity in all directions.

That was what we were doing as Operation Liberation got underway. I still clearly remember that we had gone to the fish market that day to buy emperor fish (Viḷāy mīṉ in Tamil) so that Am'mā could make her mouth-watering fish curry.

Appā loved emperor fish. It can be found in coral reefs and moderately warm waters. Point Pedro coastal region was the perfect place for them. Truly majestic in appearance and taste, a medium-sized emperor fish with its fleshy meat comes in many shades. It is still featured as a delicacy in most luxury hotels around the world due to its unique taste and meaty quality.

Appā always went to the same lady, from whom he was fond of getting his fish. As soon as she saw him, she said, "Aiyā"—*sir*—"when did you arrive?" Appā always had time for people. He was a very personable and charming man. He chatted with her for a bit, exchanged pleasantries, and then asked for his favourite emperor fish. Disappointment hit him when she said that she was out of his fish. But a ray of hope flashed across his face when she said, "Aiyā, I will find that fish from other stalls for you." She rushed off on a land-based fishing expedition. When she returned, we could see from her smile that she had been successful.

Appā was delighted and wanted to reward her tenacity. He slipped her more money than what she asked for and looked at me and quietly said, "Don't tell Am'mā." You see, Am'mā was always tight with money, and he didn't want to get in trouble for throwing it around. That night, we had an amazing dinner as a family. I saw my Am'mā very happy as she watched my Appā telling his funny stories, as he always did at the dinner table, while sipping on arrack—a distilled alcoholic drink made from the fermented sap of coconut flowers.

That was the Ratṇavēls' last supper.

Operation Liberation swept around us like a hurricane of fire. Even grass refused to grow, scorched as it was by the heat of war. We took refuge in the bunker with a few cans of mackerel. Every family had a bunker.

That day it rained bombs. Sri Lankan soldiers were advancing. The smell of smoke and sound of heavy explosions nearby reminded us at every moment that we could be the next target. After the next massive explosion, will we be joining those already scattered on the ground in pieces? The sounds of machine guns and explosives were all around us. I was terrified. "Don't worry. We will be fine," said Appā. He must've felt my fear. But the screams and shouts from nearby soldiers got progressively louder. Gunshots and explosions were sounding closer. Debris from explosions was landing closer and closer, as we hid inside the bunker. I knew we were creeping further into the depths of hell.

The only thing that soothed my soul in the dark beneath the hot ground was the Tamil music director Iḷaiyarājā's mellifluous, soulful music, which we listened to on a tiny battery-operated Sony radio. During heavy bombardment, the songs began to sound more pained, and desperate, and my seventeen-year-old heart filled with fear. The bombs were so near the house. The smells of soil, soot, and burning; the sound of people's screams began to mock me. I knew the Sri Lankan soldiers must be nearby.

We were in the bunker all day and I quivered, overwhelmed with fear. I hoped for any kind of escape from this nightmare, anything that would take me back to the life I once knew. I tried desperately to recall happy memories. It was déjà vu played backward—and I was nostalgic for a past I hadn't quite let go of yet.

When the guns went silent in Point Pedro that day and the battlefield lay quiet, my city was a graveyard of the unburied. The corpses lay among the living. The harsh bright sun still shone, and the wind still smelled of dried fish and salt—a scent the town is known for—but many Tamil mothers and fathers, brothers and sisters would never see their loved ones again.

Stories of horror spread among the surviving families. It became clear that mercy was no longer an option. We couldn't expect it, and I'm not sure we could feel it either. Since the country had exploded in civil war in 1983, the rancid cobweb of human pain and suffering was barely noticed except by the victims' families. For the victims, it seems there can be no closure, no dignity, and no respect. There is nothing but ghastly memory in haunting desolation. The cries of the dead still speak to me with words I will never hear, and that deafening silence breaks my heart in two. They are the true faces of this sad epoch in Sri Lankan history.

As I emerged from the dark bunker, hungry and tired, I heard the boots long before I saw a large group of uniformed soldiers led by their captain, bearing the Sri Lankan lion flag. The battle was lost, the enemy had won—and his name was Captain Udugama. The fighting was over. We were under occupation by our own government.

Their first step was to imprison any able-bodied young Tamil men. Udugama seized my skinny arm. I was arrested along with many of my friends for no reason other than being Tamil. My school principal, Mr. Bālasiṅgham, made a valiant effort to vouch for his pupils. He succeeded in some cases. I wasn't lucky that day. For me, the horror has just begun.

I said a very rushed goodbye to my parents and gave them a trembling hug. They looked terrified and I was even more terrified to see them like that. We unlucky ones were forced to march to the army camp. It was on the edge of town, on the edge of a field. We all knew the field was riddled with mines laid by the Tamil Tigers to protect the town. The army knew it too, and marched us across it. We knew every step we took could be our last. Later, I heard some never made it.

Innocent boys who played in the yard with sticks, and who laughed at one another's silly tales, were now the property of the birds. They were lost forever. And I lost hope for humanity.

That was the hottest and longest day I have ever endured. We baked under an unrelenting Point Pedro sun as the dry hot wind from the Indian Ocean choked our eyes and throats with dust. Sinhalese soldiers, full of the malicious glee of the victor, beat us with the butts of their rifles if we dared to look at them or stumbled and fell behind. Hatred can only make victors evil, even toward their countrymen.

Exhausted and tired, we finally arrived at our first stop: the abandoned Methodist church, directly across from my beloved Hartley College. We were held there for the night. I could see my school's assembly hall from my vantage point. Given my new predicament, I pined for the days when I was forced to listen to a long boring speech from a teacher in that assembly hall. We all had to sleep on the main area of the church floor, caked with years of pigeon waste. All night, I could hear the pigeons and the crash of ocean waves on the shore. That was when I realized that we were going to be loaded on a ship and taken to the South.

When morning broke, that awful truth was confirmed. The soldiers locked us in groups of ten in four-metre-long iron shackles. Then they loaded us on an old cargo ship as if we were a herd of cattle. As we were prodded aboard, the indiscriminate beating and taunting continued. This was followed by six days of gruesome sailing on the high seas to the South with no water or food. People had to perform their bodily functions where they lay. I was in the lower deck, which felt like an oven, with no air, no lights. We were suffocating in a tiny space saturated with filth, fumes, sweat, stench, human waste, ravaged by thirst, hunger, and lack of sleep. Only twice during the voyage did they give us a little water and some tins of plain rice. They watched us fight over every grain of rice. Eating that made us all sick and vomit violently.

We had a burning desire to stretch out and we simply weren't allowed. In these deplorable conditions, there was no question of falling asleep, since even breathing was so difficult. It was hell. As our nightmare continued, the soldiers refused to show compassion for even our most basic human needs. Up to that point, I didn't notice one single instance, not one, of the slightest human reaction, the slightest hint of difficulty or discomfort in these soldiers who were under orders to behave as they did. Nothing. Their faces didn't reveal anything human.

They continued with the regular beatings and seemed to enjoy their sadistic games on scared children. One kid, not too far from me, passed out from pure exhaustion. A soldier ordered him to get up. He didn't respond. He barked again, "Get up, you filthy Tamil." Again, no response.

Then he kicked him savagely. When the kid still didn't stir, he unshackled him. With the help of another soldier, he carried this unconscious kid to the top deck and threw him overboard.

We were all panic-stricken, too tired to even cry. We were silent in the face of a horror none of us could ever have imagined. This was my first glimpse of the barbarism that comes with the certainty that one is on the right side of history. The fierce sun beat upon the seemingly never-ending Indian Ocean, reflecting the blinding light into a patch of darkness inside the lower deck of the ship. The sea was not calm, pulsing rhythmically with the cadence of my frightened heartbeat. All I could hear was the ocean, the throbbing of the ship's engine, and my revved-up heartbeat.

But there was one good soul on that ship. I managed to form a kind of friendship with one young soldier among all these tyrants, and he showed me some modicum of compassion. He may have been about twenty-five years old. In speaking with him on this long trip, we established that we had mutual friends in Colombo. He was kind enough to sneak in some sweets when others were sleeping or pretending to sleep. I hid whatever he gave me in my pockets and rationed it out to my shackle-mates. Sometimes when there wasn't enough, I must admit that I didn't share and selfishly ate everything.

We eventually arrived at our destination—not having the slightest idea where we were in the South. When we climbed out of the bottom of the ship, it felt like we were slaughterhouse animals emerging from the shadows of death. Then the sad procession to the prison began: starved, exhausted, fear in our eyes, we dragged ourselves along like worn-out rags. We were led to a former charcoal storage warehouse that had been converted into a makeshift prison near the infamous Boossa Camp in the southern city of Galle.

On that walk, we felt like we were fighting our own shadows under the hot sun—exhausted, mute, moving along an unfamiliar road, tied to chains like two-legged animals. The inhabitants of the town of Galle passed us by on bikes or on foot, all fresh and properly dressed and groomed, with the calm engraved on their faces that can only come from a stable, unthreatened, normal life, a state of placidity we all imagined had been snuffed out by war. And yet here that calm was among these well-fed pedestrians who would stop for a moment and look at us with mild curiosity and then carry on as if there was nothing strange happening, as though ragged prisoners could rouse no empathy in them at all.

There were about 2,700 of us. They split us into fifty-two groups and assigned each of us a prisoner number. I was prisoner #1056. The primary objective of the imprisonment was to coerce as many of us as possible to confess to being members of the Tamil Tigers. The government could then claim to the world that the prisoners were in fact insurgents, not innocent young boys. The coercion to achieve this goal came in many different forms. Intimidation and threats to our families were the mild versions. Then there were various forms of torture— severe beatings with sand-filled plastic pipes, electric shocks on our private parts, and lashings by barbed wire to the upper back. At night, some men screamed at the top of their voices, some wailed, some sobbed quietly, while others argued over sleeping space. Exasperated, driven mad, people didn't cease quarrelling and telling each other to go to hell.

If you were fit and in good shape, then you were the unlucky one. They immediately assumed that you were a Tamil Tiger who had combat training. There was one man named Āṉanthaṉ, maybe in his mid-thirties—a mechanic from our town who was well-built. They beat this poor soul to a pulp. He was bleeding through his mouth for days; he couldn't even see because his eyes were closed shut from the beatings. He couldn't walk for weeks. He had to be carried on a gurney made from an empty sack; two men grabbed the corners. And some-one had to feed him. I still think about him. He was in very bad shape. I never found out if he made it out alive or not.

I played a lot of soccer and had very pronounced calf muscles. Unfortunately, one soldier took note of that. So naturally they had to beat me with the sand-filled plastic pipe on my calf muscle. Then on my heel. Each beating on the heel left me almost blind for a few minutes. The most acute pain I have ever felt. The pain shot up my leg like fire. I grimaced. It exploded in my head with a blinding whiteness behind my eyeballs. It made me dizzy, and I gasped. It was as if my legs had been replaced with jelly and electricity wired straight into my spine.

Despite the torture, I wasn't going to sign or admit to anything. I knew who in the prison were members of LTTE, but I refused to squeal on them. Regardless of the violent probing with metal rods, each time I deftly parried with feigned ignorance. As I was nursing my wounds, I realized that I was not sure how much more of the beatings I could take. So, I volunteered to become a team leader and a transla-tor since I could speak a little bit of English and Sinhala, which helped me to avoid some of the beatings.

After a while, we were brought into a cell containing a man in a mask—a former Tamil Tiger who had turned informant, we were told. We called him Thalaiyāṭṭi in Tamil, meaning the *head nodder*. As we were paraded past him, the informant would nod his head yes or no to indicate whether the prisoner was a Tamil Tiger or not. On that basis, people lived and died. Like a gladiatorial fight in ancient Rome, the destiny of a prisoner was decided by this masked man. We were all hoping to be spared to live another day. I lived, but some of my friends didn't. To this day, I worry that I didn't do enough to help them.

At age seventeen, in this prison, I faced many humiliations and torture of all kinds. Asking permission to go the washroom was to me the lowest form of existence. Then relieving myself in shame while the guards laughed was the biggest humiliation. I preferred the beatings. I had to be vigilant against sexual advances by fellow older prisoners. I had to fight a few men on some occasions who approached me with unsavoury intentions. I soon learned that I had a lethal right hook.

When you are facing death by a thousand cuts, sometimes a machete is mercy. I was hoping for one. I can't write down how I feel about all this, even after all these years—because they haven't invented the words for it. I used to think death was a kindness, compared to what I was facing. My future was grim—because I was in this man-made hell not knowing what the future held. How they treated us was barbaric. The human spirit can endure a lot. It is very resilient; it can be broken but not easily.

But almost two months into my incarceration, I was without hope.

||

THE PHONE NUMBER

Sometimes in life we find ourselves in situations we could never have envisioned being in. I was in one of those situations: in prison, with my right bicep cut and bleeding badly. I never thought in my wildest dreams that I would have been in such a predicament. I tore off a piece of my ragged prisoner's garb and made a crude filthy bandage.

I held my hand to the slash, but no matter the pressure I applied the blood still gushed between my fingers and oozed under my hand.

Such was the army's "intelligence gathering." When my tormentors found out that my brother was no longer in Sri Lanka, they assumed he was doing combat training in India, as most Tamil Tigers did. He had moved to Denmark in July 1986. But they didn't believe me. They thought a knife would convince me to tell them he was a Tamil Tiger. A confession was considered the most important proof of one's guilt. Torture was perceived as a legitimate means of obtaining such a confession. I have the scar to prove it.

They demanded we become informants. Those who refused were beaten, and some were sexually abused again and again. I saw one poor guy's head beaten and kicked so much that blood came from his ears. He couldn't hear or see properly. For days, we didn't know what had happened to us; they just beat us. No questions were asked, only beatings and torture. We were kept in the same place but were beaten at different times. I could sometimes hear others crying as they were being beaten, and they could hear me when I was beaten. The stench of blood was all around me, conjuring the car ride to the hospital with my bleeding cousin on my lap in a never-ending series of flashbacks.

In that painful moment, huddled among my broken fellow Tamils, my blood seeping between my fingers, I was the eye of my own storm. Somehow, I achieved a moment of perfect calm and mental clarity. In the years that followed, I have paid over and over with anger and outbursts. I paid dearly, but I have no regret. Those moments cleared space in my mind for the words I had heard many times from my father: "We don't choose the times we live in. The only choice we have is how we respond."

Everyone has been influenced by someone at least once in their lives. Since I was born, from virtues to defects, my father has been a great inspiration; he stood as a symbol of strength and helped shape me into my teen years.

When Captain Udugama commanded, "We have to take your son away," Appā did not cringe or falter. He straightened his back. "He is my son and innocent."

"We will determine if he is innocent or not," shouted Udugama.

"Cigarette?" Appā offered, without giving up. The captain accepted. Appā lit up a cigarette for him while taking a drag of his own. The captain softened, now speaking man to man.

"If I let your son go, my unit won't respect me," Udugama said quietly but firmly. Then he yanked me away from him.

There's nothing worse than a defeated look in a father's eyes. Appā was powerless, outdone by goons with guns. His love for his son and the love of his country violated in a single gesture.

My father did not believe in the ideas that provided the fuel for the violence of civil war. To him, ethnicity meant next to nothing. Art and culture, yes. Language, yes. The things that elevate our minds and spirits. In these ways, he was Tamil. But the idea that one could hate someone for being ethnically different was completely foreign to him.

So, I had grown up with the idea of a post-racial Sri Lanka. In fact, our very best family friends were Sinhalese. When I was quite young, my father rented part of a house from Colonel Dudley Fernando. Soon I was calling him uncle.

Every morning, I would see Uncle Fernando in his crisp uniform and shiny shoes, looking sharp and strong as he waited to be picked by his driver, Rambandā. I always had a nervous sensation when Uncle Fernando peered down his hawkish nose at me with his intense eyes and spoke to me in his gruff voice. But his smile was as warm and infectious as his manner was curt. He could light up a room.

As my brother and I were forming our friendships with all six of the Fernando boys over cricket games and mischief, Uncle Fernando was strengthening his friendship with my father, over a few scotches while discussing the country's current affairs. Uncle Fernando would often take my brother and me to Panagoda military base, twenty kilometres away from Colombo, along with the younger Fernando boys, Suresh, Sanjaya, Sanjeeva, and Aravinda. Rambandā would drive us. Milroy and Dilroy were older than us and had other friends to hang with. Sometimes Appā would join us. We would play hide and seek or cricket on the vast grounds of the military base for hours. When the lunch was ready, we would race each other to see who got to the table first, and sometimes we would trip each other in a playful manner to gain an advantage.

That was how Tamils and Sinhalese got along among the Fernandos and Ratnavēls. It never occurred to any of us that ethnic resentment had a place in that civilized world.

We turned out to be naive. We humans like to think that all our decisions are purely based on rationality and reason. In reality, a good dose of emotion is always included whether we realize it or not. What transpired after the July 1983 riots falls into this category. Violence doesn't decide who is right; violence simply decides who is left.

But some people don't let violence decide. When violence broke out in the South on the fateful day of July 24, 1983, our family was in the North listening to the news. *Eelanadu*, a Tamil language newspaper, had screaming headlines describing the horror that was taking place, and the BBC Tamil service was blaring bad news all day. We were worried about Appā. For good reason. Many Tamils never made it home. It was Uncle Fernando who made sure his Tamil friend made it back to his family; he rescued Appā from the streets of Colombo as the thugs converged. A few brave Sinhalese like him represented civility in an uncivil nation. Any truthful account of the horrors of war and ethnic cleansing must tell the stories of the heroes who lived according to their principles rather than the mob's.

When Appā offered Udugama a cigarette, he must have been thinking that no true Sri Lankan could tear a son from his father in the name of racial hate. His vision of Sri Lanka must have crumbled as I was marched away. Udugama didn't just injure me but my father as well. He stomped on what my father stood for.

This corroded my view of the world. How could this be? In the midst of my echoing pain and anxiety, I was contemplating that it was a stupid irony that I was in prison at all. The irony was, of course, that our closest family friends were Sinhalese, the Fernando family. A military family.

"The only choice we have is how we respond." My father's words.

They left no room for despair, no room for bitterness, certainly no room for surrender.

But I had no idea what to do to escape the filth and violence of prison, and the death that awaited me there. There was no way to communicate with my parents. All communication had been disconnected between North and South. It had been bad during the best of times.

What if I died here? They would never know what had happened to me. That was not a death I could accept.

It was the prison PA that fed my hope.

One day, the prison officials announced over the PA that the defence minister's wife was going to visit. She would be coming to pose for the cameras. But somehow, I realized, she could carry my message to the outside world.

When she arrived, anyone who could speak in English or Sinhala was asked to come forward. Kindness will kill you in prison. Sometimes you need to be selfish to survive, so I jumped at the chance. "This is it," I said to myself. I put my hand up along with a few others. We were asked to form a line and wait. I was third in the line, which gave me a good shot at an encounter with her. It felt like I made the podium at the Olympic medal ceremony.

When I saw Srīmaṇi Athulathmudali, she looked like a jewel in a gutter. She was a very pretty lady. (Her looks weren't lost on teenaged me, even in prison.) I marvelled that someone like her would subject herself to visit such a place of horror. But I was happy because this was my only chance: I had to get my message out. Finally, I was lucky enough to get an audience with the defence minister's wife. My objective was to get one-on-one time with her in order to pass a message on to Uncle Fernando.

I spoke to her in my broken English, and I said to her, "Thank you for agreeing to meet. I wanted to tell you that I have no connection to any groups and I'm innocent."

"That's fine, but who can substantiate your story?" she replied.

Immediately I said, "Uncle Fernando will."

She looked a bit perplexed by my rapid response and paused for few seconds with an expression of doubt. "How do I get hold of this Uncle Fernando of yours?"

Even after all these years, I had never forgotten his phone number. She wrote it down on a piece of paper and left.

I remember thinking that she may very well not bother to call him. She owed me nothing. I might have been just another dirty Tamil to her. I had hope, but I had learned how corrosive the power of ethnic factionalism can be.

When I heard a gruff voice call my name over the PA the next day, my heart all but stopped. "Subēndraṉ Ratṉavēl to the front, now." Whenever we heard someone's name in that manner, we would never see them again. They were about to die or be released. So, understandably, I felt fear like nothing I had ever experienced.

What I saw when I got to the entrance was the same man I knew from years ago—sharply dressed in his military uniform and impeccably polished shoes. For a kid who had lost all hope, he represented a flickering spark of humanity in a world that had gone dark. He was the first friendly person I had seen in months. I immediately ran up to him. He almost kneeled and gave me a big bear hug, and said, "Welcome home, puttha," *son* in Sinhala.

Srīmaṇi had called. I later found out that when Uncle Fernando got the call and Srīmaṇi asked him if he knew me, he answered, "He is my son. Where is he?"

Uncle Fernando immediately drove many hours to Galle to release me. I could have been in his embrace forever. I had missed human kindness so much. We both teared up. And then I broke down unconsolably. Uncle said "Puttha, you are safe now. Nothing bad will happen to you any more," he continued, as he rubbed my sore upper back, like a father would to a son. It hurt a lot, but I wanted him to continue. Whenever things are bad in life these days, I still think about that moment to reframe me. It was a beautiful point in my life that will be special to me until I draw my last breath.

His new driver came over and patted my head as if he was petting a dog and he seemed moved by all this. Later I learned that his name was Uppali. I was so weak, it took the strength of both men to load me into the military jeep. I was seated in the back in my ragged prisoner garb. My body was covered with rashes from infections and with bruises from all the beatings I had received. I couldn't sit for too long because of the sores caused by months of filth. The drive to Colombo from Galle was about three hours on a terribly paved road. Every bump felt like another form of torture. At one point, I had to stand up and hold on tight, as I couldn't sit any longer.

About an hour into the drive, Uncle Fernando turned around and said, "We are going to stop here for a bit and visit someone, make sure to keep your head down and whatever happens do not leave the jeep." He and Uppali exited the jeep. I followed his instruction and kept my head down for as long as I could, but I was curious. I could hear many Sinhala voices nearby. So, I peeked. I saw many men dressed in military gear. The uniforms of Tamil oppression were going in and out of the house near to where we were parked. I got scared when I saw them, thinking that I may be taken back to prison. I closed my eyes and kept my head lower. But it's still odd to me that I never felt fearful about Uncle Fernando in his uniform.

About an hour later, they both returned. Uncle Fernando didn't say a thing. Uppali started the engine, and we were on the move again in complete silence. All I could hear was the ocean and the revving of the jeep. After about twenty minutes, Uncle Fernando broke his silence and asked, "Do you know where we went?"

"No, Uncle," I replied.

"Do you remember the officer who arrested you—Captain Udugama?"

"Yes, Uncle."

"We just attended his funeral; he was killed in an ambush by the Tamil Tigers," he replied.

Here I was alive, and the guy who arrested me and put me through hell for months was dead. I was delighted.

Then it hit me. Uncle Fernando's eldest son, Milroy, was also killed in action by the LTTE. On January 6, 1986, Major Milroy

Fernando died in an ambush in the little town of Ōmanthai in the Northern Sri Lankan district of Vavuṇiyā. Later it became the last Sri Lankan Army checkpoint that divided the government-and LTTE-controlled areas. Milroy had laid down his life for his country. His loss devasted both our families. But Uncle Fernando still helped his Tamil friend's son. Maybe his silence was him quietly reflecting on his own loss. I will never know.

But I do know that he was a remarkable man. Even as a kid, I knew that beneath the strong and tough exterior beat the warm heart of a lion with infinite humanity. He was a mensch with a sense of dignity. At that very moment in the back of the jeep, I realized the world is not necessarily a bad place if there are people like him around. I obtained such an enormous blessing I had yet to experience in my life. It was the Sinhalese soldier with a heart of a lion who protected my freedom and dignity in the end.

Humans generally accommodate and acquiesce. They hope for the best but do little to work for the best. The truth is that leaders are born, not made. They are not clones. Udugama and Uncle Fernando wore the same uniform, after all. But beneath the clothes and flag and other things that tell us we are all alike, there are sometimes special person-ality traits: a passion to lead and to be human even when politics get in the way. Colonel Dudley Fernando was one of those rare men.

When we finally arrived at his home, everything started to become very familiar; we were where I grew up. Where my brother and I played street cricket on Daya Road with the Fernando boys. All the happy memories flooded back. As we pulled up to the gate, I saw Aunty Swarṇā—his wife—coming out of the home. She had always been my surrogate mom. I hadn't seen her in many years. But she was as warm as ever and gave this dirty skinny prisoner a big motherly hug and kissed me on my forehead as she wiped my tears and said, "We need to clean you first and then fatten you up." Only a mother would say such words.

It was then that I knew that prisoner #1056 was indeed home.

I woke up to the growl of a tuk-tuk picking up speed on Daya Road. I was happy that my nightmare had been interrupted. But it was not morning. I looked at the clock on the wall. It was six o'clock in the evening. I must have slept the whole day. I was catching up on the lost sleep of the last three months. The view through the window showed that the sunlit street was bustling with foot traffic as people headed home from work. I rolled to my right and felt a sharp pain on my upper back. The everyday world carried on outside my window, but my scars were a constant reminder of the darker reality of my time in prison.

It was then that I began wrestling with something that still hasn't let me go. I had been cast in a role I never wanted. I never wanted to be a victim. I certainly never asked for it. And now, seemingly, I had no choice. I was covered in bruises and festering sores. I was exhausted and malnourished. My mind was crowded with nightmares. Those facts all told me I was a victim. But I hated the role. I bristled at the idea that my captors and torturers had the strength and power to turn me into something I had never wanted to be. That filled me with more rancour than the memory of their torments. That perversion was the greatest degradation of all. Maybe other people who have been victimized feel this way. The agony in my head was worse than the pain in my back. I couldn't rest. I got up.

The world inside our heads isn't the only reality. Just across the hall, Aunty Swarṇā was preparing dinner. I could smell the food.

Man, I loved Sinhalese food. It is as delicious as Tamil food, sometimes even better. Am'mā used to make Point Pedro dosa (thōsai in Tamil) for the Fernando boys. It is a thin savory crepe made from a fermented batter predominantly consisting of lentils and rice. The boys would put them back like it was their last meal before they got the electric chair. "If only Tamils and Sinhalese could find a common bond through food, we would not have such ethnic strife," I yearned. Oh yeah, I could eat again! I needed to fatten up, like Aunty had said. I got cleaned up. In that moment at least, I felt like I was the luckiest kid alive.

My Māmi (*aunt*), Appā's youngest sister Mālar, was living at the Anderson Flats in Colombo at that time. She arrived two days later, with her husband, to take me to her place until my Appā could join us. When Mālar Māmi showed up at the door, I almost fainted with delight. She was my kin and the first family I had seen in many months. Mālar Māmi was my favourite, as she had a soft spot for me. She and my Appā had a very special bond. Appā was extremely fond of her as she was the fifth and last child of his family; Appā was fourth in the birth order. He had one older brother and two older sisters. Because they were so close in age, these two had always been inseparable. I can still recall the way she would lovingly call my Appā, "Sinna Aṇṇā"—*littlest of the older brothers*. And Appā, in turn, would reply fondly, "Thaṅgachi"—*younger sister*. In the Tamil language, birth order is demarcated clearly with gender modifications of nouns, which corresponds to an individual's natural sex.

Mālar Māmi took one look at my frail, beaten body and wrapped me in her arms. She wept like a child. Then my aunt came unhinged and unloaded on the Fernandos: "Sinhalese are awful for doing what they did to my nephew." She put the collective blame on all Sinhalese. But the Fernandos were magnanimous. They understood her animosity. She was hurting.

This made me realize that love moves through the generations as readily as trauma does. Once she released me from her embrace, she said, "Sinna Aṇṇā is going to be devastated when he sees you." I said nothing in reply. I was tired of crying. I never wanted to cry again. Being a victim didn't suit me at all. I said goodbye to the Fernandos; they looked relieved and happy to see me united with my kin again.

But the past does not let go willingly. When I went to bed, my nightmares would keep me awake as though they were a periodically set alarm clock. Many nights I would wake up screaming uncontrollably; I would have angry outbursts. I scared my aunt many times. I was unravelling. Prison played in my head on an endless loop. My poor aunt. Weeks went by and it felt like years. My aunt's kindness was no match for the stench of evil that followed me around. My sores and bruises were going away, but the pollution of prison could not be cleansed so quickly. I couldn't sleep. My mind replayed my prison experiences all night. I punched walls, screamed for no reason. I unloaded all the woes of my incarceration. This went on for weeks.

Even though my aunt was so good to me, I longed to see my parents. But I had no idea how Appā and Am'mā were doing. There was no communication between the North and South due to decaying infrastructure caused by the war. And not knowing how my parents were doing was a constant worry for me.

Meanwhile, the war was easing up in the North. A few days before I was released, on July 29, 1987, the Indo-Sri Lanka Peace Accord was signed in Colombo. It was a pact between the Indian prime minister, Rajiv Gandhi, and the Sri Lankan president, J.R. Jayewardene. This piece of paper was meant to resolve the Sri Lankan civil war through the Thirteenth Amendment to the Constitution of Sri Lanka and the Provincial Councils Act of 1987. It granted the devolution of powers to provincial councils and declared Sinhalese and Tamil as national languages while preserving English as the linking language.

The peace deal was to be monitored by Indian troops. When the Indian Peace Keeping Force (IPKF) moved into Northern towns with their tanks, Tamils cheered them and threw flowers on the route of their convoy. They were meant to be the saviours to protect us from the brutal Sri Lankan armed forces. Roads were reopened between North and South. Life resumed to *almost* normal. But the scars of war lingered throughout the country, just as they did in my head.

One day, Appā showed up unannounced. Though I was excited to see him, it felt like I was seeing him for the first time. My Appā was a slim man, six feet tall, and athletic. He had a striking and chiselled facial structure. He always sported a well-groomed moustache, and his wavy dark hair was always meticulously swept back with Brylcreem.

He had always spoken thoughtfully and carried himself with a dignity that was impossible to ignore. He walked quickly, and his long strides carried him everywhere. Always impeccably dressed, he looked like an Indian movie star. Am'mā used to tell me that he was quite the ladies' man in his day.

But that was not the Appā I saw then. He looked gaunt. I could see at a glance that worry had aged him in just a few months. As soon as he saw me, he pulled me close and engulfed me in a tight embrace. He ran both of his hands up and down my back as though he was inspecting the sharp edges of my spine, looking for damage inflicted during my time in prison.

My body heaved, reverberating into his arms and chest, but I kept silent, not yet knowing how he would react. There was little warmth in my body. As we pulled apart, my hands stubbornly lingered on his for a moment, clinging. I wanted the embrace to continue. He wiped his eyes as quickly as he could, hoping I wouldn't notice his tears. I felt guilty for not experiencing a similar surge of emotion. Strangely I was unaffected by all this. Maybe because I refused to be a victim any longer.

Appā had a place on Hampden Lane, not too far from my aunt's place. Despite the short distance, it always took longer to travel in the city of Colombo due to the juxtapositions of very narrow roads and slow-moving wicker vehicles. He asked me to pack my things. I packed what little I had in a tiny bag, leaving less behind. We said goodbye to Mālar Māmi and hopped into a taxi and headed to Appā's home.

For the majority of my life, my father had commuted, living in Colombo while we lived in Point Pedro, and it had been my Appāppā (*granddad*) who acted as an influential male figure for me. I wouldn't say that I saw him as a father necessarily—but, he stepped into the role in the absence of my Appā. I loved Appāppā. He was a disciplinarian, but kind. I learned about my own father through my Appāppā. He spoke of him very fondly, highly, and proudly.

My grandfather had shown me what a true family bond was. He taught me values. He taught me the value of hard work and instilled in me the importance of community service by making me volunteer at Hindu temples alongside him. Together, we would clean temple grounds, like a professional lawn maintenance crew. Then he would reward me with sweets. My father and grandfather had a very respect-ful but formal relationship. Appāppā was the patriarch of the family. His words carried a lot of weight during times of family conflict.

If my Appāppā walked into room, Appā would immediately stand up like a soldier would when a high-ranking officer walked into the barracks. Appāppā was a deeply religious man—a devout Hindu. He didn't drink or smoke. My Appā, of course, did the opposite. He drank and smoked and scoffed at all religions. But he would never dare to do any of it in front of his Aiyā (*sir*). That's how he addressed him. It was very typical of Tamil father-son relationships of that generation. Appāppā's death in January 1984 really moved Appā—even though he died of natural causes at the ripe young age of ninety. It was a life well lived. But it took Appā years to come to terms with it.

When the taxi arrived at his place, Appā tapped my shoulder and grabbed my almost-empty bag. "Let's go," he said. His cigarette was lit the moment he was standing on the sidewalk. He had a decent-sized place. Living by himself all those years, he had learned to cook. He made dinner for us that night by successfully replicating Am'mā's signature Point Pedro fish curry. He was drinking and smoking as he cooked. By the time dinner was ready, he was inebriated. He went to bed without eating. In the days ahead, I saw that this had become a daily pattern. I was worried for his health, as he was becoming thinner and thinner by the day.

My own troubles continued as I grappled with the effects of my incarceration and torture. Sores of my body kept score. My nightmares bled into the daytime. Then the news came that Appā's sister, my aunt Mālar, had been diagnosed with a life-threatening illness. He loved her so much. He was upset, isolated, and he became unhinged. He drank even more. It was hard to watch.

I wanted to go back to the North and stay with Am'mā, but I was afraid to go. Strangely, I was enjoying my time with Appā. Perhaps I felt that our grief was bringing us closer together. It felt as though there was no way we were going to heal unless we were to heal together.

But things would get worse. Shortly after I arrived, Appā received a telegram from the North with news that dealt him another blow. My cousin (Appā's brother's son) Navanīthan had died by suicide. The same cousin of mine who had agreed to help with my electronics project. The same cousin who had been injured severely by the bombing, the same cousin I had helped to transport to the hospital. His injuries had never healed. Infection had set in from the dust and debris the bomb had shredded him with. His doctor told him that he needed to amputate one of his legs, perhaps both. Navanīthan couldn't tolerate that loss. He left behind an infant daughter and young wife, as well as a wider family that felt a new kind of grief in a war that had already laden us with suffering.

I could feel these deaths were swallowing Appā whole. He found his solace in a bottle. Appā looked wounded, exhausted, despondent. His problems were stacking up in life and at work. He abruptly left his senior role at the private company that dealt with railway-related service. When Queen Elizabeth visited Sri Lanka in 1981 on her second visit, his company made the custom car for her railway travel to certain parts of the country. Appā was given the task of delivering it. The delivery was broadcast live across the country. All of Sri Lanka saw him, smartly dressed and striding confidently, wearing a tie that Uncle

Fernando had given him from Pakistan, which he bought while there for a military training mission. He was very proud of that. I was too.

Without the routine and purpose of his job, more room opened up for despair to rush in. Appā's face reflected it. As he drowned himself in more alcohol, he looked as though he was slowly dying inside. I've never forgotten those days, or the toll grief took on the man I admired above all others. It was so vivid to me because his normal worldview had always been optimistic. He often used to tell me, "You don't have problems; you have opportunities."

Whenever I was down and out, he would say, "There are two types of problems in this world, son—yours and everyone else's. No one will fix yours. Fixing your problems is your own responsibility." He would quote his favourite Tamil lyricist Kaṇṇathāsaṉ's song "Mayakkamā kalakkamā" (which means feeling let down or worried); the lyrics loosely translate to *Life has a thousand struggles; there is pain at every door. Whatever the sufferings are, if you stand there defeated, the problems won't run away. But if you have the heart to endure it all, there will be peace to the end.*

After singing those lines, he would proclaim, "Mortal man, immortal words." That same Appā finally looked defeated. He was often a proud and unapologetic man. This was not without reason. In this period, however, his body language and words exuded a deeply felt angst—an almost painful sincerity. An acceptance. I confess I sort of liked it. I liked seeing my stoic Appā's vulnerable side.

"There is no future for you in this country, Mahāṉ (*son*)," Appā said a few weeks later. "I want to send you away. Canada might be that land of opportunity."

"I don't want to leave my family, Appā," I protested.

He came closer, a bit agitated. I thought he was going to hit me. That would have been strange. In my entire life, I could not ever recall him laying his hands on his boys. He was always gentle. As he got closer, he said, "You are my son. You are my legacy." He stroked my hair gently with his left hand as he took a deep drag of the cigarette in his right. "I want you to get a better education and a better life than I'm able to provide to you here." By that time, I had not seen the inside of a school in almost two years.

His decision marked a defeat for a man who had always believed in his country. A proud, faithful Sri Lankan now appeared unsure. He was a refugee in his own country. That probably hurt him more than anything.

"Why can't we all leave?" I asked.

"No, I was born here, and I will die here," said the stubborn man. "I have spoken to Uncle Mahēs." My Am'mā's youngest brother was already in Canada by then. "He agrees and wants to help." Well, I knew there would be no more discussion on this subject. I knew my old man too well.

My hope of staying with my family rested with the peace accord that had ended the bloodshed. I was thinking perhaps there would be no need to leave Sri Lanka. All that changed within a few months.

When news leaked out that seventeen LTTE prisoners, including two area commanders, had died in the custody of the Sri Lankan Army, the war resumed with a new bitterness—the bitterness of betrayed hope. The LTTE blamed the Indian Peace Keeping Force for allowing it to happen. But more betrayal was on the way. The IPKF had not been expected to be involved in any significant combat role. But the renewal of hostilities convinced the Indian high command that a new approach would be required. The new plan was to disarm the LTTE militants, by force if necessary. The LTTE had a new enemy. This spark ignited the flames of a new kind of war: the IPKF turned their guns against the very people they had come to save.

From that moment on, Tamils called them the Innocent People Killing Forces (IPKF). Thīpāvaḷi (*Diwali*) day—October 21, 1987—came to be regarded as an especially dark day for Sri Lanka's Tamils. It was the day when the IPKF fired on the main hospital in the Northern town of Jaffna. The next day, they collected all the dead bodies and burned them. A total of sixty-eight innocent Tamils were killed.

Appā and I were watching this on Sri Lankan state TV, Rūpavāhini, with unease. Am'mā was in Point Pedro by herself. Appā was concerned about her. And he was concerned about me. The emergence of a new persecutor only steeled my father's resolve to send me away, out of this "cursed island of blood and tears." He showed me a letter that he had drafted to the High Commission of Canada on his trusted typewriter. It was an emotional letter, I thought, even though I didn't understand most of the words on the paper. Appā was a prolific writer. "This," he said, "will decide your future," as he headed out the door to the post office. I remember it was raining.

Months went by. Appā anxiously waited for the postman every day. Time moved like molasses for him. To pass the time, he would take me to the beach in the evenings. As we walked, the hot sand warmed our bare feet, then the foam-covered waves crashing onto the shore cooled them before sliding back into the sea.

I got the feeling that watching the waves and having a cigarette calmed Appā's nerves. The crashing sound of strong waves competed with our conversation. He would always buy me an ice cream, which I'd eat with one hand, holding my shoes in the other. Afterwards, we would go to Galle Road and have my favourite Kōthu rotti for dinner. Kōthu (*chopped*) rotti is a spicy meal of vegetables, chilies, meat, and eggs. It is cheap workers' food—filling and delicious.

I secretly wished that a reply would never come, that I would never be torn away from Appā. I had missed him growing up. I always yearned for his attention. Now, as a teenager, I had it. A positive reply from Canada would put an end to all our time together.

The end finally came in the form of a letter from the Canadian embassy. I was granted an interview. He was proud of his work and had a spring in his step—as if he had gotten a vitamin B shot. The night the letter arrived, he took me to the Oberoi Hotel for dinner to celebrate his small victory. Though we still didn't know if I would be given a chance to actually go to Canada, we had a glorious dinner. No Galle Road peasant food. It was an unforgettable father-son moment.

After dinner, he bought me ice cream, and we walked the charming promenade along Colombo's Galle Face Green. I enjoyed the ice cream, and he, a celebratory cigarette! But whenever I felt like sharing some of ice cream with my spoon, he didn't protest. He had a penchant for sweets.

The mock interviews soon began. Appā played the visa officer like a drill sergeant, marching me through vigorous English verbal exercises. My posture and answers were meticulously choreographed by Appā as if I was trying out for a part in a Broadway play. He wasn't going to leave anything to chance.

I felt enormous pressure. The night before the interview, I slept badly. But when the sun rose, what I felt was relief. I couldn't take my father's coaching any more. Still, he made sure I was dressed to his exacting standards. He had bought me a nice shirt and pants for this auspicious occasion. Appā was a good dresser. And he paid special attention to my shoes. He was always well-groomed and always had gleaming polished shoes. Even today, I catch myself shining my shoes for Appā; the sheen is a mirror to my past.

We emerged on Hampden Lane like we were going for a movie shoot. We were both dapper. Appā whistled, and an empty taxi made a U-turn and stopped in front of us. "To the Canadian High Commission," Appā barked at the driver in Sinhala and then followed with some driving instructions. The road to the embassy was chock full of traffic: cars, motorcycles, rickshaws caught together in the heat. Appā was chain-smoking, nervous to be stuck in traffic. Meanwhile, I was choking from the cloud of smoke he had created inside the taxi. Throughout the ride, he kept tapping his feet, with excitement or nervousness I couldn't tell. I was calm.

We finally pulled up to the front gate of the High Commission of Canada. He slipped the driver some money, and we got out. Two uniformed police officers were posted outside the gate. Only a few months after my time in an internment camp, I was afraid of anyone in uniform. I didn't want to make eye contact. My memory replayed footage of my march to the army camp from my house. But Appā showed them our IDs, and they let us in without any hassle.

Behind the frosted door waited a short owlish-looking Sinhalese woman with an icy stare. She could barely bring herself to be civil. Maybe she was having a bad day or, more than likely, she just didn't like Tamils, I concluded. Her attitude was colder than the air-conditioned room.

My interview was set for 3 p.m. The clock on the wall told us it was 1:30. There was no way Appā was going to be late for the opportunity of a better life for his son.

The reception area was mostly filled with Tamils. I could see that from the moustaches the men were sporting. The blur of smiling, anxious, intense faces were tilted toward the interview rooms. We found two empty chairs and parked our bums in them. The wait began.

Two tall white ladies walked in speaking to each other in French. After checking in with the owlish woman, they sat nearby. They continued to chat with each other in French. Appā said something in French to them, and they responded in a friendly manner. I hadn't known Appā could speak French. I learned that day that my father's mysteries ran deeper than I'd ever suspected. Am'mā was either one lucky woman or a very unlucky one, I thought.

Appā was a voracious reader, always hungrily operating on the margins of a potentially greater harvest of knowledge and wisdom. His bookshelf had no empty spots. He devoured books. He wrote notes in the margins of each book with his own thoughts about the paragraph he had read. He would always read two English daily newspapers: *Daily News* and *Daily Mirror*. Then the *Sunday Observer* on the weekend, after lunch. He read every section of it. He wrote letters to the editors frequently. He had ongoing written debates with other readers with opposing views. And he was obsessed with crossword puzzles.

He enjoyed Reggie Michael's columns; he respected his comments and thoughts relating to complex global issues and considered him a credible, critical commentator of contemporary political events. He often made me read sections of some random column in the English newspaper. To make sure I didn't skip over some parts, he made me read aloud in front of him.

My thoughts were interrupted by a masculine voice calling my name (pronouncing it with great difficulty, I noted at the time). I didn't have the same jitters I had when I heard "Subēndraṇ Ratṇavēl" in prison. This felt safe. I spotted a tall brown-haired man with a file folder in hand across the seated crowd. As I approached him, he smiled and shook my hand. The first Canadian I ever met. The immigration officer's name was Robert Orr. (It was only much later that I learned how remarkable it was to have met someone with the same name as the hockey player widely acknowledged as one of the greatest of all time.)

Mr. Orr asked me a variety of questions. The initial ones were procedural: name, date of birth, address. This was followed by a skills assessment to see if I understood English reasonably well. We spoke in English the entire time.

"Do you speak French?" he asked.

"No, but my dad does," I replied proudly.

"But your dad didn't apply for a visa to Canada," he came back snappily. When I recall this today, I chuckle. He was right. What does my dad speaking French have to do with me? I guess I was proud of him and wanted the world to know.

Then the questioning turned to dark matters. War. Imprisonment. Torture. The friendly disposition of Mr. Orr and the home-like atmosphere of his office made it a lot more comfortable for me to share personal information that I might otherwise have held back. His job was to rattle the cages of the demons that haunted my nightmares to see if I was lying about my incarceration. By that point, I was slowly becoming resilient and brave enough to look into these dark recesses of my brain and examine my stored ugly memories. Not too long ago, I brushed past them, as they filled me with a repugnant anxious feeling.

He asked if I could provide evidence of the treatment I had received at the hands of the army.

I took off my shirt and revealed my upper body. There was plenty of evidence.

I don't know what he thought or how he felt. I had no idea what my back would have looked like to someone who had not come from the no man's land of a civil war. What could I have seemed like to him? The strangest thing, though, is that my father and I had put such care into what I wore, but what interested this Canadian was what was hidden underneath.

I saw him taking copious notes. Then he asked me to put my shirt back on. We spoke for a few more minutes, and the interview concluded. It probably lasted forty-five minutes. My father and I headed home, anxious and not knowing if I would be granted a visa to Canada. But unlike on our way there, he looked relaxed, happy, and hardly smoked.

On our way back, Appā decided to visit one of his good friends, Quintin. To take the edge off, I bet. He had been wound tighter than a two-dollar watch all day. They had been buddies for decades and loved meeting up from time to time for drinks and deep discussions. Also, they loved playing bridge, along with other friends. Uncle Quintin was happy to see Appā and me. He cracked open a bottle of Mendis Special—a premium aged coconut arrack. Appā certainly liked opening that on special occasions. This was a very special day for Appā— and Uncle Quintin knew it well.

Appā and Uncle Quintin were up to their usual antics: laughing, exchanging silly jokes, and taking strips off dumb politicians of the time. They both had a special hate on for C. Rājathurai, the Tamil MP from Batticaloa—Uncle Quintin's hometown. This politician was famous for switching parties to land cabinet posts, and he betrayed Tamils for his personal benefit along the way. Appā thought he had the IQ of a plant. They shared a few rounds of rants as they imbibed a few rounds of Mendis. I was delighted to see Appā happy again. That's the Appā I once knew—and he had been absent for the last few months. He had been resurrected.

Then Uncle Quintin looked at me and said, "I'm sorry to hear that you were sent to prison." Appā's smile turned into a glare; he was visibly annoyed by his friend's comment. "Tell me about your experience," continued Uncle, heedless of the warning in Appā's sudden change in body language.

"I don't want to bloody know!" Appā snapped in a very loud voice. I had never seen him speak to others in this manner, least of all his friends. His outburst was followed by a painful silence.

But Appā wasn't done. "Why the hell do you want to know, Quintin?" he shouted.

Uncle Quintin realized he had stepped on an emotional land mine. He right away made a course correction and said, "I'm so sorry, just forget it. My apologies." That was that.

I had always wondered why Appā never asked me any details of my time in prison. He pretended it had never happened. I realized then that he didn't want to relive my nightmares. Maybe he didn't want to add more to the inventory of his own demons.

Almost a month went by before that dreaded letter from the High Commission of Canada arrived. It was addressed to me. Unlike the last time, Appā didn't want to open the letter. "You open it," he said, as he lit up a cigarette. I opened it nervously.

"Read it out loud," he prompted. I started to read the letter. "Congratulations," I began. But I could get no further. My concentration was distracted by Appā pounding the tabletop with both of his hands in jubilation. His wish had been granted by Canada. The only thing silencing him from his own elation at his son's shot at a better future was the deafening crack made by his own clenched fists. The sound filled the room. The letter was signed by Robert Orr.

Now some administrative tasks lay ahead. The first of which was a full medical examination to ensure that I didn't have any longer-term issues that would make me a burden on the Canadian health care system—a legitimate concern. This worried me a bit. I had just gotten out of prison. Who knows what I had contracted? Plus, I once had typhoid. I had cracked my head open three times, clowning around. I had fourteen stitches to prove it. These were my silly concerns. But I was cleared. Everything was good with my body.

The plane ticket to Canada was booked—Colombo, Amsterdam, then Toronto was the chosen route. Everything was diligently organized by Appā.

"Now we need to get you a suit," said Appā.

"Suit, why?" I was surprised.

"No son of mine is going to Canada without a suit," he replied.

I had never owned a suit and liked the idea of having one. Appā was aware of the psychological fact that the first few seconds of meeting a person influence their impression of you. He always wanted to make a good first impression. He used to repeat the Tamil saying "āaḷ pāathi āadai pāathi"—literally it means *half person, half cloth*. Off we went to his favourite haberdasher, A.G. Pauli's in Macan Markar Arcade, which faced Galle Face Green esplanade. I got measured up and Appā picked the material, a light-grey colour. I liked it too. It was sharp. A few weeks later, I had my first custom-made suit. My love for suits was born. I still have that suit. But it doesn't fit me any more.

I wanted to say goodbye to my friends and Am'mā in the North. I asked Appā if I could travel there. He said yes. A few days later, I hopped on a bus, as there had been no train service between the South and North for some time. A full day later, I was back in Point Pedro.

The Indian Army was everywhere. But things were quiet on the war front. Am'mā had not seen me in six months, and she was happy to see me. She started to do the mom thing: cook, cook, and cook some more for me. She proudly paraded me around to her relatives' homes to tell them I was off to Canada. One of her relatives, known to be somewhat of a curmudgeon—with terrible manners and a horrible outlook on life— said, "Indra," which was Am'mā's name, "this guy is a failure here. What the hell is he going to do in Canada?" This absolutely crushed my confidence in one swipe. What a horrible person, I remember thinking.

Before I said my final goodbyes to my friends and neighbours, I asked Am'mā if she could make lunch for all my friends. A party, perhaps. She agreed and made her famous Sri Lankan noodles and spicy chicken curry. Whenever I think of that lunch combo, my mouth runs like a busted pipe, even to this day. My friends enjoyed it too. We all hugged it out. And we promised each other that we would meet again. Am'mā and I left for Colombo the very next day. I would never see my friends again.

On the day of my flight, around eleven in the morning, I went to say goodbye to Uncle Fernando and Aunty Swarṇā. They were happy to hear that I was off to Canada and asked me to have lunch with them. I never turned down Aunty's meals. She was an amazing cook. And she did not disappoint me that day. Appā had already gone to my Aunt Mālar's place with Am'mā. After lunch, I headed to Anderson Flats to meet everyone. Appā's older brother and wife were there visiting. I saw my luggage; it had been packed with my name and address already written on a tag—Ratnavel, 6 La Peer Blvd, Scarborough—in Appā's neat handwriting. Well, it was time for me to say a final goodbye to everyone. I gave Mālar Māmi a hug, and we were off. We headed to Colombo's Katunayake International Airport.

In the taxi, it was eerily quiet. Appā, Am'mā, and I sat muted as the taxi fought through the Colombo traffic. It was an uneasy silence; I remember breathing the air blowing into the taxi through the open window. My parents didn't know what the future held for me. Even though my arrest had been out of his control, at some level, I thought Appā felt that he had come up short in providing for his son. It was very clear to me that I was more important to him than anything else in this world. But here he was put in this position. The silence inside the taxi was broken only by the honking of all variety of horns and the nervous beating of human hearts. The loudest sound I ever heard in my life.

We finally arrived at the airport. There was security check after security check. The number of airport guards seemed like an attempt to achieve full employment and to showcase the military prowess of this morally bankrupt nation. One dumb-looking soldier with sweat patches on his uniform rifled through my luggage and inspected my passport with menacing calm. I stood absolutely still, in an attempt to make myself invisible. I did understand the tight security: war was still on.

Finally, I arrived at the check-in counter of KLM. Everything went smoothly. No issues. Excitement and sadness flooded in all at once, a mixture of emotions that made me feel happy and anxious. I was excited about my first actual overseas trip. But concerns about leaving my parents and the accompanying sorrow wiped out any excitement I might have had in a different scenario. But this had to be done. Appā's orders!

My Appā was pushing the luggage trolley. I stood there watching him, as he placed my luggage on a scale. The luggage was underweight, same as me. I saw a random airport worker put my luggage on a cart along with others and watched it disappear in the direction of the plane. It was time to say goodbye to my parents. April 18, 1988, is a date that will forever be etched in my memory. It was the first time I had ever seen my father openly cry. I didn't know that he even had the ability to summon tears in public. Like most Tamil men of his generation, my father strived to live the stoic ideal. He was the breadwinner of our tiny family, the rock against which the family could lean. But not that day. Once we were inside the airport, Appā came apart at the seams. I will never forget that moment. He was no doubt experiencing a complex mix of emotions too. He was happy to see me leave for safety and a better future, but sad to see me leave him. Maybe it would only be temporary, for a couple of years. Or maybe it would be forever. But Am'mā held it together. She was tougher than Appā that day.

The final parting words from the faithful Sri Lankan, as he gave his last hug: "In Canada, you will have opportunities that I never had."

"Yes, Appā," I replied quietly.

"Don't squander them away. Study hard. Work hard." He didn't stop. "Do what the locals do to assimilate." Then, as he presented me with a beautiful blue striped tie, a heartfelt request made in a trembling voice: "Throughout last year, I've asked you to do many things. Therefore, it should surprise you little that I have another thing to ask of you. I ask that you live."

Then came a stern warning: "And, whatever you do, do not ever embarrass the family by living on handouts. Fend for yourself and be proud." And how could I forget the tears running down his cheeks as we hugged one more time.

The heels of my shoes were clomping against the floor as I walked toward the bus to take me to the plane. And the overpowering noise of airport announcements filled me with fear and even annoyance. I waved to my parents as the crowded bus headed toward the tarmac. Appā peered through the glass and waved his final goodbye to me. I couldn't bear to look at his saddened face. The bus eventually came to a stop by the plane. I climbed up the stairs and entered the hull of the aircraft. For the first time, my feet were no longer on the land I was born in, eighteen years ago. The flight attendant, in a signature KLM light-blue uniform and neat cap, directed me toward the back of the plane after inspecting my boarding pass. I went around people as they were loading their luggage into the overhead compartments. The flight was on time—and I had a window seat.

The plane started taxiing, took an about-turn, started increasing speed exponentially. The roaring jet engines thrusted the plane forward. Wheels up. My mind was racing with untold sadness and apprehension. I clenched my seat belt in my hands. I looked out the window at the land of Sri Lanka, the motherland I was leaving behind. I could see the tight winding roads, the vehicles on them, and homes along the way—and an island in a sea of pain. I saw the curvature of the Earth. Fear clouded my mind as the plane pierced through the clouds, and my heart pounded like a drum. I had no idea what was waiting for me on the other side.

While I do not remember everything I felt at that time, I do remember thinking that I needed to start a whole new life, make new friends, and adapt to a new language and culture. I was thankful to my Appā for preparing and guiding me for what I was about to face, alone. My heart was filled with love, positivity, and his great words of wisdom. I loved and respected him so much. I swore that I would live by his wise words as Sri Lanka faded away beneath me.

"Welcome aboard Royal Dutch Airlines to Amsterdam. We are delighted to have you with us on this flight," said a soothing feminine voice over the PA system as we reached our cruising altitude.

I settled back and closed my eyes, as I closed an important chapter of my life.

III

THE FAITHFUL SRI LANKAN

My Appāppā had taught me the importance of fate. He was a devout Hindu, and Hindus believed in karma. Karma, the baseline of our existence, metes out our suffering and our share of opportunity. It lays out our destinies. From the time I was little, fate has been the driving force in my life.

Appā thought the idea of fate was completely misleading. He used to repeat the Tamil proverb "Vidhiyaiyum mathiyāl veḷḷāḷam"—*Even fate can be overcome by the mind.* His actions taught me that he believed with all his heart that we can alter the path destiny has put before our feet. But Appā also taught me that Shakespeare showed how the power of fate can sweep aside all our plans. *Romeo and Juliet* is not a story of love; it's a story of fate.

So I wonder, was my fate my own to create, or was it predetermined? Does fate play an important role in life? If yes, then would it suggest that life events are unavoidable and unchangeable? I'm not sure. But maybe those are not the right questions. Does anyone really believe they have no choice at all? Could anyone actually live that way? It seems to me that *fate* has a subtler meaning. What we *believe* is our fate. Our minds and our hearts are our fate.

The inflight announcement woke me up. I had no idea how long I'd slept. I could smell food. Flavours that I didn't recognize. Definitely not Am'mā's aromatic curry. How I missed her curry! What did

Western people eat for their breakfast, lunch, and dinner? I was sure curry wasn't their staple. So, how would I get curry in Canada? I had seen Western movies and always saw people eating bland-looking sandwiches. Would I be eating that in Canada? Even on the threshold of a new life, a teenager will think about food.

I opened my window shade. It was night somewhere below us. Appā had handed me one hundred U.S. dollars at the airport. I checked it. It was nicely tucked inside my passport holder.

"Excuse me, Miss, how long to Amsterdam?" I asked the nearest flight attendant. She smiled and said, "About ten hours." I had slept for three hours. Man, how would I kill that much time? I thought. Well, I had had worse. Bunker. Cargo ship. Prison. I could sit on an airplane for a few hours.

I saw the drink cart down the aisle, a few rows ahead of me. I thought I should probably try a cold beer as I'd seen a commercial on the giant inflight screen for Heineken. The frothy beer looked inviting. I had had a few drags of cigarettes here and there, but I'd never had a beer. Had a bit of local toddy on a few occasions.

Toddy was a common drink where I grew up; it's made from the fermented sap of a palm tree's flowers. In my case, it was a Pālmerā tree—a cousin of the palm tree—that is mostly found in Northern Sri Lanka. I had never been intoxicated from toddy. You had to drink a lot of it to catch a buzz. Maybe I have good drinking DNA. I thought I should try this beer. I was flying Dutch Airlines, so why not a Dutch beer, right? Plus Appā told me to "assimilate" and embrace my new society. Don't white folks drink and love their beer? I was executing my old man's orders, like the good son that I was.

Those were the good old days when free booze flowed in economy class. I wasn't about to dip into my one hundred dollars. No way! The cart pulled up at my row. "Heineken, please." The flight attendant had no clue what I had just said. She looked bloody confused. I knew I had screwed up the pronunciation. Appā could have been a great help here.

He was Mr. Pronunciation. Always busting my hump every time I slipped up. I once witnessed him trying to help a guy say "tongue cleaner" to no avail. The guy kept saying "rung cleaner." Appā got visibly annoyed.

I didn't want to embarrass myself again. I just pointed at the green can. I heard that pop sound, and seconds later, I had a cold one in my hand. I was eighteen. She never asked my age or for my ID. I guess there was no age limit in the sky for adult beverages. I took one sip—and I didn't enjoy the taste. But I grew up in a world where you don't waste anything. I worked hard on that one can. I got the beer down my throat with a sense of accomplishment. It was a great sleep aid. When I woke up from the Heineken buzz, we had started our descent into Amsterdam's Schiphol Airport. About a half hour later, touchdown. Just like that, I was in a foreign land.

The airport was buzzing with people from all corners of the world, all in a hurry. There were skin shades and hair colours I had never seen before. Languages I'd never heard before. I was intimidated and avoided making eye contact with anyone. I was out of my comfort zone. With great difficulty, I found the gate for my connecting flight. My layover was about seven hours, so I started walking around. I did some window shopping. A pair of Adidas sneakers caught my attention. A few minutes later, I had only fifty U.S. dollars in my passport holder. I think Appā would've approved my purchase as he believed that life is not only a series of experiences but also a series of moments and we must live moment to moment in order to be happy. I just lived in that moment. I was hungry, but I didn't want to spend any more money. I was excited about my new footwear, but I was less excited about the wait. I checked the giant clock: I still had four hours to kill. How did time pass so fast in prison? I was never bored but almost always in pain. I would happily take boredom.

I found a place to sit not too far from my gate. The magnificent rays of the early morning Amsterdam sunlight were beaming through a clear glass window. As the sun warmed my face, I closed my eyes and listened closely to the world around me. The heat from the sun was cooled by the light breeze of every passing body. The incomprehensible announcements, partly in Dutch, were drowned out by the sounds of planes taking off to unknown locations, the loud screaming of unruly children, and the faint harmony of people conversing. Why do humans wage war? Why can't we be at peace? The war was what got me here. Otherwise, I would have still been in Point Pedro, instead of in this strange place. Destiny lies as much in how you respond to ordeals as it does in the ordeals themselves. I opened my eyes to the announcement that my Air Canada flight to Toronto would be boarding shortly.

I headed to the gate. A long and annoying wait later, I was on another plane to another foreign land—my final destination. What kind of Canadian would I be? My thoughts were in an endless loop of, what can I do? What should I do when I got there? How could I survive without Appā's guidance? What if Am'mā's curmudgeonly relative was right? Life was a bloody mystery. But I knew my anxiety about what problems I might encounter in Canada wouldn't be fixed by obsessing. Nevertheless, my feelings of insecurity and uncertainty were overwhelming. On and on. Never-ending noise. Plenty of questions were bouncing around my head, with no answers.

For another eight hours, I was cramped into a window seat of a Boeing 747. I had always thought it was a beautiful plane; it was nice to finally fly in one. On this flight, I heard more passengers speaking English. The accent was a lot different than the way Sri Lankans spoke English. Much smoother. More refined. Would I be able speak with this North American accent? My natural enthusiasm to expose myself to adventure was being tested on this too-long trip. My thoughts jumped around: When would I see my parents again? I already miss them. Would I ever see them again? One moment, I felt like the hero of an international adventure. The next, I was a scared skinny kid far from home. I was exhausted and sad. I fell asleep again.

"Good afternoon, ladies and gentlemen, this is your captain speaking. We have started our initial descent into Toronto." Yes! Finally. I was delighted. Out my window, I saw the iconic CN Tower I had heard so much about. There it was, piercing through the low-lying clouds. A symbol of prosperity and humanity's ingenuity. In a matter of minutes, we touched down with the sound of the squealing tires.

The day I landed at Toronto's Pearson International Airport was April 19, 1988. I was eighteen years old.

Inside the terminal, the first thing I noticed were the uniformed officers staffing the airport's security and customs desks. Arriving from Sri Lanka, a country where members of my Tamil community are routinely abused by the country's police and army, I had learned to associate such uniforms with terror. When I saw two burly Canadian police officers walking toward me, I tensed reflexively. But as we passed by in the corridor, they merely looked at me, smiled, and said, "Good afternoon." It was at that moment that I decided to become a Canadian.

I presented my papers at the customs desk. The officer spent a few minutes examining my passport and immigration papers for authenticity. Everything checked out fine. "Do you have anything to declare?" he asked. "I have nothing" was my response. It was no exaggeration.

I arrived in Toronto during the time when Tamil gangs were smuggling drugs through Pearson International Airport. A few months before I landed, a few Tamil guys had been busted. So, naturally, I was profiled. The officer sent me to a line where a few people were already waiting to get their bags inspected. I had no worries. I had nothing to hide. My turn to open the bags, and the drug-sniffing dogs were hard at work. One of them took a whiff of my bag and sat down. One of the gloved officers rifled through my suitcase and pulled out a bag full of Jaffna Tobacco.

Was I in trouble? I was worried. Then it hit me. Someone Appā knew had given him this tobacco to pass on to his father who was living in Toronto. This variety of tobacco was grown in the Jaffna Peninsula and had been exported to the U.S. in the 1930s. It grew to over six feet in height with large leaves averaging eighteen inches wide and up to thirty inches long. The plants average twenty leaves per plant and have the highest nicotine content of any tobacco. Older men in Sri Lanka preferred to handroll this cured tobacco leaf into a cigar and smoke them instead of cigarettes.

The officer said, "This is not allowed here. You should have declared this." He may have been right. But in my defence, I didn't know it wasn't allowed and it hadn't been my intention to sneak it into the country. After speaking to his manager, he came back and said, "You are free to go, but we need to confiscate the item." I said, "No problem." I couldn't care less if some old Tamil man wouldn't have his stupid tobacco. But I was rattled. I didn't want to be sent back due to this innocent infraction. I worried for months about this. Thankfully, nothing came of it.

My Uncle Mahēs was waiting for me. I hurriedly repacked my bag and headed toward the exit door. As the sliding doors parted, I scanned the crowd to spot uncle. There he was with a big smile. I hadn't seen him in probably over half a dozen years. He was my maternal uncle and the youngest of my three uncles. I called him Kutty Mam'mā (*small uncle*). He was a very generous uncle. He was the first to buy me a brand-new bicycle, as a reward for passing the GCE O/L exam. It was a big thing in Sri Lanka, almost akin to someone buying a car for someone in Canada.

He was a very ardent family guy. A gem of a man. Here again, he stepped up to help his sister's son by sponsoring and taking full custody of me. But he, too, was a newcomer to Canada, and I knew I couldn't be dependent on him. Appā's parting words were ringing in my head: "Do not ever embarrass the family by living on handouts."

The temperature was very cold for this kid from the tropics. Maybe not for someone who grew up here. It was about zero degree Celsius— something I had never experienced in my entire life. I was used to weather in the mid-thirties. Once in my uncle's vehicle, I lowered the passenger-seat window as he drove out of the parking lot, and suddenly the cold air stung my cheeks. I noticed people were carrying on outside like it was nothing. By Canadian standards, it may have been a nice day. "It gets a lot colder than this," said Uncle from the driver's seat as he fought through the traffic, heading east toward Scarborough. Colder than this? Seriously? In addition to all my challenges, I will have to contend with this weather too? This was not a place for everyone. Definitely not a place for someone like me.

But I was in awe of the highway system. Such an extensive road network could solve Sri Lanka's traffic congestion and deafening noise pollution. It seemed like a maze with multiple lanes of traffic and unfamiliar kinds of cars orderly directed by the signs along Highway 401. Hardly anyone honked despite all the traffic complexity and high speeds at which the cars travelled. All this had existed all along while I had no idea. About thirty minutes later, we arrived at my uncle's place, 6 La Peer Boulevard, just like on my luggage tag. It would have taken a lot longer to travel such a distance in Colombo.

There was a birthday party for someone at my uncle's. I can't recall who the party was for. I took a shower and then crushed my second beer like a champion. It was way easier to drink my second can. I spoke to a few folks and felt back in familiar territory. It was a relief to see Tamils and speak in Tamil again. But I was tired. I had dinner and then hit the rack. Lights out!

I was out for about two days from jet lag. Falling asleep at the wrong times, I was a mess. Every time I went to bed in my uncle's basement, I would say a prayer for Am'mā and Appā's safety.

I remember being awakened by a knock on the door. When I opened it, I saw Uncle Mahēs was standing in the hall. He didn't look right. "Please come upstairs," he said. He turned and left. I threw on some clothes and ran upstairs. It was maybe ten at night. My uncle and cousins were gathered in the living room. They all looked sombre.

Uncle cleared his throat as though he was going to give a long speech. But when he finally spoke, his message was brutally short.

"Your Appā is dead."

As his voice trailed off into silence, I didn't ask for clarification. My lips were locked together. I didn't ask how. Or when. I didn't react other than to sink into the leather sofa beside me. The news pushed me into the cushion like a crushing weight. My heart was consumed with unexplainable, overwhelming grief. I was utterly alone.

I didn't cry. I had told myself I wouldn't cry any more.

It felt like someone had hit me with a two-by-four right in the face. I was absolutely gutted. But I didn't cry. Everyone in the room had become background noise to me. My cousins had faded away.

After a few minutes, I said, "I'm going to bed," and left. It was a rough night in the basement. When I closed my eyes, I could see Appā, as immobile as those who had preceded him.

At the tender age of eighteen, I had lost the man whom I admired most. He was abruptly taken away from me. I lay still in that dark cold basement room, full of grief. My heart was shattered into a thousand pieces. I felt like half my soul had left my body. Then I overcame it with denial. "No, not my Appā, he wasn't killed; it must be a mistaken identity." I kept saying to myself that it was a mistake. I closed my eyes and slowly reopened them; I wanted someone to tell me that this was all a bad dream.

Memories flashed through my mind like a skipping record.

Who was this man I realized more than ever that I loved so much?

Appā was a man of principle and did not shy away from speaking his mind, especially if he thought something was wrong. His barometer for bullshit was extremely sensitive. Many people learned not to take him on when it came to debating—because you simply could not win. He also could never say no to those who reached out for assistance and frequently drew from his own wallet to help others.

He railed against the caste system. When labourers came to do chores around the house, it was customary to offer a meal to them in addition to paying them. They always sat outside on the floor and ate. They were not allowed inside the house, especially not at the dining table. Appā despised this. He always made sure they sat just like we did at the table—like human beings with dignity. He was a different man for his time. He always had a well-defined sense of what was right and wrong. Nonjudgmental while being judgmental.

I know that his open-heartedness touched others. I had seen it. One of Am'mā's aunts, a widow, had no kids of her own. She battled severe mental illness. People were either dismissive of her or very cruel to her. Appā was always very kind to her.

Appā would come to Point Pedro for Thāy Poṅkal, a two-thousand-year-old festival to thank the sun god, which is observed in the month of January (Thāy). The festival is also considered to be the Tamil New Year: the end of winter solstice and the start of the sun's six-month-long journey northward. Poṅkal means *to boil, to overflow* and refers to the traditional dish prepared by boiling rice in milk with jaggery (*raw sugar*).

Am'mā's aunt made Poṅkal on her meagre or nonexistent budget just for Appā. She carefully carried it for a few blocks from her place in a coconut shell cupped gently in her hands, as she really didn't have any possessions. Also, she had showered that day, put on clean clothes, combed her hair, coiled it neatly in a bun, and accented it with colourful tropical flowers. I only saw her do this when she visited him. She brought her Poṅkal for Appā that day.

She asked Am'mā with authority, "Where is Marumahāṉ?" (*son-in-law*).

"Māmi, good to see you," Appā responded as he came out to greet her. With a wide loving smile, she presented her tightly guarded coconut shell full of Poṅkal to him. He sat down and invited her to join him to eat the food, while dishing out generous compliments on her cooking. He made her feel important and special. He dignified her. He was one of the few individuals who was kind to her. She knew that. This was their ritual and tradition, every Thāy Poṅkal. For him, being nice to someone was like being gracious to God.

Appā would often say, "Going with the crowd isn't courage." He was an amazing storyteller who loved holding court—reciting funny stories or recounting historical events, while enjoying an adult beverage with a lit cigarette in hand. He loved Laurel and Hardy, the comedic duo. And he intently observed other people and learned to mimic them, especially historical figures. And he lived in a world of black and white. The trouble was that he decided what was black and what was white. He was a man with a great heart but with many flaws, and he never forgave! In retrospect, I think he had "Tamil Alzheimer's": he forgot about everything, except his grudges.

He was a lover of literature and languages—especially Tamil and English. I learned the nuances of the Tamil language from him during our numerous chats. Tamil is a complex, rich, ancient language with 247 characters. He would dissect Tamil grammar based on its masculine singular, feminine singular, high-class plural, lower-class singular, and lower-class plural in an effortless in-depth discussion about Indian Tamil poet and lyricist Kaṇṇathāsaṉ's work. Appā spoke English with his mind, but he spoke Tamil from his heart.

He was proud of the fact that Tamil was one of, if not *the*, oldest living language in the world—a classical language along the likes of Hebrew, Greek, and Sanskrit. The earliest period of Tamil literature, the Sangam era, is believed to date from circa 300 BCE to 300 CE. Today, Tamil, a Dravidian language, is spoken by about eighty-seven million people around the world, including the folks in my household. This is mainly due to the widely disseminated Tamil diaspora spread across the globe, including Malaysia, Singapore, Fiji, Myanmar, Mauritius, South Africa, United Kingdom, United States, Canada, Australia, and Western Europe.

Tamil is an official language in the state of Tamil Nadu in South India, Sri Lanka (despite its fractious history), and Singapore. Tamil words have influenced the English language. More than one hundred words in the *Oxford English Dictionary* have Tamil origins—words like *cash, catamaran, mantra*, and *pariah*. Appā admired the Tamil language and culture, but he smugly denounced the LTTE, the Tamil separatist group. He despised the LTTE's tactics, especially when they eradicated other rival revolutionary organizations in a violent take-down by killing their own people.

He was a staunch Sri Lankan and believed firmly in the idea of a unified Lanka. Especially after my arrest, he doubled down on this and blamed the LTTE for it all, despite Sri Lanka's blatant violations against the Tamil people. We had many heated arguments over this. He thought the LTTE leader was a rube. I was a supporter, even more so after my imprisonment, and had a thirst for revenge. But Appā and I never agreed on this. Never! I had even considered joining the Tamil liberation movement a few times and attended recruitment meetings. Unlike my friends, I chickened out. One of my Hartley College school-mates Ravishaṅkar joined the LTTE, and many others followed him. Despite my father being very proud of his Tamil heritage, Sri Lanka needed more men like him.

But for all his progressive, generous ideas, my Appā held to the belief that the parent was always right, no matter what. My brother and father had many disagreements. Instead of a bridge, they built a wall between their relationship. Aṇṇā could not tell Appā anything because Appā had been Aṇṇā's age and had lived longer, therefore he was right and knew better. He always gave Aṇṇā a look of disapproval. I really felt for Aṇṇā. They were unable to share their true feelings with each other unless it was anger or frustration. This was one of the chief reasons my Aṇṇā ran away from home at a young age and never came back. It changed Appā's emotional substrate forever. He never forgave Aṇṇā for that. They never spoke again.

Before Aṇṇā left for India, en route to Denmark, in 1984, he was rounded up in the town of Jaffna by the Sri Lankan Army and was sent to the same Boossa prison where I was later imprisoned. When Am'mā found out, she begged Appā to use his influence to help to release their son, my brother. Appā callously refused to help Aṇṇā, because Aṇṇā ran away from him and disobeyed him. He felt Aṇṇā had insulted the family. She pleaded. He was stone cold. He was emotionally unavailable, inaccessible, unresponsive, and indifferent to his first-born son's predicament. Am'mā was so upset at him. Rightfully so.

In Appā's world of black and white, there was no room for grey. Weeks went by and he didn't budge. But I could hear him at night, quietly sobbing in his room alone. All this was very confusing to me. Luckily, one of my Am'mā's cousins in Colombo passed the message to Colonel Fernando, who turned to his son Milroy to help my brother.

When Appā heard the news of Milroy's death, he was devastated. He had brought Milroy with him once when he visited Point Pedro. For him, had the death of his friend's son been a blow every bit as cruel as the loss of his own—since brave, gentle Milroy was the person who had saved his first-born? I would never know. I do know Appā's dislike for the LTTE was further deepened for the crime of killing someone so close to his heart. But I resented the inhumane way he handled my brother's situation. Even after all these years, I still get angry at him thinking about it. So often, our most inhumane acts of cruelty are meted out on those who deserve them least, and when we feel most certain that we have right on our side.

Appā enjoyed the works of Bengali poet Rabīndranāth Tagore and of Irish playwright George Bernard Shaw. He was also a big fan of Shakespeare. Once I asked, "Appā, what will you do when you retire?" He replied without any hesitation: "I will go to Point Pedro and tutor English to the kids in the North for free."

He loved to read and study in English. He always maintained that the Sri Lankan school system moving away from the English language to teach in the mother tongue of the pupils was a colossal mistake. He felt that Tamils were coming out of university with degrees but unable to properly express themselves in English. He said, "English is the language of business. You can have the best idea, but if you don't know how to express that idea to others, then you have *no* idea."

While I was living with him, he would come home after a long day of work to teach English to university students, who were mostly Tamil. I would watch him passionately unpacking the literary works of many great English authors to his students—as always with a drink and cigarette in hand. Some students couldn't afford to pay him. He didn't care and he wasn't doing it for money. He wanted Tamils to learn proper English.

I remember an England versus India cricket match being played in South India. I was listening to the cricket commentary over the radio in Tamil. He quickly came over and changed the radio station to the BBC's English feed and yelled, "English please!" He believed it was good for me to learn English every chance I had.

Appā was my first English literature teacher; he possessed a very deep knowledge in this area. He taught me *Hamlet*. He would refer to my Aṇṇā, Ravi, as "his Hamlet" because my brother ended up in Denmark—and presumably because their relationship was so fraught. When I once asked him why he wouldn't speak to Aṇṇā, he said nothing, only gave me a stone-cold look that sent shivers down my spine.

Appā was fascinated with one of the most quoted and iconic lines in all of Shakespeare's work: "Alas, poor Yorick! I knew him, Horatio: a fellow of infinite jest, of most excellent fancy: he hath borne me on his back a thousand times; and now, how abhorred in my imagination it is!" He thought this speech, delivered as Hamlet holds a human skull, was the central scene in the entire play because it drew together so many of Shakespeare's themes—death, decay, and despair—in a graphic and dramatic way.

I felt Appā was experiencing despair and decay of his own. Once, for a poetry recital contest at school, he taught me William Blake's poem "Piping down the Valleys Wild" during a long bike ride over the sounds of grinding gears and our own laboured breathing—in, out, in, out, in, out. I got second prize. A kid who had recently joined the school from Papua New Guinea named Kārthikēyaṉ beat me. He spoke with a British accent and had better enunciation.

Thinking of my failures as a son, I finally fell asleep.

The next morning, I came to know of all the details of Appā's death. He had been shot by the Indian Army in cold blood in our ancestral home in Point Pedro, where I had been standing only days earlier. Am'mā survived because she had been in the other room and the soldiers hadn't known that she was there.

Neighbours had heard the shots, but everyone was too scared to come out and help. The animals who shot Appā were shooting anyone they saw moving about. So, everyone hid, out of fear. Am'mā had to deal with her grief alone. I was told she sat there next to her husband's lifeless body for four hours. No one was able to come to her aid for that long.

I used to think the Sri Lankan Army was the most ruthless force imaginable—until I heard what the Indian Army could do. During their short stay in the region—on a peace mission, mind you—they killed more Tamils and raped more women than the Sri Lankan soldiers ever did. The soldiers who made up the Indian Army were intentionally selected from the Northern parts of India so that they didn't have any language, religious, or cultural kinship with the people they were governing. It is estimated that the thirty-two-month presence of the IPKF in Sri Lanka resulted in the deaths of six thousand innocent Tamils. I knew a few of the victims: friends, neighbours, and now my father. Statistics are human stories with the tears washed off, I remember hearing once. Appā was one of those stats, but he was not unique in this.

It has been thirty-five years since I saw him at the airport in Colombo—the last encounter of my life. It was April 18. He died three days later on April 21, 1988, killed by a single bullet. He was only fifty-three. A single bullet made his soul depart to the celestial planes, to walk with his ancestors. A piece of me gone, my flesh and blood, my father, myself.

A faithful Sri Lankan and a proud Tamil.

IIII

THE IMMIGRANT

A few days later when no one was home, I was sitting in the kitchen at my uncle's house, feeling suffocated by the news of Appā's senseless murder and yearning for a past that I hadn't come close to letting go. The moments we had shared played in my mind like a slide show. Watching *Ben-Hur* at the Savoy. Walking along the promenade of Colombo's Galle Face Green together with ice cream in hand, discussing literature.

I fondly remembered running into his long hairy arms whenever he arrived in Point Pedro, even when his hands were empty. In that, he was a rich man. I miss the little things about him, like the way he mimicked historic figures. His favourite was Benjamin Disraeli, the first Jewish prime minister of U.K., for his fiery words. I miss seeing those impersonations. I miss the cigarette smell. I miss his sharp wit. Our conversations are still a constant noise in my ears, though even then my memories began to fade as I desperately tried to recall them.

Ever since I lost my dear Appā, I have been trying to fill a hole. The hole in my heart was so big I didn't think it would ever close. Walking around Toronto in the first few weeks after his death, with my body and mind numbed by the shock, my eighteen-year-old brain just kept thinking selfishly, My Appā is not dead. It is someone else's dad who died, and the news I got was incorrect. Everything's going to be great again.

But I was wrong. Of course. When it was finally confirmed, the ultimate weight of reality hit me, and I was crushed. Wrapped in my own arms, my body tried its best to reject the onslaught of emotion. It was at that moment in my uncle's kitchen that the hole inside me began to burst open. When I finally accepted Appā's horrible death, I sobbed uncontrollably, clinging to the kitchen countertop as if it was a life preserver. Tears flowed. Anger rose. I couldn't breathe.

From that moment on, my most cherished wish has been for revenge.

That is not to say that I think revenge is a good motive or a healthy goal. But reason has no chance against emotion. I was engulfed in resentment and rage. While other eighteen-year-old boys were chasing girls, having fun, and preparing for university, I was struggling to come to terms with my father's death.

His death stole everything from me except my memories—his mischievous grin, his confident smile, our bicycle rides. These memories made me smile fondly even in the midst of my overwhelming loss, reminding me that somewhere in that tragedy there would always be the life it represented, an echo I no longer heard but swore I would never forget—who I was and what I needed to do as his son, as a human. I decided—not at once, but over days and weeks—to honour the memory of my father. I was committed to spending more time thinking about how he lived and less time thinking about how he died. I cherished the time we had together and stopped asking "What if?" or playing the victim. We both deserve that.

My father's untimely death left me with the feeling that I had to live for two people. I thought that if I did well enough in life, somehow I could make up for the life he should have had. He sent me to Canada to give me a life that he never had. I would honour his life. Perhaps we all should try our best so that our kids won't feel that way when we pass on. It changed me fundamentally. It moved me to the core. The intense suffering put me in constant pain. It hollowed out part of my soul.

But pain also showed me the way out. If there was one thing I took from my loss, it was that you could find strength in vulnerability. My father's death made me more resilient and stronger than before. I wanted his death to be meaningful.

I never imagined something beautiful and positive could come out of the darkest and most painful experience of my life. But I realized I had to develop strength instead of weakness. His death motivated me to *strive*.

There are two kinds of pain in this world: pain that is no more than suffering, and pain that changes you. Pain that alters the direction of life. Now, I don't even know if fate exists, but if it does, can pain become fate? A power that predetermines events; the inevitable events predestined by this force. Some people wait for fate to reveal their paths. I didn't have to wait. What defined me had just happened. My fate was laid out in front of me, if I was strong enough to follow it.

I had to change. What was in the way was now the way. A sign of living. A daily salve for my red, angry, and unhealable wounds. I thought of a line from Appā's favourite Shakespeare play, *Hamlet*: "For in that sleep of death what dreams may come." My old man's dream must become my reality. I made myself that promise. That was my resolve. I had to turn something awful into something amazing. That is what my father would have wanted for me in life. It was what I would strive for.

When I had arrived at Pearson, I was far from Canadian, but my hopes and dreams were recognizably Canadian. Like immigrants from everywhere else, I was determined to overcome my tortured past and build a new life, so that the next generation would never have to endure the sense of terror that I associated with my ancestral homeland. I gained the gift of freedom and safety in Canada. A prosthetic for my amputated soul.

Immigration is never only about the pursuit of a better life; it is a struggle on behalf of people you may not even know yet. That is, it is a challenge that immigrants take up for the betterment of the next generation. To make my way in Canada, I left behind not only the brutality of a long civil war but also the country of my birth, soaked with the blood of friends, neighbours, and now my father. The only collateral I had was a strong back and the hope of a better life—which my father had passed on to me. I would not misuse those gifts.

The weight of grief could not crush me, I realized, as long as I carried it wisely. Cheery optimism that things would work out one day could never help me; I might wait forever. And pessimism could never lead anywhere I wanted to go. The only thing that could get me out of my uncle's basement in Scarborough and help me achieve my father's dreams was ruthless pragmatism. I needed that to win in life here in Canada. I had to deal with reality on reality's terms. I came across this quote long after Appā died: "Your thoughts become words. Your words become your action. Your actions become your character, and your character becomes your destiny."

In other words, fate is not what happens to you. It's how you allow what happens to you to shape you. For a man who didn't believe in fate, Appā's death was all the more senseless. He couldn't do anything about it. I still believe that. Fate had cut him down. He was born in Sri Lanka, and as he wished, he died there! But he had lived his life with everything he had.

And so would I. I still wanted to go on and change my own destiny, because "what is in the way is the way." That was what my old man would have said to me. I was determined. As he said to me before I left, "There are two types of problems in this world, son—yours and everyone else's. No one will fix yours. Fixing your problems is your own responsibility." How could I forget that? I never will.

Am'mā was by herself in Sri Lanka, where the Indian Army was continuing to commit blatant atrocities on Tamils at will. I decided to bring

Am'mā over to Canada. I had to. But I could barely fend for myself. To honour my mother and father, I would have to venture out into the cold in Scarborough and go to school.

I registered at L'Amoreaux Collegiate Institute, a high school at Warden and Finch. A new school. A new beginning. No Hartley College friends. No cricket at lunchtime. I was forced to restart my life, while suffering from anxiety about what may lie ahead and enduring my fear of being rejected. This school's students were mostly new to the country, and mostly from Asia and Africa, with white students being the minority. This was not particularly strange given that the neighbourhood was inhabited predominantly by newcomers to Canada.

They put me in the English as a Second Language (ESL) class because I was a newcomer. You've got to love bureaucracy. There were people in my class who didn't know the English alphabet. Meanwhile, I knew *Hamlet*. Not to brag, but I didn't think my teacher knew *Hamlet* as well as I did. School was boring.

My problem was I had no confidence and spoke in a quiet, trembling voice with a difficult-to-understand accent. People couldn't understand. I was a mess.

I met a kid from Jamaica, Winston—a nice guy, about my age. He was in my class and drove an old black Trans Am. We hit it off. During lunch hour, we used to go in his car and buy Jamaican patties somewhere not too far from school. We used to eat a few of those bad boys for lunch and wash them down with Orange Crush. He always paid.

I had no money, except that fifty U.S. dollars, which I wasn't going to touch. I said, "Winston, you have a car and you buy me lunch. Are your parents rich?"

"No, mon, I work. School is just part-time."

None of it made any sense to me, but I was intrigued. I asked him what kind of job he had.

"Factory," he said, as he took a giant bite of his beef patty.

Now I was really intrigued. "So, can I get the same job?"

"No," he said flat out. "But I know a place that is hiring. I will get dem details, mon."

A few days later, Winston delivered. He gave me a phone number to call. I did. I spoke to a man who owned a small packing factory in the Concord area, north of Toronto. He said if I had a social insurance number and I was willing to work, then the job was mine. Check and check. But it was a day job, he told me. I dropped out of school.

From then on, I took high school courses on evenings and weekends. During the weekdays, I stood on an assembly line, applying spray foam with a special glue gun. A board would come by on the belt, and I would spray it, while listening to 104.5 CHUM-FM. That radio station was always on, blared all day. That was my introduction to English-language music. Def Leppard became my favourite rock band. "Pour Some Sugar on Me" from the 1987 album *Hysteria* was my favourite track. It was hard for me to escape into the total awesomeness of the song. Making money was my priority. I was focused on getting Am'mā out of the hellhole. I had to show steady income for that to happen.

The monotony filled me with dread every day. It was a small factory with about dozen workers, all men. The powerful scent of glue intermingled with the body odour of the workers. I was the youngest at eighteen. I was making $3.50 an hour. I'm not even sure if I was being paid the legal minimum. I took any overtime that came my way. Some days I would work for fifteen hours. I was still not making enough money.

I did my best to spend little. The factory was located north of Steeles. Bus service north of that street cost an extra sixty cents. So, I decided to walk it both ways. It was about a two-kilometre walk, and it took me about fifteen minutes. It was an uninspiring walk along the light residential and heavy industrial area. I would do that walk to save 35 percent of one hour's wage. Except it was a very bad move on cold wintery days. Those Adidas shoes from the Amsterdam airport were no match for the Canadian winter. I was hungry, tired, and just wanted to get home.

It wasn't long before I experienced my first Canadian snowstorm. I was inside the factory the whole day. Head down, glue gun up, for fifteen hours. After my shift ended, when I stepped out, it appeared as if Mother Nature had draped the earth with her very own crystal-white gown. I stepped out of the smell of glue and sweat into a winter wonderland with the intense smell of pine cones. A winter storm had hit Toronto. I was absolutely gobsmacked. The freezing cold air punched my face with its fist like a heavyweight boxer in round one. I had no warm layers, just a plain jacket I had bought at BiWay and a T-shirt. As the Scandinavians would say, "There is no such thing as bad weather, just badly dressed people." I was certainly badly dressed in that moment. Totally ill-prepared for my first Canadian winter experience.

The white blanket of snow covered the trees, ground, and structures, everything glistening with drops of dove-white snow. I was surprised by how quiet it was. The only sound I could hear was my Amsterdam Adidas crunching in the snow, as I plodded due south on Keele Street—and my huffing breath as I plowed through the snow to the eastbound bus stop at Keele and Steeles. Sixty cents at stake. Two kilometres and about fifteen minutes to the goal. Between the physical cold of that bitter wintry night and my money-saving expedition, it was challenging to keep my thoughts coherent—and to keep my core warm. But I did ask myself, over and over, why didn't Appā choose to send me to Australia?

Snow made my walk take longer than fifteen minutes. The coldness ramped up and spread all over my body from the stiffness of my frozen toes all the way to my head in a blinding agony faster than I could blink. But I wasn't going to let a storm defeat me. I had endured actual torture. This was nothing. I must brave this, I thought. Can't give up. The agony slowly faded into a dull throb as I marched on. To the drivers on the road, I may have looked like another Canadian teenager walking around aimlessly in the cold in sneakers with an open coat.

The hourly wage I was making at the factory wasn't enough to get my Am'mā to Canada. I barely had money to feed and clothe myself.

So, I decided to get a few side gigs. I joined a cleaning crew through a connection of a Tamil friend of mine. At night, I cleaned tall office buildings in downtown Toronto. I remember being inside 44 King Street West, the Scotiabank building at King and Bay; it was part of our cleaning route. Yes, folks, I had finally made it to Bay Street, the financial power centre of Canada. The Canadian version of Wall Street. Not bad for a skinny kid from a funny country who had arrived in Canada only a few months ago. No stopping me now.

As I cleaned the posh offices of big shots, I kept hoping I'd have a break one day so I, too, could have success—and realize my Appā's hopes and dreams. Some offices had pictures of happy families displayed on desks for people to see. Husbands, wives, a few kids, and even dogs. Sometimes I would stare at those photos, reflecting on the happier times of the Ratṉavēl clan, my eyes welling up. I was all alone in the echo chamber of my pain. One of the most destructive feelings I have ever felt. I still faced an undeniable truth: the way of life that I'd enjoyed in Point Pedro for years was gone. It would never be the same. I would often think of Appā. I was having a constant internal conversation with him.

He never left my thoughts. His memory fuelled my motor, daily. It thrust me forward despite any hardship that life threw at me. He instilled in me the idea that there was dignity in hard work. And to take pride in any and all tasks. He would often quote *Āthichūdi*—an old but very popular collection of single-line verses written by great Tamil poetess Avvaiyār. These 109 sacred verses, expressed in simple words, were always used as the first Tamil lesson for kids learning the language. In addition to teaching the Tamil alphabet, it also aims to inculcate good habits, discipline, and deeds.

Appā would quote one in particular: "seivana thiruntha sei"—*do things with perfection.* It used to annoy me. He would often make me redo a task until it was perfect and to his liking. So annoying. I hated him for that. I felt he was watching over me cleaning and criticizing me if I didn't clean the office to perfection, giving me his signature gesture of disapproval. For him, the greatest sin was mediocrity!

I was an ignorant youth when he died. With my role model gone, I was forced to re-evaluate the direction my life was heading. I needed to re-examine some of the lessons he had taught me through the years. I needed to become a man, not remain a boy.

What it meant for me to lose him—no one will ever know. I was a teenager without a father. I would take his criticism happily all day if I could be with him, for just a few moments. If I could, I would redo tasks all over again. When he died, I realized I had never taken the time to truly appreciate him. It taught me, in the most difficult of ways, to be thankful to people who are kind to me. He was the one who explained to me the difference between zero and one. One is your family and loyal friends. Zero is everything else. The best advice I ever received.

With the factory job and cleaning gig, I still needed more money. So, on weekends, I had a third job as a security guard. My shift would start Friday at midnight and go to Saturday noon. Then again from Saturday midnight to Sunday noon. Then back to the factory on Monday. Also, my education was reaching a critical moment. I signed up for night school to complete my Ontario Academic Credits (OAC)—also known as grade thirteen. (This was phased out in 2003.) With three jobs, I hardly had time to study. At least at the security guard job, I could study a lot during my twelve-hour shift.

I wasn't assigned to a permanent location, and I hated that uniform. It was a few sizes too big for my skinny little frame. I looked ridiculous. Like a noodle-armed choirboy. I was so embarrassed for myself. I looked like a brown version of Steve Urkel—minus the dorky glasses. I used to take the bus to my shift wearing that uniform and hoped I would never run into anyone I knew.

I always hoped to be assigned to a construction site, because there wasn't much to do. I would sit in the trailer and study most of the time. I would do a patrol every two hours, and call the dispatch and report in, as I was required to do. But these construction sites were scary. They were usually located in some remote desolate area with no one around. Bad actors were always gunning for copper wires and pipes to steal and sell on the black market. The only weapon I had was a flashlight. Yeah, as if that would come in handy during a confrontation with bad guys. This made my night shifts all the more terrifying. I was scared shitless.

One of the trailers I was in had a tiny TV with bad grainy reception. I decided to watch whatever was on just to pass the time. I caught some show midway, and in one scene, a security guard was choked to death by a wire. I quickly turned off the TV. I was so scared after that. I didn't want to leave the trailer even to take a piss. I would just hop up on a chair and piss through the one window the trailer had.

One night I was terrified by a loud voice outside the door. "Roy! Roy, wake up!"

(I had changed my name to Roy. Nothing good ever happened to Subēndraṇ. I needed a new name, I thought. Roy means *king*, and that worked for me. To this day, I hate anyone calling me by my birth name. Only my very close family and Tamil friends can call me that.)

Someone was banging on the door. I must have fallen into a deep sleep. I was blissfully unaware that a small fire had started. Not sure how. Luckily, Rick the supervisor had driven to the site around the same time. Supervisors periodically dropped by unannounced to make sure all was well. Rick saw the fire and called the fire department. Only then did he come to the trailer to wake up the kid in his ill-fitting uniform.

I knew none of this when I opened the trailer door, pretending to be wide awake. "Hi, Rick. What's up?"

"Fire is what's up," he replied. It was clear he was not pleased. Fire trucks blaring with sirens arrived a few minutes later and put out the fire. I felt embarrassed for being negligent. Once everything was under control, Rick said, "Try to stay awake this time, eh kid?" as he walked toward his car.

I was sure I would be fired the next day. I felt Appā disapprovingly saying, "Do things with perfection." But Rick spared me. Rick was always nice to me. Sometimes when my shift was over and he happened to be going in my direction, he would give me a ride to my place.

By this time, I had left my uncle's place and moved to the east end of Scarborough to Wingarden Court, near Finch and Neilson. Kutty Mam'mā wasn't happy about me moving out, but he understood. He knew I needed my independence. He had always been a great guardian in the absence of my parents. An amazing uncle. I had never seen him upset. Always agreeable. Loved him to pieces. Still do. One of the hardest-working, nicest people I've ever come across in my life. Always willing to help. I will always be indebted to him for sponsoring me to Canada.

At my new place, I shared a room in a small townhouse with two other guys, Sathā and Janakan, to keep my rent down. Sathā is a distant relative of mine and I met Janakan through him. They were both students at DeVry, a private university. Both were Sri Lankan Tamils but spent their preteen years in Dubai. I only ate once a day, at dinnertime, to save money. I had to get Am'mā over to Canada. Janakan made decent dahl curry and Sathā made an edible chicken curry. Of course, there was always the Tamil staple: white rice. Dahl and chicken curry with rice, we called it "the standard." I would call from wherever I was and ask, "What's for dinner, boys?" Sathā would without fail reply, "The standard."

I would return home very late at night and everyone would be sleeping. I never cooked. Didn't know how to. But I was a self-proclaimed amazing cleaner. I still don't know how to cook. But I'm still an amazing cleaner. Even when I could afford a cleaner, for the longest time, I resisted. I loved cleaning things, making them pretty and shining again. It was therapeutic. I was trying to make my life pretty again. I was trying to clean up the mess. To shine again. I still find shining my own shoes therapeutic. Just like I used to shine Appā's shoes. It is still my Sunday-night ritual.

One time, I was assigned to the Skymark II condo building at Don Mills Road and Finch Avenue; I would spend the night operating the gatehouse. That was a rough shift. I had to open the hanging-arm gate every time a resident drove into the property. No time to study or to take it easy. Plus, I had to walk across every other floor of this twenty-nine-floor building with a punch clock device and go to the corner wall, where there was a key permanently attached to the wall on a chain. I had to take that key on its chain and punch it into this silly device that had a clock in it. Every two hours. That confirmed to the bosses that in fact I had done the patrol, while parading around in that ridiculous uniform.

Every resident's car had a green sticker, usually on the driver's side windshield. My orders were to not allow anyone in without that sticker. In the absence of a sticker, they had to have a pre-approved visitation pass. One night, a sleek Benz pulled up. No sticker. I didn't press the open button. The white man behind the wheel put down his window. "Open the gate," he shouted.

"Sir, are you a resident?" I calmly replied.

"Yes, you stupid fucking Paki." The *P*-word. Wow, my first racist. You never forget your first one.

Well, I was from Sri Lanka. Not from Pakistan. I didn't think he was in the mood for a geography lesson. But I wasn't in the mood to accommodate a bully. I had a chip on each shoulder. In that sense, I was well balanced. A battle of wills ensued.

"Sorry, I don't recognize you." He wasn't going to rattle me with this "Paki" shit. He had no credibility as a racist. He couldn't even get it right. A failed racist, in my opinion.

I'd had electric rods up my nuts. This guy was nothing. His racist insult was nothing. Fuck this guy. I was determined. That was that. I refused to let this asshole in. Maybe he was driving a new vehicle or someone else's car. I wouldn't let him in until his wife came down and showed me the sticker. He looked frustrated and rattled as he sat in the car. The skinny brown kid in his ill-fitting uniform had won the day.

Sure, there are many assholes in the world, but there are very nice, decent people as well. The former mayor of York, Alan Tonks, whom I met during my security posting at one of the buildings he used to frequent, was one such person. He was such a pleasant man. A gentleman. He always came and said hello to me and asked me how I was doing in school. He made me feel good. I loved his friendly disposition. I had learned early on to separate the assholes from the amazing people.

If you looked at the world only through the lens of racism, you would find it everywhere you looked. They will say hurtful, dumb things. But it didn't make a huge impact on my ability to make a difference and make a positive contribution. In fact, I preferred having a few racists around, because they kept my skates sharp.

Throughout my journey, I have had obstacles. I have also had many supporters, doubters, and haters. The man who turned away from me when I entered the elevator. The woman who avoided eye contact as I greeted her on the street. Being resilient and having my own goals in clear sight helped me triumph despite any distractions in my way. Boors like the guy in the Mercedes are no more than a distraction. Screw what others say—it's not their life. Be you and do you! That's the only thing that matters in the end because that's what creates happiness. Be a victor, not a victim.

The real question was not whether there were unpleasant people in the world. What I had to ask myself was, can I be a victor if I'm operating a glue gun for minimum wage? I was standing there with my glue gun, next to a guy in his mid-fifties on the assembly line. I forget his name, but he just stood there muttering to himself all the time

One day I asked him during our morning break, "How long have you been doing this?'"

"Twenty years."

And I had a vision of myself turning into that guy if I stuck around in this glue joint. I knew I had to get out.

I remember reading somewhere that the greatest weight on the human heart is the regret of unrealized potential. I didn't want to bemoan the way things were—because the Ratṉavēl family wouldn't be exactly the same way again. I knew that inherently.

I had seen enough death to appreciate the value of life. I wanted a life. A proper life. I knew that a dream doesn't become a reality through magic. Canada gave me a second chance on life. And I wasn't about to squander that away. My motor turned on. The greatest gift you can have is a motor. I had that gift. I had a crazy motor. How many heartbeats do I have left? Nobody knows. So, I wanted to take every heartbeat of mine as a very big deal—and go for it.

I was like Jake LaMotta in *Raging Bull*, after Sugar Ray Robinson punched him mercilessly. "Hey, Ray, I never went down, man! You never got me down, Ray! You hear me, you never got me down." Life kept punching me in the face mercilessly, but I never went down. Sure, I was on the ropes. But I never went down, and I never will. That would be a sacrilege to my father. Appā didn't send me here to survive; he sent me here to live. His death, my life.

卌

THE MAILROOM BOY

So I decided to leave the factory job, along with the cleaning and security work. Quitting isn't easy when you have close to nothing, but my cousin Jan inspired me. She is the sister I wish I'd had. Jan had been very loving and endlessly kind towards me since I arrived in Canada. It was she who encouraged me to rethink my life's direction. But before I could quit those three jobs, I have to find a better one first. My boss at the factory was kind enough to strengthen my sponsorship application with a letter guaranteeing Am'mā a job upon her arrival. Now I just needed to be able to support her.

But when I told my boss that I would be leaving the factory for an office job, he wasn't exactly encouraging. He was sympathetic, but he left little doubt what he thought of my chances of making it in the corporate world. In his view, I had none. I didn't have the skills or the background. I wasn't corporate material. I suppose I can see why he thought that. I guess he didn't see many skinny immigrant kids pass through his factory on the way to desk jobs downtown. But he didn't get under my skin. I immediately thought of Am'mā's curmudgeon relative. Another doubter!

"Fixing your problems is your own responsibility." Appā's words echoed in my head. Only carefully considered action would solve my problems—not thoughts, prayers, or any amount of hoping. Hoping was not a good strategy. It was time for action.

My seven housemates and I subscribed to one daily newspaper, the *Toronto Sun*. If I am honest, I would have to admit that we never read it. Basically, our subscription was for a daily glimpse of the Sunshine Girl on page three. If my old man had been alive, he would have made me read the entire damn newspaper out loud in front of him. These were the days before the internet. If you were looking for a job, you either asked around, or you looked in the classified section of the newspaper.

After one particularly long shift at the factory, I arrived home late. That night, instead of flipping to page three, I went straight to the job listings. And there it was: "Office Help Needed. $14K." I applied by calling the number and leaving a message—even though I didn't even know what *K* meant.

A few days later, I received a call. "We would like you to come for an interview," said a woman on the other end. The time was fixed, and an address provided. I was nervously looking forward to the second interview of my life. My very first job interview.

"Oh, by the way," she said, "please bring your updated resumé."

What resumé?! Dammit, I didn't have one. If I were to type one out, it would only list my name, address, and jobs in factory work, cleaning, and security. I decided against a resumé. I was going to go with my skinny good looks and Ratnavēl charm.

I left home early. "Show up early, be punctual," Appā would always say. I took the train to St. Clair Station. I had never been to this part of town. When I emerged from the underground station, I saw a river of well-dressed people, everyone moving in all directions, never stopping. I felt like I could be anyone or perhaps no one at all. I felt that I wasn't dressed well and looked out of place. I had never been claustrophobic before, not even on the cargo ship to prison, but in that non-stop flow of humanity, I felt the panic rise in my chest. Even in the bitter late-January cold, I felt the warmth from my sweat. I slipped into the crowd, full of adrenaline-pumping nervousness. I wouldn't trade this anonymity for anything. The buildings towered on each side.

I arrived early at the midtown office building at the intersection of Yonge and St. Clair. "Hi, I'm Roy Ratṉavēl, here for the job interview," I said as I checked in at the reception. When the receptionist checked my name on the list, she told me I was an hour early. She probably thought I didn't know how to tell time given such early arrival.

I took a seat and looked around the reception area to pass the time. It moved slowly. I tried to remain calm. No matter how much I tried to be a lion, my heart trembled like a lamb's. My meekness was my weakness. I lacked confidence. The more I sat there watching other candidates come and go, the more my confidence slowly chipped away. I was terrified. I could see into the adjacent office tower where people were busily at work; it felt as if I was seeing a glimpse of a future that could be mine.

Just over half a dozen people sat in the small, badly lit waiting room. I could smell them, the body odour and overapplied cologne. They were mostly newcomers applying for entry-level jobs like me. Unless they were all early like me, we could not have applied for the same job. They all looked anxious and serious, and no one said a word. Their anxious faces reminded me of the Canadian embassy's waiting room in Colombo. We were all waiting for a chance at a better future. But I could feel a sense of adventure and excitement woven into my nervousness. I had no way of knowing how the interview would go.

"Roy, follow me," said the receptionist, holding a file folder. I wondered what was in the folder. I had never submitted a resumé. What could possibly interest them enough to write down and file? She led me into a drab room with threadbare carpet and scuffed furniture. I began to wonder whether the office life was what I really wanted. Would I be working *here*? Did I want to? Still, I had to nail this interview. This could be the launchpad to the "proper life" I was longing for.

This was my chance to live a life for two. For Appā and me. A life he never had, and a life I desperately wanted. But first I needed to earn that life. My internal monologue was interrupted by a well-dressed, slender lady. She walked in and introduced herself. "Hi, I'm Lauren. Nice to meet you, Roy."

She opened the file folder. It was empty. "Where is your resumé?" I should have known. I mean, they did tell me.

It was not a promising beginning to the interview. Though she asked a few questions politely, I could see that my missing resumé had left me at a fatal disadvantage. At least she was honest. "You seem nice," she said as the short conversation sputtered to an end, "but I don't think you have the required skill set for this job."

"This is an office help job?"

"No," she said. "Mailroom."

"Okay, I can do that. Just give me a chance, and I will work hard for you." That I could say confidently. I meant it.

"We are not the ones hiring," she explained. "We are screening candidates for our client." That's when I learned there was such a thing as a headhunting firm. This was all new to me. "The thing is, you just don't have enough work experience in Canada." A response every new immigrant must have heard at least once, I'm sure. She shook my hand warmly. "You are a nice kid. Good luck." I wished she thought that I was an asshole kid but had given me that opportunity to have an interview with her client. I was dejected.

As I was leaving, I could hear the receptionist speaking on the phone. "Yes, the address is 401 Bay Street . . . The Simpson Tower, twelfth floor . . . *Yes*, Universal Savings for the mailroom job." She was clearly exasperated.

I may not have had much Canadian work experience, but I was very motivated. The receptionist was talking to someone who had passed Lauren's screening interview—and the genius couldn't even figure out the address of the company waiting to interview him.

My Point Pedro risk-taking gear kicked in. Why not just go to that address and try my luck? What did I have to lose? I suddenly felt a surge of confidence that I might be more skilled than the candidate they had sent over. I was willing to bet that I would at least be able to find the office.

I hurried back to the subway station, chanting that address like a mantra: "401 Bay Street, twelfth floor, 401 Bay Street, twelfth floor, 401 Bay Street, twelfth floor." Those words were the directions to a new life. I asked the ticket taker in the booth, "How do I get to 401 Bay Street?"

"Go to the southbound platform, and take the train to Queen Station," he said.

I hopped on the next train, working on my plan and keeping the address on a memory loop. I had no plan. I was acting on adrenaline. I arrived in about ten minutes. I ran out and asked the man in the booth, "How do I get to 401 Bay Street?" He pointed to a flight of stairs and said, "Go up those, and then go left to Bay Street. It's the building in front of the clock tower, the old City Hall." I ran up the stairs and found the building right away.

Appā once shared with me D.H. Lawrence's famous poem about self-pity: "I never saw a wild thing sorry for itself. A small bird will drop frozen dead from a bough without ever having felt sorry for itself." "What an amazing thought," Appā said, marvelling at this poem. "In the natural world, self-pity doesn't exist. Self-pity is unique to humans. It's our burden—and the locus of our self-destruction. Self-pity is the fastest way to destroying yourself." Appā was adamant on this.

I recalled the lines as I was about to walk into this office unannounced: "A small bird will drop frozen dead from a bough without ever having felt sorry for itself." Better to be that bird than a self-pitying coward. I wanted to stand up with a stiffer spine as if I was going to draw a bow! I did not wish to go home defeated while pitying myself. That's how I found myself at 401 Bay Street, uninvited, just one block north of the Scotiabank building that I used to clean.

One of the greatest freedoms I gained from growing up amid war was that I no longer worried about what was going to happen tomorrow. I was just happy to be alive on any given day. I had already danced with death twice by a very young age, and I was still among the living. People often shrug and ask, "What's the worst that can happen?" I knew the worst that could happen. I knew it all too well. But I also knew it wasn't going to happen at 401 Bay Street. Knowing the worst made me more resolute. Being rejected by a job agency was certainly not going to break me. Rejection only strengthened my resolve.

I hopped on an elevator from the brightly lit lobby and took it to the twelfth floor. Through the glass door, I could see the company sign on the wall behind reception. "Universal Savings," it read. The receptionist's name was Juliette. It said so on the name plate that rested on top of her imposing desk. "May I help you?" she said warmly.

"I understand there is a job for a mailroom clerk," I replied.

It was a dark, cold, snowy, winter day in Toronto. I was drenched in snow, now melting off my BiWay jacket due to the sudden heat generated by my body, as if I had caught a high fever. My body was on full overdrive. Adrenaline!

"Did the agency send you?" she responded.

I admitted they hadn't. I didn't admit that they had deemed me unworthy.

"You have to come through the agency," said Juliette apologetically. But I wasn't going to leave.

"Can I at least speak to the hiring manager?"

No, she said, I couldn't.

And yet I couldn't leave. No way forward, no way back. In my agitation, I asked again. Juliette had the same answer.

A white lady in her thirties popped her head out and said, "Hi, I'm Gail, the manager. Can I help you?" Her office must have been within earshot of reception. She must have heard the commotion.

The opportunity I had been asking for had just materialized. "I know you have a vacancy in the mailroom; I want that job. I will work hard for you and you will never regret it," I said in my accented English.

She hesitated. Her face was an expressionless mask. I allowed the smoky ember of hope to flicker into a flame. Just a little. "Follow me to my office," she said coolly, as she turned to walk down the corridor. She was probably hoping to avoid a scene.

I happily obliged. Once in her office, she said, "Why do you want this job so badly?"

This was my chance. I gave her the *Reader's Digest* version of my story. By this time, I had sponsored Am'mā and I wanted a permanent job so I could look after her. I told her that too. We spoke for at least half an hour.

At the end, she caved. "I have a brother who is about your age," she said. "I wish he was as responsible as you."

What was she getting at? My hope was getting warmer.

"But you still have to come through the agency. We need to honour our contract with them. I will take it from here. Welcome to Universal," said Gail. I was in!

A week later, I received a letter in the mail. It was dated February 16, 1989, and signed by Lauren, who had interviewed me at the job agency.

[Job agency name], acting with the knowledge and approval of Universal Savings, is pleased to put forth to you their offer of employment as Mailroom Clerk.

Your starting salary as advised by Universal Savings is $14,000 per annum. You commence employment on February 20th, 1989.

We feel confident that your association with Universal Savings will be mutually beneficial. We wish you continued success in your career.

Your signature below will confirm your acceptance of the above position.

Yours truly,

Lauren

Life doesn't give people like me chances, if you hadn't noticed. Maybe life doesn't hand them out at all. Asking for one is certainly a waste of time. You have to fight for it! I always fought fiercely for opportunities in life. I won many but also lost a few. I will go to great lengths to achieve. Steamroll others if I must. It is the more primal side of me, stemming from my deep desire for survival. This has made me a very polarizing person, all my life. People either absolutely loved me or loathed me. No in between. Black or white, just like my Appā was.

The letter was signed, sealed, and sent. And that day I learned that *K* means *thousand.*

That job was a turning point in my life and ended up teaching me in a most painful way that not only was life unfair—which I already knew—but that it could never be fair. It also taught me that the world was grey. Life will give you what you fight for, once and for all, if only you could find out what you were capable of—and I did. I never negotiate when I'm on my back foot; I always hit first. That's how I landed this mailroom job. I always refused to allow circumstances to define me and my dignity and destiny. I didn't allow it on that day, for sure. Maybe Appā had been right about fate and destiny?

If you are capable of becoming this person, life is going to give you what you fight for. Stop backing into everything. Stand up. Stiffen your back a little bit. Be like that little bird and have no self-pity. Become the best version of yourself. Do it in your own quiet way—and radically change yourself if you must. In life, you don't get what you deserve; you deserve what you fight for. My intentions created my own reality. The last freedom a person has is the right to choose their own actions. My offer letter dated February 16, 1989—thirty-four years ago—now hangs in a frame proudly in my office.

‖‖‖ ‖

THE MENTOR

I was looking forward to the first day of my office job. I wanted to work with pride. Bet on myself. Be fanatically loyal to Universal Savings for taking a chance on a kid. Be passionately productive. And I didn't want to let anyone down. I thought how I dressed could have a big impact on my self-esteem and confidence. If I dressed in a way that made me look like I was at the top of my game, I would be more likely to feel that way too. So, I took a little bit of money out of my small savings and bought myself a tie and a dress shirt at Stitches.

Monday, February 20, arrived. I was ready. I made the short walk down my narrow tree-lined street through the sleet to the bus stop. I joined a half a dozen people already waiting for the Finch 39 bus. The bus stop itself was nothing more than a pole stuck into the concrete with a small sign on top that read "Route 39." The traffic rushed by as we hunched our shoulders and shivered in the cold. Anyone who has ever taken transit in a Toronto winter knows the thrill of relief that arrives when you see the signature Toronto Transit Commission white-and-red bus approaching in the distance. As the bus hissed to a stop in front of me, I hopped on and noticed it was empty. My stop was the first of many on the way to the subway. It would take me almost an hour.

I sat on one of the many vacant seats. The long bus ride was my morning meditation, a chance for my thoughts to greet the nervous energy and fear I was feeling. The bus slowly became crowded as it picked up more morning commuters, each preoccupied with their own thoughts and going to their own jobs. They all looked unhappy to see the end of a weekend and the start of a new workweek. Finally, the bus arrived at the station. All that remained was a straight train ride from Finch down to Queen Station. A long way from home. This was to be my daily routine. It was the beginning of something new.

My gut was all tied up in knots as I nervously approached the twelfth floor that morning. I wanted to make a good first impression. My palms were sweaty, and this thought kept swirling in my head: Don't screw up and don't just do my best, but do Appā's best. You need this job. Jane, a pretty blonde young lady with a very friendly disposition, greeted me at the reception and showed me to the mailroom. She had me sign some forms and complete other formalities.

I was shown my daily responsibilities. Collecting and delivering mail. Filling in orders of marketing materials and couriering them. Mailing trade confirmations. Taking overnight trade transaction tapes to brokerage houses and bringing back their tapes to our office. Computers didn't talk to each other back then; this was before the internet. They needed human intervention. Waiting around until the last minute of the business day for any mailing or couriering that needed to be done. And running urgent deliveries from building to building in the downtown core. I was known as "the runner."

The buildings were heavenward-looking skyscrapers made of metal and glass. Appā once took me to Ceylinco House, Sri Lanka's first-ever skyscraper and one of the most enduring landmarks in the country. These buildings made Ceylinco House look like a small hut. I was eventually able to figure out the underground PATH system, so I didn't have to endure the punishing Canadian winter aboveground. I would walk between buildings below ground with a giant black box in each arm, each carrying a few large round overnight trade tapes inside. The weight was too heavy for my skinny arms to tolerate, and the boxes would almost drag along the floor. But the sound of passing footsteps, as a mob of people willingly chased sweet success in the business district was music to my ears. To me, this was better than standing for hours plying a glue gun. I was employee number twenty-five. The lowest man in the hierarchy. I knew that because my phone extension was 224; the CEO's was 200.

At the end of my first week, I decided to visit a Tamil friend of mine on my way home from work. His mother would occasionally cook food for me. I was always up for a free home-cooked meal. I missed Am'mā's cooking. This was close enough. A lot better than the standard.

On that Friday, a pretty girl with an infectious laugh was there with my friend's sisters. It turned out they were schoolmates. I had never seen her before. I was intrigued by her. She was stunning. From the time I got to Canada, I was too busy to even talk to girls.

My friend's sister introduced her to me as Sujantha (Sue). I wasn't sure if she was a Tamil or if it was even a Tamil name. I couldn't say for sure. She looked Mediterranean or Latina.

I was smitten. Her well-defined beautiful features were commanding the attention of this skinny mailroom boy. I couldn't take my eyes off her. Her midnight-dark silky hair shimmered under the light and accentuated her beauty. Those dark-brown eyes stared back at me and pierced my very soul, as if she was reading something legible only to her. We shook hands and said hello.

On my way home on the bus, I could think of nothing but that beauty with the huge laugh. I hadn't even been that funny. I was always in awe of people who could laugh like that. It was often in short supply with me. I enjoyed having people around me who laughed. It gave me hope. Her laugh sure did.

I thought there had been a spark. Maybe? I was pretty sure her eyes had mirrored something in mine. Maybe my funky tie from Stitches got her attention? The lethal Ratṇavēl charm? Or maybe she looked at me once, and it was over. I did not know. But I did know that she had a great personality. She also possessed many of the other qualities prized by a superficial guy such as myself. I felt pretty damn good that night going home, for the first time in a long time.

Weeks went by and things were progressing well at Universal Savings. I was starting to get into the groove with the daily work routine. One day, a handsome, athletic, friendly-looking guy, probably in his late twenties, walked into the mailroom to drop some mail in the outgoing box. He saw me, immediately walked over, put his hand out, and said, "Hi, I'm Bill Holland."

Eyes often reveal a great deal about a person. I learned this in prison. I learned to trust, or distrust, people based on their eyes. I look into people's eyes deeply. Not in a creepy way, I hope. Bill had an expression full of kindness and compassion, as well as confidence. I could immediately see that he was intelligent, inquisitive, and an alpha male. A lion! He looked like someone out of a *GQ* magazine. He was dressed impeccably and had shiny shoes like Uncle Fernando's.

"I'm Roy Ratṇavēl," I said meekly, followed by "That's a great tie!" It was sharper than the tie Appā had received from Uncle Fernando. I bonded with Bill over our shared love of designer ties. Not that I could afford them, by the way. He was one of the company's rising stars, I later learned from others. Already VP of sales, he was what is called a wholesaler. He didn't sell to retail investors setting aside money for retirement. A wholesaler sells to stockbrokers and financial advisors who then moved these products into the right retail portfolios.

A few weeks later, I found a shopping bag on my desk in the mailroom. When I opened the bag, I saw designer ties—Armani, Brioni, Canali, and Zegna. Bill had given me the ties that he wasn't using any more. Needless to say, after that, I was the best-dressed mailroom boy on Bay Street.

When Bill returned to the office after a business trip, he would often drop by the mailroom to chat. He was endlessly curious about my background, my progress in night school, and Sri Lanka. "A young guy like you should be in school full-time," he would often lament. He took a shine to me and a keen interest in my well-being.

Though he was much younger, he reminded me of my father with his sharp dress sense, mannerisms, and sensibilities—minus the curly dark hair, skin colour, and the lit cigarette in hand. Perhaps I wanted to see him that way. Do grief triggers tend to pop up when you least expect them? Maybe it was yearning, which is a very common grief reaction. Whatever it was, I was delighted by his kindness and earnest interest. Bill gave me dignity the same way Appā gave it to my Am'mā's mentally ill aunt. I wasn't mentally ill. But I was just as lost as her at that point. Bill anchored me. To be honest—he probably didn't know that was what he was doing.

In 1989, Universal Savings was a privately owned asset manager with only a few hundred million dollars under management. It was a tiny company, and it was slowly becoming my family. Everyone I met was very warm and nice, except for one lady. (There is always at least one in every family, no?)

Robert C. McRae was the founder and CEO of the company. He was a war veteran and a former airline pilot. A soft-spoken and generous man. Some bosses demand an outward show of respect. Then there are people you just can't help respecting. That's how we felt about Mr. McRae.

Then there was Ray Chang. A very nice man. He was Jamaican born with Chinese heritage. He was a very slim tall man, looked Chinese, and spoke with a Jamaican accent. I was so confused when I met him for the first time. Back then, he was the chief operating officer. All the letters from his degrees would not fit on his business card: B. Eng., C.A., M.B.A., C.F.A. He was no dummy. The man had many professional designations. He was also incredibly kind.

He used to smoke around the office, which was not all that uncommon back in 1989. I would sometimes smell the smoke in the corridor, and it would immediately remind me of Appā and his cigarettes. I would be distracted for few seconds. Then back to work. By then, I had also picked up a smoking habit. I would smoke three times a day—with morning coffee, at lunchtime, and after work.

The work was getting busy. I felt I was doing enough work for two people. But I wouldn't ask for help. I was too proud. I didn't want Gail to think I had failed. No way. I was not about to fail. I was swamped with all kinds of menial tasks on top of running between buildings and my main job of packing marketing material and couriering it. The important stuff was starting to slip.

Gail stormed in one day. "Are the marketing material orders up to date?" She sounded agitated, as she grabbed the two-inch-thick stack of order forms. "Oh my god, Roy, you haven't filled these? You are *months* behind." She was really mad.

Do things with perfection—Appā's words resonated again in my head.

"Goddammit, Roy, why didn't you tell me you were behind?" She wasn't slowing down. "Bill is super pissed. We have to hire someone to help you." She stormed out just as she had come in.

I was devastated. I had disappointed Gail. And Bill too. Maybe Lauren at the job agency was right to say that I didn't have the right experience. I felt like a fraud.

I was so upset at myself. I ran into the washroom. I went into one of the empty stalls and sat on the seat. My mind was racing. "How am I going to fix this?" Was "hiring someone to help me" a euphemism for "we are replacing you"? These paranoid thoughts were going through my head. I found the courage to get out of the stall after few minutes. I walked up to the mirror and saw that lamb again. Scared and lost. There was no lion.

I went back to the mailroom. I started by finishing up the daily mail, courier, and other routine matters of the day. It was five o'clock on Friday. Time to punch out for the weekend. I was ready to go home. I could hear the elevator activity picking up as people were heading home for the weekend. I grabbed my jacket and I was out the door. I saw that the elevator was packed with people. I squeezed my skinny frame into one of the gaps and fled the office.

But as I was walking toward Queen Station, something wouldn't let me go.

Do things with perfection. Take pride in what you do.

Appā's voice wouldn't let me walk down into the subway. I turned around and went back. Back up the empty elevator, back through the quiet reception area, back to the silent mailroom. I took off my jacket and started filling those orders. I told myself, I don't care how long this takes. I will not go home until I fill every order and complete all the labelling for the courier so it will be ready for pick up on Monday.

I worked for seven hours, nonstop. I was done around one in the morning. I stood there in the silent office and admired my handiwork for a few minutes. I was proud. A lamb would have gotten on the subway. A lion got things done. I lit up a cigarette, alone on the twelfth floor, feeling as though I ran the place.

Sometimes marketing materials are not just marketing materials.

Am'mā was about to come to Canada. Her visa had been approved. There was good news and bad news. The good news was that she could get out of Sri Lanka and away from the IPKF's killing and raping spree. The bad news was that I wasn't sure how I would support her. Her ticket was $1,500. I had only five hundred dollars saved up. I had to borrow one thousand dollars from a Tamil loan shark to make up the difference. I didn't have credit history. No banker in his right mind would ever lend money to a guy like me. And I didn't blame them either.

I was living in two realms. I wanted to build a new life in Canada. But my heart was with my widowed mother in Point Pedro. My survival instinct was not yet sure what to make of the safety and stability that defined my new life. I was attuned to danger, and yet it was my mother who was at risk now, not me. Steeped in Sri Lankan fear and anxiety even in the safe streets and quiet offices of Canada, I worried about her. I needed to resolve that. That's what Appā would've wanted. That aspect of my life was highly imperative in my situation, whether I was inside or outside Sri Lanka. My new job was the source of my income, which barely kept me fed and with a roof over my head. But I also had the other realm to contend with.

The next day, the phone rang. It was Sue.

She had found my number through her friend's brother, my friend. After the week I'd had, I was happy to speak to her. She spoke fluently in English; me, not so much. I had an accent. I wanted to come off like a lion, not a lamb. I mustered up my courage to ask her on a date. After all, she had called me. The adrenaline was pumping through me as if I were about to jump out of an airplane. I wasn't sure what she would say.

She said, "Let's do it."

I didn't have a lot of money for a lavish date. I didn't have a car. We took the bus to a Chinese restaurant in Scarborough at Kennedy and Ellesmere. If you know the neighbourhood, you'll know that we dined that night on MSG-laden dishes served on a stained vinyl table-top. The food was absolutely awful, as you might expect when you spend five dollars on a dish. I still can't believe she stuck around for the entire duration of the date with this cheap guy. She couldn't resist my Ratṉavēl charm, perhaps? It certainly wasn't the best strategy to lay a foundation for future dates with her.

Sue was dressed for the date. The most beautiful girl I had ever laid eyes upon. Absolute perfection in heels. Her dark-brown eyes glistened under the dim restaurant light like a glossy pearl on the shore of white sandy beach. Her cherry-red lipstick went well with the tight black dress she was wearing. She looked like royalty visiting the humble villagers in a place like that. I couldn't blame her for dressing up. She may have thought I was going to take her to a classy restaurant.

The dim light shone on her just enough for me to admire the lus-cious curves of her body. She smelled nice, even over the powerful smell of food emanating from the kitchen. For me, growing up in Sri Lanka—a country of monolithic despair—the fear I remembered most clearly was feeling the shocks from bombs, each one getting closer and more intense, while lying on the floor thinking that I would never have the chance to fall in love, feel the gentle touch of a woman, be a father, or grow old.

In that restaurant, sitting across from Sue, at that very moment, I felt I was the luckiest guy on the planet. What the hell is she doing with me? I remember thinking. I was a high school dropout with no clear path to success. But it didn't matter that I was punching above my weight dating a beauty like Sue. We had a blast. We laughed, joked around, and had an absolute fun time. One of the best moments of my life. A very high return on investment. An asset manager's dream, I might add. Maybe I was cut out for this asset management business after all.

Not long after that, I found myself at Pearson International Airport, waiting for my mother, standing in the same crowded, echoing cavern where my uncle had waited for me not all that long ago. Now I was waiting for Am'mā.

I was nervous about her arrival. I was eager to see her, of course. But I wasn't sure if I would be able to take care of her. It was only a few months ago that she had been taking care of me.

It's hard to lie to yourself when it also means hiding something from your mother. I tried not to think about it too much, but by this time, I had picked up enthusiastic drinking and smoking habits. I know she hated Appā for that. She would ask him to stop, but he never did. I knew my new habits would put me on a collision path with her. But I understood my responsibility as a son.

My Am'mā was short, slender, maybe five feet tall on a good hair day. She liked dressing in nice clothes. She paid a lot of attention to her external appearance, like Appā did. She always hurried and did all the household chores. Am'mā had golden hands when it came to cooking. She looked after my brother and me extremely well when Appā was away, working in Colombo.

Appā met Am'mā, after a few failed romantic relationships, when he was a young man on holiday from Colombo visiting his parents in Point Pedro. Am'mā and her family had just moved in next door to his parents. He saw this young lady and it was love at first sight. Appā was nine years older than Am'mā and a foot taller. Appā was six feet tall, which was very tall in those days, especially in Sri Lanka. I wouldn't say they had the best of marriages. They were two very different people. And they had very different interests in life. Beyond the physical attraction, they had not much in common. Appā craved intellectual stimulation. Am'mā wanted attention from her husband.

He drowned himself in booze and books. She hated that. But they made it work for the kids' sake. She was eighteen when they got married. A teenager. At forty-four, she was a young widow.

The flight arrival monitor at Toronto Pearson International confirmed that her flight had landed. When I saw the sliding doors split open and she came walking out, my heart also split open. A young mom in a strange land. She looked absolutely confused, out of place, and now dependent on her nineteen-year-old son for survival. Is this what Appā had in mind for his legacy? Instead of being overjoyed to see her after a long time, my heart felt heavy. I was gutted. It felt like I had to now live for three people. Living for two was already one too many.

Am'mā and I hardly spoke on the ride home. Uncle drove us in his car, just as he had driven me when I landed in Toronto. I was now away from all my boys and that daily visit of Sunshine Girls from the *Toronto Sun*. I was with Am'mā. I knew there wouldn't be any more standard meals of chicken and dahl curry with basmati rice.

She would cook amazing meals for me every day. And she had been plucked out of danger. Like any son, I felt relief and joy. But I knew it came at a price. What nineteen-year-old wants his mother to move in with him? Riding in the cab with my Am'mā that night, I realized that while I had moved to the other side of the planet, I hadn't fully moved to a new life. I yearned for all that my new world offered me, but leaving my old world behind was out of the question.

My very first office Christmas party was scheduled for only a few days after her arrival. I had never been to such a soiree in my life. I was excited. I bought myself a cheap suit from my favourite clothier, Stitches. When I said goodbye to Am'mā, she said, "At what time you will be home?"

I was pissed. She used to ask Appā the same question every time he left the house. Am'mā always showered me with affection. But she also saw too much of Appā in me. All her actions toward me were as though she finally found someone in the image of Appā that she could control, in a way she was never able to with him. But I didn't like being controlled any more than he did, especially after my imprisonment. "I will be home whenever," I barked, and I stormed out.

The party was held at the Sheraton Hotel in downtown Toronto. I had been to Christmas lunches with Appā in Colombo at his Christian friends' homes. As kids, my brother and I used to light fireworks with the Fernando boys on Daya Road. I always liked the festive season. But this was my first formal Christmas party. It was nice to see my work colleagues outside of the office setting and to get to know them personally. They were all dressed for the occasion. Most arrived with their spouses and significant others. Few were single, like me. Every woman wore a fancy dress and jewellery. Men were in nice suits and colourful ties. The dainty colourful lights added more colour to the parade of people. The sweet melody of music from violinists and harpists at the end of the ballroom drifted through the crowd.

We were all served cocktails as we mingled. I was still a lamb, slowly trying to become a young lion cub. I was so overwhelmed by all this. I kept hammering the booze to calm my nerves. Then Bill asked me to sit at his table during dinner. I was so honoured.

I drank so much that night. I was lit up like a Christmas tree. Even in that polluted state, I wanted to make sure that I didn't make a fool of myself. Mr. McRae and Ray Chang were there too. At one point, I realized I had had way too much alcohol; I made the wise decision to disappear and pulled an escape act like Houdini.

A taxi home would have cost me sixty-five dollars, so I decided to take a series of buses at that late hour from downtown to Scarborough. I got home very late and went to bed. I woke up a few hours into my sleep, ran to the washroom, and threw up. Am'mā saw everything. And in me, she saw a younger version of her husband. It wasn't my proudest moment.

A few days after Christmas, I received the news that Uncle Fernando had passed away. I had already lost Appā, and now this man who had once driven many hours to release this mailroom boy out of a horrible prison. I respected him like a father. They just don't make men like him any more.

Just like that, Uncle Fernando was gone. The man who gave me another chance at life. I know he fought against Tamils, my people. But I don't have to agree with someone to like and respect them. He was a patriot who served his country honourably without losing his humanity while doing so. To me, he was humanity in a military uniform—a Sinhalese colonel who protected my freedom and dignity with his own great personal sacrifice. What an amazing, beautiful soul that man had. I wish I could speak to him now.

Though I knew I would never be able to repay him, maybe I could show a similar kindness to someone who crossed my path in life—so that his legacy could live on through my kindness.

It has been said that a man isn't defined by his enemies. He is defined by his friends. Our relationship was woven together by a thousand tiny threads of humanity, friendship, and loyalty. Our national identity, allegiance, devotion to our family, and deep loyal friendship was what brought us together.

My nightmares were hounding me. They were becoming increasingly vivid and violent. I was struggling to sleep at night. Nightmares always followed me to bed. It has been written that I should be loyal to the nightmare of my choice. The howling wind rattled the window-panes upstairs that night I learned Uncle Fernando had died. I twisted and turned under my thin covers, thinking of Uncle. I couldn't sleep. Whenever I closed my eyes, I saw my Appā murdered in his own home, or the woman in Point Pedro whose eye had been blown out of its socket by a bomb. My heart would thump hard within my chest.

This happened every night, after I turned off the light in our basement apartment; my mother was probably seeing and feeling the same things in the next room. I never stopped seeing the war. In the silence of the night, I continued to hear the screams. The smell of death and war. The constant rattle of gunfire and the shrieking of jets.

I wasn't sure whether I was winning or losing. One moment, I would feel as if I was conquering the world, sipping cocktails with millionaires, or rolling up my sleeves in the office and getting noticed. Only hours later, I would be cowering in my bed, unsure if I was awake or asleep as I heard attack helicopters circling above. Surviving wasn't a crime, but I was beginning to think maybe it was a life sentence.

I was not here to survive; I was here to live. Even humble mailroom boys have some say in their destinies. The Friday night I spent packing marketing materials changed mine.

On Monday morning, Gail came to say hello. When she saw more than one hundred packages ready to be shipped out, she stopped in her tracks.

"Roy, did you do all this?" she asked.

"Yes, Gail." I was proud. She was over the moon.

"We have to pay you overtime. How many hours did it take you?"

I refused. "Gail, I don't want any pay; it was my job to do them in the first place."

She gave me a hug and left, shaking her head and smiling. I guess Bill heard about this and a few hours later he showed up and said, "You should be in service, not in the mailroom," and gave me two thumbs up in approval.

The positive things thus far in my life had always come when I faced life's biggest challenges. In fact, I could hear my father saying, "It is your habits that decide your future."

It wasn't long after that morning that I was out of the mailroom for good. Bill influenced the decision makers to get me out of the back office and into administration. The promotion came with a five-thousand-dollar salary increase. That made a huge difference to someone making fourteen thousand dollars. But to be honest, I would have taken the new job without a raise. I just wanted to get out of the mailroom and learn more about the asset management business.

I admired Bill and wanted to be like him. Dress like him. Exude confidence like him. Fit in like him. Speak like him. Be a man like him. Not a boy. A lion, not a lamb. I'm not a fan of copying from *C* students. I like to copy from *A* students. Success leaves clues. And this guy was on a solid path to success.

In administration, I learned about buying and selling mutual funds, how trades are settled, and how to make trade adjustments—essentially how mutual funds are priced every day. I learned that a mutual fund is a type of financial vehicle made up of a pool of money collected from many investors to invest in securities like stocks, bonds, money market instruments, and other assets and managed by professional money managers like the ones at Universal Savings. These managers allocate the fund's assets and attempt to produce capital gains for the fund's investors for an annual management fee. That's how Universal Savings made its money while offering small or individual investors access to professionally managed investment portfolios.

While searching for more knowledge about the industry, I found out that the first modern mutual fund was launched in the U.S. in 1924. But mutual funds didn't really capture the attention of Canadian investors until the late 1980s and early 1990s when investors realized that there may be incredible returns to be had. My timing in joining the industry and Universal was impeccable as the overall mutual fund industry was rapidly growing. Perhaps it was my destiny?

I absolutely loved learning about all this. It was a new world for me. I craved to know more. I would go to the library after work and read up about stock and bond markets. Whenever I had the chance, I would ask Bill a bunch of questions about these topics. I was learning and loving every minute of it. Not too long ago, I had been inside a factory with a glue gun, inhaling fumes for ten to twelve hours per day.

Universal Savings was growing rapidly. We couldn't keep up with the workload. There was plenty of overtime available, and I needed more cash. I stayed back after my regular eight-hour day. Appā's mantra had always been, "There is dignity in hard work." I would work until ten p.m., for twelve to fourteen hours per day. The company paid double hourly wages on overtime, provided dinner, and gave us a cab ride home. Not a bad deal. I was hammering home some decent biweekly paycheques. My schoolwork was suffering, but I did manage to finish high school.

Universal Savings reached one billion dollars in assets under management. Mr. McRae was thrilled. We were all thrilled. It felt like a collective win. I was especially happy to be part of it. I was starting to feel like I was on a winning team. By now, we had grown to about fifty employees. To show how much we had contributed to the company's success, McRae took money out of his own account and gave each one of us a crisp one-thousand-dollar note. I had never seen a one-thousand-dollar bill. He gave one to everyone, regardless of title. The CFO got a one-thousand-dollar bill, same as the new mailroom person, who had started two weeks prior. Then we hit two billion in assets under management quite rapidly. This billion came faster than the last. At that point, there were over seventy-five employees. Another crisp one-thousand-dollar note from Mr. McRae.

While the one thousand dollars was nice, I was a bit conflicted. Were these handouts? I was under my old man's orders to never accept handouts. But I reconciled it by reminding myself that I was part of the team, the same as everyone else. Performance-based pay is the opposite of a handout, right? It should be fine to take the money. In any case, those bonuses made us work harder for Universal Savings and Mr. McRae. That was a second lesson in leadership for me. Celebrate the success and reward the team. The first lesson was to show empathy to your people. That I learned from Bill.

With the rapid growth of Universal Savings, management decided to rename the company as Canadian International Group Inc., which later became CI Investments.

Mr. McRae was nice, but I'm sure he had a tough side when it came to business, which I had heard about. But he was good to me. He had a great line about public speaking—and he was certainly a captivating speaker. He said, "Leave when they want you to stay." Something I try to follow to this day. He fought in the Second World War and in the Korean War; like me, he had seen the terrible things that humans can do to each other. But he was always smiling and helping others. I thought I should also learn to smile. He used to say, "If you do your job, you go up. If you don't, you go out." That got my attention. That was something I never forgot.

I was working so late every night that I barely saw Am'mā. I also worked weekends at CI to clear the backlog. I never slacked off from hard work. I was determined to win this game with pure tenacity and dedication. Meanwhile, poor Am'mā didn't know anyone other than family and was stuck in the dark basement apartment. I thought maybe getting an apartment in a high-rise would help, as I saw sadness in her eyes more and more often. Finally, I got a place not too far from the condo where I had worked as a weekend gatehouse security guard in the horrible ill-fitted uniform, where I'd encountered that racist guy. Am'mā and I moved in.

Bill visited me frequently to see how I was progressing in the administration department. "Now that high school is done," he asked, "when do you plan to enrol yourself in university?"

I tried to avoid eye contact and change the topic but wasn't successful.

"You will do well in university, and you must find a way to do that while working. You came from a culture that values higher education, and you must fulfill your dad's wish." He knew perfectly well that he was deploying an argument I would never be able to resist.

Bill always pushed me. He was always blunt and painfully candid. Very similar to my own father. It was hard to listen to such blunt talk. I remember one time with Bill in an elevator, I was speaking very softly and avoiding looking at his eyes—a practice regarded as polite and respectful in traditional Tamil culture. Bill interrupted me and said, "Speak up! The world will never hear you otherwise." He wasn't criticizing me or Tamil culture. He was coaching me on how to get ahead in Canadian business. And I took his advice seriously. Immediately. And guess what? From then on, I spoke up. Maybe a little too much, if you ask some. Today I give the same advice to aspiring young Tamil professionals. Speak up, especially when you need to say something people may not be ready to hear.

Still, I often bristled at his coaching—even when I knew his comments were justified and true. They sometimes hurt my feelings. But he believed in me more than I believed in myself. Soon I learned to recognize that just because my feelings were hurt, that didn't mean he was wrong.

But CI wasn't my only life. I lived in two worlds.

Like many in the Tamil diaspora, I was thinking about my homeland on May 21, 1991. Former Indian prime minister Rajiv Gandhi had been assassinated at a rally in Southern India while he was campaigning for re-election. He was killed by an LTTE suicide bomber named Thaṉu. It was a revenge killing for the atrocities of the Indian Peace Keeping Forces.

Between July 1987 and March 1990, they had killed many innocent Tamils, including my Appā. They had maimed and seriously wounded many more. IPKF committed unspeakable acts of sexual violence on everyone from prepubescent girls to elderly women. Their cruelty against Tamils knew no bounds. Crushing people with their tanks, gang-raping women while husbands, sons, and brothers were forced to watch. They made the Sri Lankan Army look like Mother Teresa. All this happened under Rajiv Gandhi's watch.

Of course, they also suffered many casualties at the hands of the LTTE, and they withdrew in humiliation. Many Tamils viewed the LTTE as the only group to offer effective resistance against what amounted to subcontracted butchery and recreational sadism. Thanks to the IPKF savagery, popular support for the Tamil Tigers grew exponentially. India, the regional superpower, couldn't subdue the Tamil Tigers. It was India's Afghanistan moment.

When Sri Lankan Tamils heard of Rajiv Gandhi's violent end, many of us secretly rejoiced—including me. I personally held him responsible for my father's death. "Fuck Rajiv Gandhi," I said to myself, as I cracked opened a beer to celebrate the news. "It's settling the score, buddy," I remember telling a friend of mine, though I am not proud to admit it now. Rationality goes out the window when you are consumed by a lust for revenge.

(Ironically, I felt the same when Lalith Athulathmudali, Srīmaṇi's husband and the former minister of defence, was assassinated in April 1993. I was somewhat conflicted about this because through Srīmaṇi, I was able to pass the message to Uncle Fernando, who then saved my life. In that respect, I felt some loyalty to her, and I was sad to see her made a widow, just like Am'mā was, at a very young age of forty-seven.)

It took me awhile to realize that the score wasn't even close to settled. Rajiv Gandhi's death didn't change my day-to-day life. Everything was still as it had been: my father was still dead; my mom was still a widow. The war in Sri Lanka and the one in my head were still going on. Revenge solves nothing.

It was also a huge political miscalculation by the LTTE to assassinate Rajiv Gandhi; even LTTE leader Vēluppiḷḷai Pirapākaraṇ admitted as much. He called it "a regrettable event." Then U.S. president George H.W. Bush called the assassination "appalling and a loss for world order." Years after Bush Sr. left the oval office, under the Clinton administration, the LTTE was designated as a foreign terrorist organization in 1997, which was the beginning of the end for the LTTE. Still, they had earned the undying support of the Tamil diaspora and had a successful run for another twelve years in Sri Lanka.

And as the war ground on, the diaspora grew. I was starting to observe more Tamil people around Toronto. I could see at a glance that more Tamils were leaving Sri Lanka for a better life in Canada. Why wouldn't they? War and blatant discrimination against our kind was on the rise in Sri Lanka. It only made sense to seek greener pastures. I could recognize the look of terror on their faces.

Many appeared lost. What a tragedy to our people, I thought. A once proud people chased out of their own country to a faraway land and an unknown culture. And now they were clueless, just as I had been.

But what could I do? How do you live in one world and try to change another? Like some of my classmates at Hartley College, I felt the instinct to fight. But my life in the country I'd made home went on, as if peace reigned around the world. The office at CI went on humming with everyday concerns. The phones rang. The faxes poured in. The bike couriers came and went. A noble victim complex wasn't going to get me anywhere. I couldn't transfer my trauma onto people who hadn't in any way contributed to my pain.

"A lack of focus could be very costly for you when there is so much at stake in your new role here," Bill said to me once. He was absolutely right.

I had to make things work. I had to claw through, no matter what— I was determined.

But it is not easy to live in two worlds, especially when one is a land of peace and prosperity, and the other is a battlefield of ethnic violence. Even as life seemed to be offering me everything my family hoped for, my nightmares were finding a way to manifest themselves into the daylight.

Few places in my new home felt as far from the scorched earth and misery of Point Pedro as the hustle of Yonge Street near Dundas. The shops, small and large. The tourists, the buskers, the oversized signs that together announce prosperity. But even here, the weight of the past could pull me down. One day, I was walking through the chaos of Yonge Street when I heard a helicopter above me. It immediately took me back to the Point Pedro war zone and I became a terrified fifteen-year-old again. My body started to convulse with confusion and fear as I crouched under the awning of the nearest building. It was lunchtime, but everything went black.

I was brought back to reality by a passerby, who was hovering over me. "Buddy, buddy! Are you okay?"

I snapped out of whatever spell the roar of the news helicopter had put me under. I lied to the concerned passerby. I told him I was fine, and I darted away.

But I wasn't fine. Incidents like these were becoming all too common. My mind was like a scary neighbourhood that you don't often visit. You can't screw this up, Roy, I would keep reminding myself. I had to fight through it all. It had been almost two years since I'd moved to the administration department.

We are all products of our past, and certain words and actions can be our triggers. It is perfectly normal. It's like accidentally picking a scab, exposing the wound, exposing our enduring vulnerabilities for that moment. When this escalates, our unpleasant past experiences can interfere negatively with our present experience. This is normal as well. It can never be eliminated because it is deeply rooted in our wiring and buried in the fibre of our being. We must learn to manage its impact to minimize the negative effects on our future.

I had spent time in prison, where I had no say in any matter. I had to do what I was told. I hated that. I was robbed of my independence. I deeply resented that. I still do. So, when someone asks me to do something, especially when I don't want to do it, I react very negatively. Am I just being overly sensitive? Probably. I was indignant and combative to my own detriment. I had a massive chip on my shoulder. To a certain extent, I still do. It is deeply ingrained. It's my default mode. It was starting to affect my relationship with Sue.

From my perspective, I had grown up in misery and had to work through my pain and suffering without complaining. But others did not recognize this. Then again, why is it their problem? It was my subjective reality, not theirs. Why couldn't I separate good intentions from deliberate insults? It just meant that my feelings got hurt. In the grand scheme of life, it was so trivial. I recalled my old man's lesson: "There are two types of problems in the world—yours and everyone else's. No one will fix yours. Fixing your problems is your own responsibility."

I did not want to waste any mental energy worrying about what might happen. I thought it was better to put all my efforts into making sure things happened. I alone am responsible for my behaviours—especially the ones that make the biggest difference to my success, like smart, efficient, productive activities. I never wanted to make excuses, list reasons, or point fingers. Unless, of course, I was pointing them in my own direction. I was willing to do whatever it took to ensure things turned out the way I had planned—and accept final responsibility.

Excuses stopped mattering. I knew I had to tackle my own imperfections and blind spots in order to win in life. I would often tune myself up to that end and then find myself going back to my default factory setting.

I had started to notice a change in Am'mā's behaviour. There was a look of emptiness in her eyes. It had been three years since Appā's murder. I found her at night walking around. She seemed paranoid and kept telling me that someone was trying to hurt her. I thought she needed a companion. She was lonely. I was unable to be there for her 24/7. She was in the early stages of her grief, with rawness at her fingertips. Dunes of emotion dominated her psyche, as she oscillated between howling sadness and stunned silence.

Am'mā was always by herself. Sometimes I would get home very late and find her in a dark corner, shivering and thinking someone was going to get her. She always put a cloth over her head, only revealing her eyes. I never understood it. Was it the war that made her this way? Or was it something in her DNA? Would I end up like this one day? There were many questions.

My Am'mā's paternal aunt, the one who made Poṅkal for Appā every year, had similar issues. Would Am'mā be like her in a few decades? I was concerned for Am'mā. I would console her and then she would be fine. It became a routine—a routine I hated. It would break my heart every time. I didn't want to see Am'mā in shambles like this. So, I would tie one on at a cheap bar before I got home, just so I could deal with this. I was turning into my Appā—minus my knowledge of literature, Tamil, and English. I loved him so much; it was only natural I became like him.

Then Am'mā was diagnosed with schizophrenia. Her mild symptoms were pretty familiar to me: she was hallucinating and having delusions, as well as disorganized thinking. I could see it; she would often tell me that someone was following her and trying to hurt her.

All the stress had caught up with her. I was gutted when I heard the doctor tell me that; life had handed me another shitty hand. Just when I thought I could see clearly and I could raise my head above water, *bam*—bludgeoned in the head. God is a heartless asshole, I remember thinking. Hadn't my family suffered enough? My anger and resentment toward the world rolled right back in. I was back to my factory setting. I drank a lot that night to forget it all.

Despite her new medical diagnosis, the pain in her heart, and the nightmares that played in her head with clockwork predictability, Am'mā did her best to lead a fulfilling and meaningful life by making and retaining friendships, even making some new friends. Somewhere in this tragic epoch, she embraced life for what it was. As a son, it was heart-wrenching as well as heartwarming for me to witness.

She was primal in every thought and movement as she attempted to rise each day and put one step in front of another, despite the ongoing battles in her head. Her strength was equal only to her heart. She enjoyed travelling to faraway places like Europe and Australia to see family—especially for important occasions such as weddings. It was a much-needed reprieve from her justified melancholy.

How could I have ever understood how she felt in the aftermath of the tragic death of her husband, my father? Not even the passage of time could numb how horrible she felt. As hard as I had to work, I knew I was lucky. I was in control of my fate. I had responsibility, yes, but I had the strength and the opportunity to live up to it. How could a young man understand that Am'mā had lost not only the world she had built for her family but also her role within it? It must have been a unique kind of torment to be such a young woman in the care of a young son. Still, there was something that would always bind us. My father's murder forged something unbreakable between us, even if our day-to-day lives were sometimes difficult.

In one conversation, I gently suggested to her, "You should probably marry again and carry on with your life."

"Shut up!" she shouted. She refused to speak to me for weeks.

It was taboo in the Tamil culture of that generation to do that. Though the cultural attitudes have slowly changed for the better in this respect, once the husband died, ladies of Am'mā's vintage would never deign to remarry, fearing the condemnation of Tamil society. "What would people say?" was their overriding concern. Like my pops, I never was worried about what others thought.

But Appā had been forward-thinking, and I thought he would have been okay with it. Plus, the great Tamil poet and social reformer he most admired, Pārathi, was always for the emancipation of women.

I tried convincing her weeks later. "Forget what other people think. None of them understand your struggles anyways." That was my last-ditch attempt. But there was no chance of changing Am'mā's mind.

By then, I had moved into customer service, again with the help of Bill's recommendation and guidance. He thought I had learned as much as I could in the back office. I needed front office experience, dealing directly with our clients—the financial advisors. My manager was Lorraine Blair. She put me on the phone and taught me how to have a professional conversation with clients. Her boss, Dave, was a very smart man. I would often walk into his office and ask all kinds of questions in an effort to learn the business quickly. Though he was a very busy man, he made time and tried to explain things to me. Sometimes he would jokingly say, "Don't take this personally, but fuck off." Code for come back when I have time.

My job was to take incoming calls from financial advisors from across Canada. I was starting to really understand the Canadian mindset and what I needed to do to succeed in this country. I generally felt that people didn't really care that I spoke with a slight accent or had a non-Anglo-Saxon last name. All they cared about was my ability to help them solve a problem and to help their business.

Coming from Sri Lanka where everything was divided along racial lines, I found this meritocracy to be rather refreshing, which further galvanized my Canadianness. I knew I could thrive in this environment if given the opportunity.

A variety of people called. All kinds of different accents. Happy people, funny people, rude people, mean people, and rushed people. I was slowly starting to learn to deal with different personalities. I was slowly becoming confident in my conversations—and understanding the business better. I became quite good at customer service. I was reliable and quickly fixed problems regarding trade and administrative errors. Bill introduced me to some of our top clients. I was soon the go-to guy for this elite group of financial advisors. I felt I may have found my calling.

Bill's influence extended much further than advice on ties and navigating the corporate ladder. Every chance he had, he told me to enrol in university. The man was relentless. His father was a professor at the University of Toronto. He arranged a call with his father, who helped me apply as a mature student. I enrolled at U of T in September 1993. I did it for Appā. He had sent me to Canada to obtain a degree. Now it seemed I couldn't avoid getting one.

Not that it was easy. Between work and taking care of Am'mā, every hour was accounted for—though I stole every hour I could to see Sue. In fact, the only thing that made me feel better, in the midst of all this, was Sue. She was partway through completing her own degree at U of T but had started working full-time at an investment management firm and switched to night classes. We took some courses together. I missed most of them due to work. But Sue was a diligent notetaker. I would meet her on the weekend and we'd study together.

When others were crowding onto the subway after work to head home, I would be heading to U of T. One evening, I pushed my way onto the southbound train to St. George Station, and in walked Mr. McRae. He saw me and said, "Aren't you the fella in customer service?" (I'm sure he knew who I was, but everyone looks a little different away from work. And anyway, there were only a few brown studs with Bollywood good looks roaming around the downtown core back then. He was correct to confirm.)

"Yes, Mr. McRae," I said with great respect.

"So, you live this way?"

"No, Mr. McRae," I said with the same respect I would show to my grandfather. "I'm taking courses at U of T, at night."

"You mean to tell me that you study at night?"

"Yes," I said timidly.

"Are we paying for this?"

"No, Mr. McRae."

"Come to my office tomorrow with all your receipts," he said as he got off at Union Station.

(I learned later that Mr. McRae took the commuter train to the suburbs, where his driver would pick him up. He could certainly afford to be driven the whole way, but he was a very down-to-earth man. Not that he was above a little Canadian luxury. Someone in the company told me he had a heated driveway. I thought that was a pretty fantastic idea. You flick a switch, and the snow melts away? From that moment on, I dreamed of a driveway I wouldn't have to shovel.)

I knocked on Mr. McRae's office door the next day.

"There you are," he greeted me. "Do you have those receipts?"

I said yes. "To be honest," I continued, "these are just the copies as I have already claimed them as a deduction on my income tax."

"I don't care," he said, as I approached his desk with absolute reverence. He looked at them and added them up. Then he reached over and grabbed his chequebook and wrote me a cheque.

When he handed it to me, I said, "Mr. McRae, you have no idea what this means to me."

"Yes, I do," he said. "Better education is what it means." When I looked at the cheque, I realized it was for double the amount on the receipts.

"Mr. McRae, this is more than I submitted."

Mr. McRae responded before I finished my sentence. "This is for your future tuition fees. An educated employee is an asset to this company."

Was this a handout? Was I letting my father down? I struggled to come to terms with what had just happened. This man had just written me a cheque for half of my yearly income. (Tax-free!) I was moved beyond words. Some guardian angel was certainly looking after me. My loyalty to the company deepened. That was the only way to ensure that this generosity wouldn't be a handout.

Now I had no excuses. I had to work hard—and study even harder. Bill got me into university, and Mr. McRae had just paid for a good chunk of it. I would stay after my customer service shift was over to work on my assignments. Ray Chang's office was only a few feet from my little cubicle. He often worked late, sometimes until ten. One time, while I was working on an abstract algebra assignment, I felt a tall frame hovering over me. And I could smell the smoke as well. The cigarette certainly wasn't a Bristol, like my pops used to smoke. It had a stronger smell. Du Maurier, perhaps? I liked Du Maurier. Ray did, too, it turned out. He offered me one.

He pulled up a chair. "Let me see your assignment," Ray said as he took a puff. "I'm embarrassed for you." He mock-frowned. "Let me show you the trick." It turned out Ray was a math whiz. I was impressed. I had sat and stared at the page for a very long time. Ray did it in a few minutes. Once he finished, we sat back and had another cigarette together.

"I understand your mom is here and you moved into a new apartment."

"Yes, Ray," I said as I took a decent drag of my cigarette to keep up with him. Ray always took generous drags of his cigarettes.

"Have you furnished the place?" Ray asked.

The apartment had two bedrooms. I gave my mom the larger of the two, with a decent closet. I had a box spring and a mattress. I bought a queen-sized bed for mom. Beyond that, we had some pots and pans.

No TV. No anything. No wonder my mom went off the deep end. It was a minimalist existence. Plus, I was never there.

"No, Ray, I can't afford to," I said, sounding like the lamb I was.

"You mean to tell me that you do your assignments on the floor?" Ray asked with an anxious tone.

"Sometimes, but that's why I study at the office. It's easier."

He said goodnight and left.

I walked into my cubicle the next day and saw an envelope from Ray. Inside was a cheque for five thousand dollars. A note accompanied it: "Your furniture fund." I knew this was a handout.

I walked into his office and saw that he wasn't there. A few hours later, I went by and spoke to him. I said, "I can't accept this—but I need this, badly. But I would like to repay you biweekly, one hundred dollars." He said yes to make me feel proud of myself. I took the money and furnished the apartment. It took me twenty-five months to pay that interest-free loan.

I considered myself blessed to have men like Bill, Ray, and Mr. McRae. Were they helping everyone in the company or just me? I would never know. Why did these three try to help this fucked-up, angry kid? I remember once I had asked Appā, "Why are you teaching English to these people for free?" He replied by quoting a Tamil proverb, which loosely translates to, "If I feed the village children, my children will grow on their own." Perhaps he had it right. I still believe to this day that I have benefitted from Appā's good deeds. Good karma!

On June 20, 1994, CI Investments went public and issued an initial public offering of twenty-five million dollars—at eleven dollars per share. Sue and I bought as many shares as we could afford in the IPO. We pooled all the money we had, and we borrowed from her dad and the bank. Why wouldn't I bet on decent, hard-working people with a clear vision? Maybe it was risk-taking DNA from my Point Pedro days? Since then, I have felt like an owner and saw CI as an extension of myself. As a result, I did what others would not do—because no one washes the rental car. I behaved like an owner and took genuine owner-ship and pride over my work at CI. I couldn't quit on myself.

But just as I lived in two worlds, there were two Roys.

Even as I pushed myself to succeed and invested heavily in the future, the past clung to me. Perhaps I tried to outrun the past by fleeing up the corporate ladder. That's better than going down, I suppose. But I could not tolerate anything impeding me. Not with the past at my heels.

Of course, that's not how I understood it then. Back then, I was just angry.

Even with all the good things happening in my life, I was consumed with anger. I was angry at the slightest delay in my ascent. I wanted more. More responsibility. More experience. More *work*. But my new manager was not on my timeline. I asked for more. I demanded more. I was chafing. No one likes to be told how to do their job by a subordinate. My manager was complaining to Bill that I didn't take instruction. I thought I was trying to help the company. My manager thought I was a pain in the ass.

I let my anger take precedence over everything else, that was my weakness. I thought like a victim and behaved like one. I couldn't keep it together. I just couldn't. And it all ended up on Bill's plate.

Finally, Bill had had enough. We had it out in a fiery exchange. This was the guy who had given me one opportunity after another, and I was angrily demanding more. Crying never helps. It never does.

"I think you have outgrown the company," Bill told me. He said I should quit or that he would fire me. I was too proud to get fired. I gave my resignation letter the very next day.

"This is why I like you. You don't screw around," Bill said.

I always acted decisively and quickly. But I didn't always take the outcome into account. I never cared about consequences. Sometimes, that backfired.

I had a car by then, a British racing green Mazda MX-6. After I quit, I drove it to an empty lot and parked. I considered where my anger had got me. Maybe I had hoped that Bill would refuse my resignation. Now reality came rushing in like the tide. Having a job was one of the things that stabilized me. How would I take care of Am'mā and myself?

Would this job loss bring out the worst in me? I had seen Appā go through that. I was afraid of that. I was always aiming to be a better version of myself, because even I didn't like myself at my worst. How could I rebuild? This was my failure, and it was painful, but I deserved it. I had so much fun at CI. When we went public, Mr. McRae had given us all another one thousand dollars. By then, we were about 150 employees. What a generous and fun place to work.

I also remembered when we moved to our new location at 151 Yonge Street. Lorraine, our customer service manager, would take us out to the pub Growlers right behind our office building. We would all get smashed on Thursday nights. Then after last call, we would try to bribe the bartender with a hundred-dollar bill to stay open, which never happened. We had a weak sales pitch, I reckon.

One night, instead of going home, I decided to stay downtown—but not in a hotel room. I dropped a dollar and grabbed a newspaper from the newsstand, spread the paper on the sidewalk next to the office, and slept in my suit. Then after a few hours of sleep, I awoke hungry. I remember stealing a loaf of bread from the truck that was delivering bread to the Cambridge Suites hotel. I ate that on the street like a vagrant in a suit. But I was the first one in the office and ready for work while my head pounded like a drum. Would I ever find a family like this again? Those were fun memories I would miss. But here I was in my car in an empty parking lot, with a heart that felt just as empty.

I didn't work again for two years; I attended the University of Toronto.

Once I completed university, I applied for many jobs, but nothing panned out. My Ratṇavēl charm wasn't working on anyone any more. I was starting to lose hope. On a cold, dark Thursday morning, the sound of the phone ringing woke me up. I looked at my digital clock; the red numbers read 9:30.

"Hello," I answered in a sleepy voice.

"Is this Roy?" said the voice on the other end.

"Yes, who is this?"

"Bill Holland."

I was stunned. How did he get my number? What did he want?

"Why haven't you kept in touch with me?" he said.

"Well, you are a busy man and I didn't want to bother you," I said nonchalantly.

"Do you have time for lunch?" he asked.

"When?"

"Today, Cambridge Club at one o'clock," said Bill without hesitation. That was the Bill I'd always known. There was always a sense of urgency. He moved faster than other people.

At that point, I hadn't shaved for a month or more. I got up and got a straight shave from the nearest barber. After changing into some decent clothes, I was on my way to see Bill for the first time in more than two years. I still owned those CI shares.

We met at the club restaurant. Bill looked prosperous; I looked poor. I felt out of place at this private club with many successful businesspeople around me radiating confidence. Bill was attentive and engaging. We had a good chat over lunch. Exchanged pleasantries.

"Congratulations, you graduated."

"Thanks, Bill."

"Do you have any work lined up?"

"No, Bill." I answered like a lamb.

"Well, then, you start Monday at CI as a sales associate," he said as he leaned back on his seat.

My eyes welled up.

"By the way. I'm not head of sales any more. And I'm not going to be there on Monday. So, get there early. Tell them I hired you."

When I arrived at seven on Monday, Gloria, the receptionist, greeted me warmly and took me up to the sales floor. My new boss arrived a bit later. His first words were "What are you doing here?" Bill hadn't hired me for a specific position. He hadn't even told the company he had rehired me. It would be up to Peter, the new head of sales, to create a role for me. That felt even better than being recruited for a particular job.

It's rare to find someone in life who believes in you even more than you believe in yourself. I was incredibly fortunate to have found that in my former CEO, current executive chairman of the board, motivator, disciplinarian, friend, and cheerleader—Bill Holland. A man who taught a young, scared, skinny boy from a war-torn country that the world is not necessarily a bad place and who proceeded to make a man out of me. I wanted to emulate someone who was living and having success in their life. Bill was all that. I was obsessed with how he held an audience, how he was stylish and confident. I would study his gestures intently. Every move. Of course, watching and doing are two different things.

I believe effective mentorship happens organically. It happens without you realizing it; it must be natural and not forced. Everyone has at least one person they admire—someone to look up to and learn from. Someone who walks alongside us and guides us on what we can do. I think Bill saw something in me worth saving. I was owed nothing, but I got a second chance. Now it's up to me to decide what I'm going to do with his offer.

To paraphrase American trumpeter Miles Davis, it can take you years to learn how to play like yourself. I had finally figured out how to play myself and be myself. I had the fire in me, but it was dormant. I had a crazy motor and it needed fuel. It needed a direction. I had no direction. Bill gave fuel and direction. My Appā, who was very thoughtful, had given me a basic understanding of how a society functions and prepared me for life in Canada. Bill continued that education by showing me the nuances of business life.

Yes, he is still my mentor.

༈𝍡 THE TRAVELLING SALESMAN

Bill wasn't the only one who took a chance on me. In fact, the day I rashly quit CI was the day Sue pushed all her chips into the middle of the table.

While I was cooling down and second-guessing myself, I was also waiting in my little Mazda for Sue to finish work. She was working for an institutional money manager and making more money than I was.

I had no plan when I quit. I needed one in a hurry. And I couldn't do that without Sue.

She had a plan immediately. She said, "Go to school full-time. I will support you." Just like that. I thought she would be annoyed by my impulsive decision to throw away my career and everything I had accomplished. She had been annoyed in the past by my hasty and reckless ways. I grew up with the unconditional support of both my parents, and with Appā as the strong centre in my family. Without him, I lacked confidence. Leaving CI, the place that had anchored me in Canada, left me rudderless. Sue was my rudder.

When you grow up in an awful war environment like I did, nothing in this world happens by coincidence. That's for sure. Sue was always supportive of me. Next to Bill, she was the only person who could make me listen to reason. She was the common denominator in my success. I knew it from the very first time we met; I knew she was the one. During this vulnerable phase of my life, Sue's support lifted me. I am forever thankful. I will never forget who was with me when no one else was.

I've always appreciated strong women. And Sue is tougher than a night in prison. When she said she would be there for me in my weakest moment, I knew I wanted to be there for her forever. "I want to talk to your parents and tell them I'm interested in you." She agreed, though I thought she looked a bit nervous.

The date was set to meet the parents. As in my first job interview, I knew my resumé wasn't going to help me. No degree, no job, no prospects. I wasn't fooling myself: I knew I wasn't a great catch. Still, I didn't show up unprepared. I brought a cake for Sue's mother. And I ran a sales clinic on her father. Sue was their only child. I was expecting a full-on battery of tests.

Her father opened the door to greet me. I had been fretting all night. I put out my hand and introduced myself.

"I hear you are interested in my daughter," said the man who looked like he was very capable of burying my skinny ass in the front lawn. He was tall like Appā and physically fit. Though I was a cocky guy, I was a bit intimidated by him. Then he invited me in. The approach Sue and I were taking was not traditional in Tamil culture, at least back then. Traditionally, parents would be the ones discussing such matters and arranging the marriage. I left my Am'mā out of this. She wasn't happy about that. But I wasn't going to let anyone control my future. Not even my own mother. I was a control freak in a lot of ways.

Sue's father was ahead of his time, like my Appā would have been in this situation. He gave me his tacit approval. I suspected that Sue had already lobbied him on my behalf. His friendly manner and gestures indicated that he approved of me seeing his only child and daughter. Then he excused himself as he went off to play bridge with his friends. I thought if my Appā were alive, they would have made great bridge partners. Just thinking of the future reminded me that I would be going through it without my own father.

Sue's parents turned out to be more modern than I could have imagined. Soon I was living in their basement to save money. They had a nice-sized home in the city of Markham. Am'mā had moved to Denmark to be with my brother for six months. When she returned, she moved into a basement apartment, not too far from us.

Sue's mom was a great cook as well. I loved the fish buns she used to make. They reminded me of my childhood days at Hartley College. Sometimes her dad would cook. He was not bad either. I would eat upstairs and return downstairs again. I was studying full-time with Sue's support. We were becoming a family without making anything official. I wanted to make it official.

I had already spent everything I had on a ring. I was going to ask her to marry me. I was guarding that ring with great care. It was only a question of when and where. It would have been out of character for me to wait long. I just wanted to get the ring on this gal's finger.

I may not be fond of planning, but I did plan this. I took her to Jamaica. We hadn't been there long before I found the captain of the daytime crew at the hotel and asked him if he could organize a sunset cruise for the two of us. He obliged. But said, "It's not allowed, mon. Dem, don't allow dis." The hotel prohibited its staff from doing business directly with the guests. Still, he was all aboard to help. He reminded me of my good buddy Winston from L'Amoreaux. He was warm, just like my pal from Scarborough. "You want to axe har de question?" said the man.

That evening, there was a knock at the door just before sunset. I opened it to find a young man ready to take us to the boat. This was it. My future was about to be decided. Sue may say no, I reminded myself. My heart settled in my throat.

As we walked along the beach, the sun was bathing everything in the peach light of late afternoon. The brilliant blue ocean stretched out to the orange of a cloudless horizon. Most of the vacationing white

folks we saw all had coconut-brown faces. Some were still working
on their tans. They were trying to get to our colour. They had to work
hard at it. We were the privileged ones; we were born with a brown
face. Brown privilege!

The salty tang of the breeze and the squabbling of the gulls took
me back to Point Pedro Ocean Road and my bike rides with Appā in
the evenings. Would Appā have liked Sue? He'd always wanted a
daughter. Would she be the daughter that he never had?

The captain was already on the boat in his civilian clothes. I have
to admit I was a little disappointed by his humble vessel. I had imagined something a little more glamorous. But the fellas had brought
music and flowers on the boat. We stepped quietly on-board for what
she thought was no more than a sunset cruise.

I couldn't help fishing nervously around in my pocket to make sure
that the ring was still there—to ensure the presence of this simple thing
that in a few short moments could determine my future. It was ready
to be put on the finger of the woman I loved and cared so much for.
And hopefully there it would remain, continuing to gleam on that
beautiful brown finger.

We set out to sea. The sun slowly stitched itself into the ocean's
horizon, hemmed by the glowing clouds. That was my cue to go down
on my knees and ask this beautiful girl (both inside and out) to marry
me. If only I could find the strength to say the words out loud.

I knelt. She had to have known. Her deep-brown eyes shimmered
under the sunset. I took her soft hand, gave it a little squeeze, and
pitched my case.

She said yes. I was bumping against the walls of heaven. Life is a
glorious mosaic!

Sue had stood by me through tough times and acted as a pillar of
strength—and now she would be by my side forever.

A year later, we got married.

It was a traditional wedding. A traditional Tamil wedding is steeped in Hinduism and filled with ancient customs and rituals—a vibrant and colourful religious ceremony of the physical, spiritual, and emotional union of two people and the coming together of two families through celebration. The religious ceremony lasts for almost three hours. Appā used to joke that the reason for this was to discourage people from marrying again. And a Tamil wedding concludes once the groom ties the thāali (a thick and elaborate gold chain) around the bride's neck. Our wedding was a big event with close to eight hundred family members, distant relatives, and friends from around the globe in attendance. That may sound like a lot, but it's not an especially large number for a Tamil wedding.

A bride is one of the most celebrated icons of the Tamil culture. Sue presented a stunning picture of bridal beauty and elegance. She was draped in a beautiful and traditional silk saree in bright red with contrasting borders and gold thread woven into lush designs. She wore gorgeous gold jewellery, primarily family heirlooms passed through generations. Her hair was in an elaborate plait and bun combination around which white and orange flowers were draped. The ornament around her waist known as Oṭṭiyāṇam (*belt*) was made of solid gold with temple designs and kept the saree border and garland in place. A Tamil bride also wears a special ornament on her Netṟi (*forehead*) on both sides of the central hair parting. Sue looked stunning. I hit the jackpot. I never imagined this was in the cards for me when I was in prison. But here I was.

My two worlds came together at the wedding. Though I wasn't working there at the time, CI was still my family. When we were planning the wedding, I got dressed as though I was going to work and made my way to the office to invite the people who had changed my life. It was weird to be back on the elevator. I had to admit I missed the place and the sense that I had been part of building something. I missed the action. I couldn't help feeling that I had dropped the ball.

But I was in love, and I was getting married. That didn't leave much room for regret.

I made my way to Mr. McRae's office to give him my news and to request his presence. His response was to growl, "And what about Mrs. McRae?"

I stammered that she was invited too. Then he produced his chequebook and wrote down a number that would basically pay for the reception. I protested. No handouts. "Mr. McRae, I can't. I didn't invite you just so—"

"Shut up—what's your wife's name? Sue? It's not for you. It's for Sue, okay?"

Mr. McRae was there on the big day, sitting in the front row with his wife. Ray Chang was there too. Bill was away. The biggest difference between Canada and Sri Lanka isn't the climate. Even that pales in comparison to the difference in the way groups interact with one another. I wasn't so shocked by the snow or by the lung-numbing cold in the winter. What bowled me over was the kindness of Canadians.

We had a nice honeymoon in the Caribbean. Then we were faced with the realities of life. Sue was the breadwinner. She went to work, and I went to U of T. I was supposed to take care of my girl, not the other way around. It weighed on me. My father had laid down the rules: no handouts. And here I was, supported by my wife. But she was my wife. That should be okay, I figured.

Sue worked for two. Never home. Always working. All I did was study. And work out. Twice a day. Sue had once blurted out that she liked men with a good physique. So, I decided I was going to put on some muscle. (I also decided to work on my swagger, but physique comes first, then swagger, that was my theory.) I was 120 pounds soaking wet. My goal was to put on seventy pounds—mostly muscle. Maybe people might take me seriously then.

I was going to transform myself. Would it work? Who cares! It was worth a try. I had signed up for GoodLife Fitness. I imposed some misery on my life. I worked out very early in the morning and again at night, every day. No break.

I was a gym rat. I had an insane daily workout routine. I followed many well-known weightlifters' routines, especially Arnold Schwarzenegger's muscle-building workouts, which included an intense high volume and frequency approach to training. It worked, by the way. I got so strong that I was able to shoulder press one-hundred-pound dumbbells with no spotter. I was doing biceps curls with an Olympic bar with forty-five-pound plates and bench-pressing 315 pounds. I gained seventy pounds, mostly muscle. I was crushing it in the gym. It was pure hard work and dedication. When I put my mind to something, I will not rest until I achieve my goal. It becomes an obsession. I liked the extremes. I never did moderation; I didn't even respect it. It's a curse and a blessing. It may not always make me a great husband or son-in-law.

Or a cheap son-in-law. I was consuming six thousand calories a day, enough for two large adults. I ate six times a day, every three hours. I often raided Sue's parents' fridge at night, like a raccoon.

At university, I was crushing it as well. I studied hard. And I was getting great marks. Financially, we weren't rich, but we were at least on a good trajectory, thanks to a strict budget. We allocated twenty-five dollars per week for entertainment. It was enough to pay for two stuffed Guyanese chicken rotis. I loved those. Plus three Coors Light beers and a movie rental. That was our Saturday night.

Everything seemed to have fallen into place. But we were still struggling with our relationship. I shouldn't say *we*. I could not have been a dream husband in those days. Despite all that I had to be thankful for, I was crumbling.

Each time Am'mā would have one of her episodes, everything would start to unravel, including my marriage. I felt helpless. I knew

I couldn't use loss as an excuse to destroy myself and my marriage. But I knew how to fuck up a good thing.

I was mad at the world and hated everyone. Even those who loved me. I became resentful. I had become a dangerous human, especially with my new-found muscular frame. Once during an argument with Sue, I put my fist through the wall. I scared the shit out of her. I didn't know how to deal with all this. I was alone and in the dark. I was resentful that I was a fatherless son, saddled with taking care of my deteriorating mother while living in my in-laws' basement. I knew crying never helped. I refused to cry. Instead, I resorted to anger. I let my anger be more important than anything else—that was my sin. I wasn't proud of it, but my resentment and anger were becoming unmanageable to the point that I was a threat to Sue. She never signed up for this.

Nor had her parents. We were living in their basement. I'm sure they heard our fights upstairs. They were probably wondering why they married their only precious daughter to this angry idiot. Once, after a huge blowout with Sue, I drove to the university and slept on a table. I was so mad that I could have hurt anyone who even looked at me the wrong way. But I also knew Sue was the only one who would put up with me. Most women would have divorced my sorry ass. She stuck it out.

I was in a very dark place. That was when I got the call from Bill. That call inviting me to lunch saved me and my marriage. When he offered me that job at CI, something that had been missing in my life fell into place. It changed the course of my life. Uncle Fernando had come at a crucial time to save my life in Sri Lanka. Bill secured my future in Canada.

Still, Bill would never have stuck his neck out for me if he thought I was going to be passive. He knew who I was and why I had left CI in the first place. I wanted to do better career-wise. Bill might have given me a chance, but I had to take it. Scared and nervous, I meekly asked my boss Peter, the new head of sales, if I could please get more responsibility in order to make more money. To my astonishment, he gave me a chance at wholesaling. It was a job for a gregarious, good-looking white man, not me. I had landed my dream job—the job Bill had when I was in the mailroom.

The position was highly sought after by all the junior salespeople. I was the only non-white hire in the department of eight or so internal sales staff. I was also the only one who didn't have a fancy network of contacts or influential parents. I didn't know how to play golf or have a membership at a private club. I never went to my parents' cottage on the weekends. I came from the other side of the planet. In that sense, I was deeply unqualified for the job.

I was certainly not set up to be successful in this new sales role without at least some of these attributes. I would have certainly stuck out like a sore thumb. That is probably why Bill, after he heard of my promotion, came in and said, "I don't believe you will be good at sales. But you are smart, and you should be an investment analyst with Gerry Coleman." Gerry was Canada's most sought-after money manager and he'd just joined CI. But I'd always wanted to be in sales. I liked the glamour of it. I wanted to be like Bill. But Bill felt that I was set up to fail given that I didn't fit the profile of a salesman. Why do people always underestimate me? I steeled myself to prove Bill wrong about this.

I'm not afraid of failure. It's hardwired into me: I will try anything. I will risk anything. I feel I have nothing to lose.

The job offer came with a catch: I had to move to Vancouver. Sue had a solid job in Toronto. I wasn't sure if she would agree. Plus, she was an only child. Would she want to be four thousand kilometres and three time zones away from her parents? When I broke the news, she said, "Mother CI has never let us down. Let's do this." I was thrilled. She was always supportive of me. I knew I'd married the right gal.

This also gave us a chance for a fresh start in our marriage, which may have been Sue's chief motive to leave Toronto, despite losing her job.

My Am'mā was worried about our decision to move. She felt like she wouldn't have any support. Despite my assurances that I would continue to support her financially, she wasn't happy. I could see her concerns, but at that moment, I had to live for me and my new family. I wanted a future. I wanted to leave my past behind. Am'mā was still living in the past. I had to take the job. I was tough. It didn't matter how hard it was emotionally or how guilty I felt.

I hopped on a plane in July 1998 by myself. Sue was going to follow me a few months after. I was on my way to Vancouver with just a sleeping bag, and I felt like a new immigrant again. I was terrified. I couldn't fail. I couldn't let Sue down. I had to prove to Bill that I was capable. I wanted to be the best at this craft. I was determined.

I had only been to Vancouver once before on a work trip. I'd met Russ Isaac, an industry veteran who owned a well-known investment dealership named Great Pacific. He was friends with Mr. McRae. Mr. Isaac was a gentleman and gave this kid some time for a chat. I remember meeting him and thinking, Wow, what a well-dressed man. He was nice too. In conversation, he told me I should be in sales. "And move out here, you will do well." That was what had started it all. He died on March 28, 2011, at the age of eighty-two. I went to his funeral to pay my respects to the man who kickstarted my sales career.

On the plane, I had a few screwdrivers to calm my nerves about the move. I had moved up from Heinekens and was ordering drinks with ease. I was looking out the window as we were flying over the Rockies. I'd never seen them before. The view was absolutely stunning: the jagged rock contrasted with the smooth contours of gleaming summer snow.

The peaks pierced the sky, but I bet the foot of the mountain was covered in fog and mist, like my life once was. But I was laser-focused now, like the arrow tips of mountain peaks. No matter where I went,

I observed nature—it was always there. It always made me calm. Growing up in Point Pedro, I enjoyed the ocean. The waves made me calm and anxious at the same time. I always had waves of emotion; when they crashed on the rocks of life, I became calm. But I found myself starting to appreciate mountains more.

Coming from the concrete canyon of Toronto, I was in awe at my glimpse of the heaven-grasping apex of the snow-drenched mountain-top in the brilliant summer sun. I know everything happens for a reason, but sometimes I wish I knew what that reason was. The early struggles of my life pushed me away from my country of birth. Then I had to quickly grow up in Canada without a father while caring for my ill mother and now struggling to be a better husband. All the while, I was suppressing my sadness and nightmares. A decade after coming to Canada, my dream of living for two people, to make up for the life Appā never had, hadn't come true yet. I had anxiety about coming up short on my promise. I often felt inadequate. Conquering my personal mountain was something I battled every day. But I could do it if I stayed focused and was not distracted by the noise around me.

As the plane descended into Vancouver, I realized I'd had one too many screwdrivers. It was Saturday evening when I got into the closet-sized condo I'd rented in Yaletown, without a single piece of furniture. I only had my sleeping bag and suitcase. It felt like I was starting all over again.

There was no going back to Toronto. I had to succeed. I had to prove anyone who ever doubted me wrong. Especially Am'mā's relative and the owner of the factory. Strangely, even Bill. It was a long list. I was going to figure out how to silence their doubts. I would push myself to the ultimate level. I would go through everything in my head—all the vulnerabilities, insecurities, flaws, sales plans—and then show my bravado and sometimes a smile.

I aspired to be the best vice-president of sales British Columbia had ever seen. I was only twenty-nine years old. I didn't know what the title meant, but my Am'mā sure was proud of me. I did have to explain to her repeatedly that I wasn't working for the Canadian Imperial Bank of Commerce, CIBC, but for CI in B.C.

Traditionally, Tamils in Sri Lanka preferred jobs in government or banking because they meant stability. Now, many Tamil youngsters are risk-taking entrepreneurs. What an amazing transition, in just one generation.

I'm not sure if Am'mā was still proud after I clarified that I wasn't working for a bank. She called me every day to tell me that she was sad that I wasn't close by. I would tell her that I needed to do this for everyone. They were tough conversations. She felt abandoned by me. It was sad knowing that.

Ever since my father's death, the pain inside of me had been growing day after day. Piece by piece, it built up a fire in my heart. I dreamed of success. My ambition to succeed in life grew stronger day by day. However, something did not feel right. The ghost of my past kept hounding me. The hole that was left in my heart made me feel so empty and lonely. So many questions were in my mind with no answers. Knowing my mom was in this condition broke my heart. She meant a lot to me, but she didn't think I cared so deeply about her. We were both from a teardrop-shaped island, and countless are the tears that we shed. I was still seeing that through my Am'mā. My past followed me wherever I went.

But it was time for me to get laser-focused.

The following Monday morning, I had my first meeting with a client. It was at his office at nine. I practised all my pitches in front of the mirror that Sunday. In the early days, I still spoke with little bit of an accent; it has since faded so as to be almost imperceptible. I would sometimes nervously alter my word choices to avoid embarrassment. Sometimes, like most Tamils speaking English, I would switch V and W, so "market volatility" would become "market wolatility." To avoid this, I would say "market fluctuations." I would diligently go through my speaking notes to replace any word starting with V.

My job required that I do lot of one-on-one or group presentations, but I was terrified of public speaking. I was self-conscious. Before the first meeting of my career, I stopped by our small office in the Scotia Tower on West Georgia Street. Only six people worked out of our Vancouver office. We had a very small operation in Western Canada. We were trying to expand there and had about two billion dollars in assets under management at the time.

"I won't allow anyone to crush my confidence, I will be strong, I could do this," I kept saying as I walked into the first meeting of my new career. I shook hands with my first client and exchanged the standard pleasantries. The topic of the morning was opportunities in the Canadian equity market.

The meeting had been set for an hour. About fifteen minutes into it, I could clearly see by his body language that the client had tuned me out. I stopped and asked him, "What do you expect from someone like me in terms of information?" in an effort to salvage the meeting. "Quite frankly, not much," he replied abruptly. Immediately my confidence was crushed. A lamb! That was an absolute gut punch.

That was the end of the meeting. My first meeting. On my very first day. A colossal failure. Where did I go wrong? Did I look too overconfident and arrogant? Was I overdressed? I was in my three-piece suit in the summer. Maybe that was it. Quite frankly, I still don't know.

What I do know is that nine out of ten human interactions are not memorable. Common sense is herd mentality; it represents the lowest common denominator thinking. We need to have *uncommon* sense to win in life. I had to learn to differentiate myself in an uncommon way, by creating unique content and using methods that were memorable and engaging. There was no point trying to fit in. Doing so would spell failure. No one ever made a difference by being like everyone else.

I needed to embrace my unique attributes to stand out—not be just another sales guy in a suit. I remembered Appā's sage advice, "You can have the best idea, but if you don't know how to express that idea to others, then you have *no* idea." Good communication skills are like laws of physics: they apply everywhere. I needed to work on this.

In other words, sales is hard.

I signed up for Dale Carnegie's sales training program to learn how to give effective presentations. I researched a lot on the subject of body language in order to better read unspoken feedback from my audience. I applied discipline to my meeting process: among many other things, my daily morning workout routine became vital to me; it put me in the correct frame of mind in the early hours. It affected my mood and productivity positively for the whole day. I was like a boxer training for a prizefight.

A boxer has to be confident, but I'm guessing he feels a little fear too. How could you not feel some fear of failure with your career and reputation on the line in a confrontation in front of a crowd? I certainly felt fear. I was looking over my shoulder. I was definitely thinking about everyone who had ever underestimated me. I was also thinking about those who had put their trust in me. I wanted to be sure they hadn't overestimated me. I was thinking of my father. I started working on Sundays to prepare for the upcoming week, while my competition was resting. Even after all these years, I still do.

My hard work was paying off. I was starting to get good traction with the financial advisor community and getting referrals. My regional manager noticed a huge improvement in my sales, and they continued to tick up.

I wanted to run my own race. To be content in life, you need to benchmark yourself against yourself—not against others. If I compare my life to others, I will always be miserable. There will always be people who are richer, smarter, faster, stronger, more successful than me. I can't try to equalize the outcome by bringing them down to my level. I win by pushing myself up to a higher level, by my own actions, if possible.

The better question everyone must ask is, "Am I better off today than I was a year ago?" If yes, then good. Keep going. If no, then investigate. Why aren't you? I set myself a rule that I never wanted to be in the same role for more than a decade. I must keep changing. To improve is to change. As the responsibility got bigger, my time in the role got closer to the upper limit of ten years.

At that time, the dot-com boom was lifting all boats. I was cooking with gas. It was a prosperous time for me and everyone in the office. We often went out on Thursday nights as a team to celebrate. Camaraderie was at an all-time high. The executives in Toronto were very happy as well. We were minting money. But I was travelling a ton to meet clients and attend investment conferences, and I didn't see Sue for months at a time. When she was home, I wasn't home. When I was home, she wasn't home. I was either on a plane or in the car all the time. Sometimes I would wake up in Kelowna for breakfast, have lunch in Victoria, and dine and sleep in Prince George. Those were analogue years, and we would leave each other yellow sticky notes on the fridge, doors, and everywhere else in the tiny condo.

My work took me to glamorous places and hotels, and some not-so-glamorous ones. I would be at the Ritz-Carlton in Laguna Beach, Santa Barbara, or Maui one day, and two weeks later at the Travelodge in Campbell River by the side of the highway next to a methadone clinic.

One night someone tried to break into my room. I was up all night. I couldn't sleep. I was slowly starting to become soft. I would catch myself complaining about the view from my room to the front-desk person, forgetting about my time in prison or sleeping in the belly of the cargo ship in filth. Then I would be ashamed of myself. The comforts of my life were starting to change me, and I had to remain on high alert to make sure I stayed grounded. The minute I realized my job wasn't glamorous, I started to become pretty well adjusted to my profession.

I also had the opportunity meet many Hollywood celebrities during my travels—the likes of Samuel L. Jackson, Robert Duvall, Ben Affleck, Sean Penn, Billy Bob Thornton, and Matt Damon. If this book were ever made into a movie, I'd like Matt Damon to play me. We are similar in stature. But he probably would have to get a serious tan for the role.

Once I was at the Coast Hotel in Prince George, and I saw a guy standing outside having a smoke. I recognized him from the movies. I approached him and said, "Didn't you play the scary dude from *Con Air*?"

"Yes, that would be correct," he replied.

It was Danny Trejo. He was in town to shoot *Reindeer Games*. We had a smoke together. He was really a nice guy, unlike the mean characters he played in the movies.

Then there were those who pretended to be nice in public but privately were horrible human beings. I met one such person in the Hotel Fairmont lobby in Winnipeg. He is a famous Canadian climate crusader, a nice guy on TV. I witnessed him reaming out a young woman at the hotel reception. He brought her to tears. This man was a bully—very impressed with himself and he had a sense of entitlement. I hated bullies.

"I guess you feel like a big man by scaring this young woman, don't you?" I shouted at him.

"Mind your business," he shouted back at me.

"I am," I said, even louder.

By now, a few people were watching us, expecting us to throw down. He came close to me. He was in my space. My wartime PTSD began playing out in my head. In my world, once that domino drops, there would be no discussion. I could never unring that bell. I clenched my fist and was about to give him one of my solid right hooks. Before I took a swing, some random guy got in between us. I'm thankful for that guy. A personal disaster averted.

That night in the room, when I looked at myself in the mirror, I didn't like the person who looked back. I was becoming arrogant and aggressive. I was losing my cool often. I was always trying to prove something. Even with Sue, my tone was rough and dismissive. I was impressed with myself. For a guy who hated bullies, I was slowly turning into one. I was treating my subordinates and my colleagues badly.

I tried to understand myself. I wanted to be a victor. But I behaved like a victim. I was always thinking that when something didn't go my way, it was someone else's fault. I argued for my weaknesses. Winners don't behave that way.

But I was always willing to learn, listen, and change. I would never convince myself of my own delusions and never try to rationalize my obscene ideas into palatable ones. So, I wanted to guard against hubris because I knew it would lead to delusions of grandeur. An audit of myself was warranted—no matter how unpleasant it might be. I had to jump through crappy hoops to get here. I thought it was time for me to get professional help. Lorraine, my former manager, a good friend, and now CI's head of human resources, recommended a psychologist in Vancouver. I started working with him to hopefully conquer my demons.

In 1999, my mentor Bill Holland became the CEO of CI. I was thrilled. The dot-com boom was still on and we had the right investment products. CI's sales went through the roof—so did mine. I was working even harder. I liked the money. I was hammering home big quarterly commission cheques. I took 100 percent of my sales commissions and bonuses in stock or options. Why? I wanted to increase my ownership in the company.

With Bill at the helm, I knew this was the right call. CI stock was on a tear. In October 2000, the board of directors approved a two-for-one stock split of the common shares of CI. Two more two-for-one splits ensued. I also invested my savings into hot technology stocks.

The guy who barely had money to buy Coors Light a few years earlier was now drinking expensive Napa vintages. Sue and I were eating at Vancouver's best establishments. Unlike in the past, we ordered food without glancing at the prices on the menu.

I could buy my own Armani, Brioni, Canali, and Zegna ties. I gave the ties I wasn't using to junior sales staff. This, on some level, made me feel like I was Bill. Made me feel good.

Every day, my report card would come in the form of an overnight sales email. Even when it was positive, I didn't feel glorious euphoria; it was more relief and then I was off thinking of how to win the next day. I was constantly paranoid.

My tech investments were up, CI stock was up, and all my stock options were in the money. I was making a lot of money. I was barely thirty and already a millionaire—on paper. I made a spreadsheet and tracked it daily.

Many years ago I was only eating once a day, because that's all I could afford. Only some time ago, I had spent my nights in a sleeping bag. Now I was money obsessed. I was living for two. I wanted to make sure I didn't lose my money. This was a hard-won battle. This one was for Appā. Getting wealthy was like a drug addiction to me. I loved the high I got from seeing my net worth increase. I doubled down and borrowed money from banks to increase my exposure to the stock market. I was addicted. I was irrational with money and had an unhealthy relationship with it. And completely unaware of the impending financial doom I was about to face.

Between 1995 and 2000, equity market valuations grew exponentially. The technology-dominated NASDAQ index rose from under 1,000 to more than 5,000 between the years 1995 and 2000. "Irrational exuberance," said Federal Reserve Board chairman Alan Greenspan in a speech given at the American Enterprise Institute during this time. That was a signal that monetary contraction was about to happen. That phrase was a warning that the stock market might be overvalued. "You

These are the people who shaped me and set me on my way, my Appā and Am'mā. Looking at these pictures now, I am struck by how different the world I grew up in was from the one I came to inhabit. But their notions of hard work and the pursuit of excellence travelled very well from Sri Lanka to Canada, even if I had my own culture shock.

The photo above captures my exuberance at the end of my first week in the mail-room at what was then called Universal Savings. I was on top of the world. The photo on the right is of one of the people there who made me feel welcome, who helped me get settled in Canada, the incredibly generous, brilliant Ray Chang, who also helped me with my math homework after business hours.

Courtesy of Donette Chin-Loy Chang

It is impossible to talk about my life here in Canada or to talk about CI without shining the spotlight on my mentor, cheerleader, disciplinarian, and friend, Bill Holland. When he was a young salesman, Bill gave me encouragement, great advice (and much-needed constructive criticism), and some spectacular ties. This was us in 1989 at the office Christmas party and now. Yes, he is still my mentor.

Our tragedies befall us out of the blue, and so do our blessings.
I can't believe I deserve a wife as wise, patient, and beautiful as
Sue—so I can only conclude that I am extraordinarily lucky. We have
been together almost as long as I have been in Canada. She is my
pillar of strength.

I saw the very worst of human nature during my time in prison—murder, torture, and the basest hatred. And yet, the man who saved me was an officer in the armed forces that brutalized the Tamils. He was also my father's best friend. Colonel Dudley Fernando was a brave, courageous man, and I grew up calling him "Uncle." His example showed me that for the truly brave men and women, human decency trumps ethnic chauvinism. The photo on the bottom left is Uncle Dudley on his wedding day. The one on the bottom right is me with his widow, "Aunty" Swarṇā, when I visited her in 2002.

Courtesy of Sanjaya Fernando

Courtesy of Sanjaya Fernando

My father taught me to go through life making a difference. Along the way, I've met others who approach the world the same way. In the top photo is Robert Orr, the Canadian consular officer who approved my application in 1988 to come to Canada. I've never forgotten him, and managed to reconnect in 2017. In the photo on the above left is Second World War RCAF combat veteran and former CI colleague Del Budd, who saw more of human brutality than I ever did, but never stopped inspiring others. We named a sales award after him at CI. And in the photo on the above right is my good friend and client Brian Hein. The only quiet thing about Brian is his immense generosity. When I started out in Western Canada it was people like him who trusted me and gave me a chance. To me, that openness is what Canada is all about.

Courtesy of Gnane Buwan Gnanendran

The top photo is of a plaque in Point
Pedro, bearing an ideological slogan of
the Sri Lankan government. My own life
shows how meaningless those words are.
The photo on the above left is the last
ever taken of my family in 1980 before
ethnic violence tore us apart forever. The
one on the above right is of my mother,
who arrived in Canada shortly after I did,
as a young widow.

I have had my mountains to climb. We all do. And whether we like it or not, our families are a huge part of that ascent. When Aaron was born, my life became focused on guiding him with the same assurance my own father showed me. The tie my father gave me at the Colombo airport the last time I ever saw him remains to this day a symbol of the challenges he set out for me to rise to. And I am proud that Aaron, Sue, and I had the privilege to summit Mount Kilimanjaro in honour of my mother on August 26, 2019. One more challenge we accepted as a family.

never fight the Fed," they say in our business, but I was too naive. I was levered up as far as I could be.

Things started to change in 2000, and the bubble burst between 2001 and 2002 with equities entering a bear market. Stocks I owned dropped as much as 85 percent. CI stock also came down drastically. My options were out of the money overnight. I was forced to sell my holdings—including Amazon—to meet my daily margin calls. That call occurs when a trader's brokerage balance drops below the minimum equity amounts mandated by margin requirements. So, I had to quickly deposit more cash or securities into my account. If I didn't, the firm could begin liquidating my positions to cover margin requirements.

Whenever I received a phone call from my stockbroker, my heart beat fast. I knew it was a margin call and I had to come up with more money to meet it. A resource I was quickly running out of. I was under enormous pressure. I was embarrassed to admit to Sue that I had lost it all. When I told her, she was remarkably calm and said, "We are young, and we can make it back." That made me feel better. But I stopped watching and reading financial news. It was mental torture. But still better than the physical torture I'd received in the prison. The market sell-off continued.

I went from a few million dollars net worth to negative net worth in a few weeks. I had a big loan at TD Bank. The loan was bigger than my CI holdings. I was broke. There is a saying in the investment business: "Bulls make money, bears make money, and the pigs get slaughtered." I got slaughtered. I was greedy as a pig. I had committed the cardinal sin of not following the adage "To become rich, you must specialize; to stay rich, you must diversify." Pigs aren't diversified.

It felt unreal as I saw everything evaporate. And my money obsession created an emotional indifference in me, replacing love and gratitude for people. It changed me. My money was a manifestation of power, and that power I felt was a manifestation of my fear, the fear of failure. So, could I be free of fear without money? At some deep level, despite losing it all, it felt liberating. It was a very strange feeling. Not that I disliked money after losing it, but I disliked the person I became in the presence of it.

On July 23, 2001, after a long day of meetings in Kelowna—a city on Okanagan Lake in the Okanagan Valley, wine country in the southern interior of British Columbia—I went back to the hotel. The phone rang. My other world was on the other end of the line. It was my good friend and former Hartley classmate Ronnie, sounding jubilant. "The Tamil Tigers attacked the Sri Lankan military planes at the international airport." It was music to my ears. These were the same flying killing machines that had rained terror on my family in Point Pedro.

"Good riddance," I replied to Ronnie.

The attack marked the anniversary of the day Sinhalese mobs killed over three thousand Tamils in July 1983, pouring gasoline on the smoldering tensions that would explode into civil war. The LTTE chose the date symbolically. Revenge was part of their manifesto. And mine too. If the Tamil Tigers wanted to blow up the aircraft that had terrorized my family, that was fine by me.

To be clear, I had no interest in revenge against the Sinhalese majority. For me, the civil war has never been an ethnic conflict—though I know that is the shape it inevitably took. It was not the Sinhalese who were guilty of the atrocities. It was the Sri Lankan government. I have amazing Sinhalese friends, especially the Fernando family who were nothing but heroically humane amidst all the hatred and violence. I knew Uncle Fernando's son Sanjaya was in the air force; I hoped he was okay. We had been pals from a young age. The Fernandos had also suffered enough from this war; it wasn't just the Ratṇavēls. I didn't want any harm done to them. I couldn't bear to see Aunty Swarṇā lose another son. Losing Milroy had been hard enough. It would break her heart. Yet, I couldn't have been happier to hear this news.

Around 3:30 a.m. on July 24, fourteen members of the LTTE Black Tiger squad, an elite suicide commando unit, had infiltrated the air base, located about thirty-five kilometres north of Colombo (my place of birth). This air base was connected to the airport I departed from in 1988 to find a better life in Canada. The airport that had all that over-the-top security. I had to go through all that nonsense to get here. How did these guys get through?

The Black Tigers had destroyed the electrical transformer to plunge the base into darkness. They then cut through the barbed wire surrounding the base to begin their assault. They used rocket-propelled grenades, anti-tank weapons, and assault rifles to attack the base. They destroyed eight military aircraft on the tarmac, including Mi-24 helicopters, Kfir fighter jets, and MiG-27 bombers. LTTE members then crossed the runway to the adjacent international airport, and began blowing up empty civilian planes.

This attack lasted for five hours. By the end, fourteen of the Black Tiger attack team had been killed, along with six Sri Lankan Air Force personnel and one soldier killed by friendly fire. No civilians were hurt. Between the cost of the destroyed aircraft and lost tourism, the total estimated economic damage was about one billion U.S. dollars. Sri Lanka was rocked! It was a national embarrassment. A total of twenty-six aircraft were either damaged or destroyed in the attack. This should stop the rain of bombs I'd experienced in Point Pedro, I remember thinking.

There can be no doubt that war and violence are deplorable. No one who has seen the fallout of grief and despair could ever contemplate war without horror. But there can also be no doubt that war and violence can be effective. Taking up arms is no guarantee that justice will prevail. But giving up without a struggle almost always ensures that the bully who starts the fight ends up winning it.

The airport attack was not only an act of revenge. It was also a towering political success. It brought the Sri Lankan government to the negotiating table, where it agreed to an internationally monitored ceasefire brokered by Norway. That opened the door to the first full-scale peace talks in seven years. This ceasefire was widely regarded as the best chance for peace there had been yet in this decades-old war, which had already cost many lives, including my father's, and severely held back the island's economy. A daring guerilla raid had proven to be Sri Lanka's best effort to give peace a chance.

I was back at the same hotel, Kelowna Grand, a few months later. I always asked for the same room every time. It was home away from home. I woke up at 5:30 to get ready for the gym. As always when I woke up, I turned on the TV. I heard the news of a "small" plane that rammed into the World Trade Center. Initially, like everyone else, I didn't think much of it. I got into my workout gear and went down to the gym. While I was on the treadmill, I saw the second plane going into the building.

Al-Qaeda had attacked America. It was a terrible tragedy that killed many innocent lives. An assault on freedom and democracy. I was horrified by the grief and trauma I knew would follow in the attack's wake. Seeing this horror unfold hit me hard. The Tamil freedom struggle I was supporting had also taken many innocent lives. I was very conflicted.

Tamils were fighting for freedom, not against it. But doesn't every armed group say the same thing? And does anyone care what their enemy's real intentions are? "If you are not with us, then you are against us"—that's how George W. Bush put it, as the U.S. prepared to fight for its freedom.

I knew full well that all armed struggles against governments would be lumped together as one. I knew that the Tamil freedom struggle was over. The Tamil Tigers would be seen as terrorists.

And let's be clear: the Tamil Tigers may have deserved to be called terrorists. Their tactics could be reprehensible too. The LTTE was a brutal organization out of necessity, and sometimes committed terrorist acts, including some of the worst suicide bombings on record, which killed innocent Tamils and Sinhalese. They were banned in most Western nations in the post-9/11 world as a result.

But there is no law in life or nature that says a group may commit atrocities against another with impunity, without consequences. To that end, I thought that sometimes the Tamil Tigers weren't ruthless enough. The law can't defend terrorists against terrorists. Throughout history, occupying forces have met violent resistance from indigenous populations, because it is human nature to resist occupation with all means available so that one can live with freedom and dignity.

Sri Lanka took on a known enemy and screamed foul when it struck back. The pain Sri Lanka had to endure was appalling, but it doesn't make a martyr of Sri Lanka, nor—much as one might like—does it sweep away all arguments about the ambiguities of Sri Lanka's participation in its own downfall. Until Tamils are granted their basic human rights and treated like human beings, the violence will continue. Anyone who thinks otherwise needs to reread their history books.

But knowing what is right, or even what is inevitable, does not undo the damage of war. It won't put one brick back on top of another to rebuild shattered towns and villages, and it won't heal wounds. It can only fuel the resolve of those who resist. This is one of the most grotesque consequences of aggression. It perverts a sense of justice into something that can only create injustice. I could see that clearly because my own life had been shaped by that corrosive violence. I had lost nearly as much as I could bear. I had been sent to Canada to spare me from the undertow of hatred that was sucking Sri Lanka into a whirlpool. But my life could have taken a different, darker path.

I had two friends involved in the airport attack. I was not sure if Sanjaya was there at the time, and I hoped that he wasn't. But my good friend Ravishankar—*nom de guerre* Charles, a Hartley boy who I'd sat next to at my tutor's and played cricket with—was the mastermind of this attack. He was an incredibly smart and affable kid. He dedicated his life to the Tamil liberation cause—rightly or wrongly. He joined the LTTE in December 1985 while still at Hartley College. This same kid, if he had made it to Canada, could have founded a billion-dollar company. Instead, he had become a brilliant military tactician and what some would call a terrorist. Our fates could easily have been swapped. He could have been sipping Opus One and riding a bull market in Canada, while I plotted guerilla attacks in Sri Lanka. I certainly don't think I'm a better person than Ravishankar.

Fourteen young Tamil men died to at least temporarily stop the reign of terror from the air. Could that be considered anything other than brave and selfless? Meanwhile, I was devastated by the losses to my stock portfolio. It wasn't even a fair comparison. I felt like a coward whining in the West, while these guys were laying down their lives.

There are no winners in war, only survivors. I'm one of the many survivors of the Sri Lankan war. Since I'd arrived in Canada, I had been living in two worlds. One with loss, grief, and endless misery. And the other with peace, prosperity, and profit. One was painful and the other, gratifying. I often struggled to reconcile the two and wondered why I'd never picked up arms like Ravishankar to fight against Sri Lankan tyranny. Killing would solve nothing, but giving up would also solve nothing. Ignoring Sri Lanka—one of my two worlds—was not an option for me any more. I had to find some other way to reconcile my two worlds and to do the right thing without taking up arms.

This got me engaged in the misunderstood Tamil freedom struggle; I wanted to be a voice in the West. In the absence of leadership, and to fit Appā's definition of courage—to go against the crowd—I wanted to shape the public narrative of the Tamil cause. Appā would have been appalled by my stance as he despised the Tamil Tigers. I started writing opinion blogs. I was engaging readers by writing letters to the editor. Appā would have been proud on that score, for sure. He had loved doing that about contentious topics of his era.

A peaceful society cannot exist until there is racial equality, or at least a genuine attempt to address the central issues, as Canada is attempting to do. When all else fails, armed response, as undesirable as it may seem, needs to take place in order to begin addressing the situation. The bottom line is this: like it or not, we live in a universe that rewards power, and power flows from confidence.

The winners of history are those who sound their barbaric yawps over the rooftops of the world, while the losers are the ones who cannot express themselves without an apology. And the one surefire way to make your life a series of defeats, miseries, and misfortunes is to constantly back away from even your most passionately held beliefs. The Tamil freedom struggle was centred on this. As a society, Tamils no longer could back away. I certainly wasn't going to back away.

I wanted to go to Sri Lanka during this ceasefire. I wanted to go and be inside the room of our ancestral home where Appā was killed. I wanted to have a conversation with him. I wanted to have the closure that I had been yearning for years. I wanted to help my people who had suffered the most during this prolonged war. Sue and I decided to visit Sri Lanka. This was a shocking decision on my part, because when I had boarded that KLM flight on April 18, 1988, and left Sri Lanka, I never thought I would ever go back to the country that had stripped away my basic rights and dignity. But I needed closure. My head needed help.

After two decades of tough times and false dawns, the foundations had been laid for a free and independent Tamil nation. As far as I could tell, the vast majority of Tamils in Sri Lanka, as well as Tamils abroad, were utterly convinced of the need to smash the oppressive rule over them—despite the Tamil Tigers' terrible tactics. Since the last big pogrom by Sri Lanka against Tamils in July 1983, they had not been able to repeat such atrocities against Tamils, fearing the Tamil Tigers' wrath.

Tamil Tigers were a deterrent, an antidote to Sri Lankan atrocities. This was the chief reason why many people like me morally supported them.

Maybe, just maybe, it was time for a string of good luck for my people, I thought as I packed my suitcase for Sri Lanka.

Would this trip finally fill my emptiness?

卌III

THE FATHER

As our plane descended into Colombo, my stomach was churning, like I'd had a bad meal. I was nervous and scared. I was returning to the land where I had been tortured at a very young age. The land where my father had been killed. I'd lived with nightmares for years. Now I was willingly walking into the landscape of my fears in waking reality.

Publicly I had criticized Sri Lanka. I knew Sri Lanka guaranteed freedom of speech—but it didn't guarantee freedom *after* speech. Sri Lanka's political opponents, insufficiently loyal followers, independent journalists, and people of the wrong ethnic background had a habit of winding up dead, imprisoned, or in exile from this "democratic" republic.

My public stance was that the Tamils in Sri Lanka were not interlopers or invaders, as they were often characterized by Sinhalese nationalists, but an ethnic group that had occupied North and East Sri Lanka for at least as long as the Anglo-Saxons had been in England. I was on the record stating, "Sri Lanka has been governed by leaders with a penchant for redrafting history. It is symptomatic of a country light years away from attaining true nationhood." This statement had made the rounds in Colombo circles. Naturally, I was worried about entering the country.

"The true greatness of a nation—like Canada—is its willingness to accord to all communities and offer status and dignity equal to the majority, in order to weld those diverse groups into a harmonious polity. In this joust, a leader with this vision is pivotal. Unless, and until, Sri Lanka can produce leaders who can realize that truth, and are willing to act on it, it will continue to be dismembered by conflict." This statement of mine could get me into real trouble. I knew that well, and Bill had even warned me against visiting Sri Lanka despite the ceasefire. This odyssey could turn deadly. I was with my young wife about to enter a land that uses rape as a weapon of war.

I didn't know how this was going to play out. This trip was partially fuelled by survivor's guilt and the need to find closure. Even though I was safely living in Canada, often I had nightmares of being captured and watching my friends die. I would feel guilty that I couldn't protect them. After my father's death, I felt I let him down. I knew full well I could not have done anything to stop any of this from happening, but it constantly punished me inside. The people who were still left standing were the survivors. I was one of them. Why me? Why not them? I often got the awful feeling that I was pitifully small, a particle caught up in a whirlpool of bad memories of my past. My hope was that this trip could in some way put an end to all this guilt by bringing closure to my tortured past. I needed to do whatever it took in order to live, like Appā had wanted me to. To live, I needed to put my past behind me.

But I didn't want to see the inside of a Sri Lankan prison. Once was one time too many. I had heard of journalists or people who spoke against the government being kidnapped in Colombo and bundled into a white van, only to be found later with their hands bound and a bullet wound to the head. I didn't want to end up like that.

The long flight from Vancouver to Singapore gave me plenty of time to think about what I'd got myself into. My mind was racing, my heart was pounding, and I started to panic on that Singapore Airlines flight.

To steady my heart, nerves, and panic, I ordered a double scotch on the rocks as I sat paralyzed in my seat. The menacing terror of Sri Lanka tightened its grip over my thoughts and sucked the very breath from my mouth. I was not scared, frightened, afraid, or worried. What I felt was beyond description.

"Are you okay?" Sue asked me as I gulped the scotch as if it was well-chilled Coca-Cola on a hot summer day. I could hardly hear her as my pulse beat loudly in my ears, blocking out her concern. My fear was a tangible, palpable force that crept over me and covered my face, immobilizing my thoughts. I'm sure she could see that. I cleared my throat and said, "I'm just fine." But she didn't believe me. She put her arm around my shoulders and said, "All will be well, don't worry."

I was really starting to understand my wife for the first time. How tough and resilient she could be in rough times. How pragmatic she could be when the chips were down. And what a pillar of strength she could be when I was absolutely gutted. She was an unrelenting woman with a strong commitment to her family. When we decided to go to Sri Lanka to take advantage of the ceasefire, there was a fire burning within her too. Her dad's brother was killed in the 1983 anti-Tamil riots. They cut him to pieces, and no one ever found her uncle's body. He left behind a very young daughter, an even younger son, and a distraught wife. This bothered Sue a great deal. I could feel it in our conversations, whenever she brought up this subject. So, when I suggested going back Sri Lanka, she was a more than willing participant.

A married couple staying together was extremely important in the Tamil community. My Appā and Am'mā had a turbulent relationship, but I was thankful they'd stuck it out for the kids' sake. Broken families tend to produce broken kids; I saw that then. If I ever became a parent, I vowed to stay together with Sue, despite whatever challenges, to raise our children together. Because government programs couldn't be a substitute for my absence as a father or hers as a mother. I would make sure to instruct my children not to focus on colour but character.

To help mould them into good human beings. Not humans who blame others. If I failed to do that, then I would have failed as a parent.

Despite these feelings, I never thought that I would actually be a parent. I never had the temperament. I never wanted to go through the motions. And, quite frankly, I never thought I could even have a kid. I had been tortured badly—I'd had electric rods used on my testicles, so I thought I would never be able to reproduce. I never wanted to confirm my worst fears by seeking medical tests. Also, I didn't want to bring a child into my world and be incapable of emotionally caring for them. I had my own issues to deal with emotionally. I was already a mediocre husband, so becoming a dad just wasn't in the cards.

Sue was more of a devout supporter of the Tamil Eelam (*homeland*) struggle than I was, even though she left the country when she was three years old. (Her dad worked in Africa and South America before coming to Canada.) She spoke Tamil with great difficulty, but in her heart she was a Tamil Tigress. When she spoke in Tamil, adult Tamils would make fun of her pronunciation. Tamils were used to the idea of the cultural mosaic and pride in our heritage by declaring that our kids are proud Tamils. But it is mistakenly defined by the ability to speak Tamil. I believe a person can honour their ancestry even when unable to speak the language.

Many young, second-generation non-Tamil-speaking Tamils I have met during my travels have exhibited a solid, quiet Tamilness that had nothing to do with traditional definitions and everything to do with belonging to a proud, rich culture. They were fierce in that feeling and did much to advance the Tamil cause. This, it seems to me, is crucial. Yes, I agree, Tamil language and Tamil identity are tied inextricably together. But Tamil, as an identity, does not just arise from a Tamil surname, the ability to speak Tamil, or a proper Tamil first name; it comes from values and pride from within. Our goal should be to raise our kids in such a way that they can move back and forth seamlessly between the dual identities and societies.

We arrived in Western nations and embraced the new ways of life to make a better future by working hard—at times by doing multiple jobs. A great sea change has happened within one generation. Tamil kids who were born in the Western world are juggling a heritage they were born into, that they were never really in tune with as offspring of Tamil parents born in Sri Lanka. And in Western countries, which they naturally belong to, they look different. Therein lies a specific kind of baggage for them. The hope is to blend the society in which they grow up with the society they would have been raised in if their parents had never left the old country in the first place.

I have always been in awe of the Jewish community and aware of the strong commonalities between the Jewish and Tamil communities. Just like Tamils, there are North American, European, and Australian Jews. Jews, just like Tamils, have been persecuted. And similar to Tamil, Hebrew is one of the oldest living languages in the world. Family values and a strong emphasis on education are hallmarks of the culture.

Tamils were called the "Jews of Asia," which to me was a badge of honour. While many Jews can't speak Hebrew or don't follow Jewish religious teachings, they are proud of their Jewish heritage and help their kids to embrace the culture without language or religious pre-requisites. Speaking the Tamil language is certainly a plus, but the absence of it is not a minus.

Despite the strong commonality with the Jewish people, anti-Semitic sentiments in certain pockets of the Tamil community were widely prevalent, and this troubled me. This may have had something to do with the fact that Israel's Mossad had trained Sri Lankan interrogators on how to extract information from Tamil prisoners. Or because of Kfir jets, an Israeli all-weather multi-role combat aircraft supplied to the Sri Lankan government that terrorized the Tamils. Or is it an innate instinct to dislike winners? Anti-Semitism is very prevalent in Western society now, and strangely, universities are the breeding ground for such hate. Despite persecution, the Jews are a successful minority.

Nothing would give me more pleasure than to see my Tamil community in a similar position one day. The global Jewish population is a lot smaller than the Tamil population. While the Jews possess a faith that can unite them; Tamils are united by language and a shared cultural and ethnic identity, but that bond is not nearly as powerful as faith. But Jews and Tamils have so much in common, both persecuted peoples from the oldest civilizations on Earth.

Touchdown. I was back in Sri Lanka. I couldn't believe it. The plane came to a complete stop. I heard the chorus of unfastening of seatbelts throughout the plane. But no one could deplane. We were informed that we had to wait for a Buddhist monk on board to deplane first. Then I noticed a bald, saffron-robed middle-aged monk exiting the first-class cabin, as Sri Lankan tradition dictates. Monks are given the utmost priority and comfort in this nation. Why is that? Isn't shaving your head a symbol of renunciation of worldly ego and possession? Isn't modesty the Buddha's purifying quality?

The reason the monks' hypocrisy irked me so much is that they had a direct hand in the demise of the country that was going out of its way to honour them like this. Just as Buddhists in Myanmar whipped up paranoid hatred against the Muslim minority in that country, they have always agitated against the Hindu Tamils in Sri Lanka. Their hate for Tamils is palpable. Their racist stereotypes and paranoid accusations helped to incite the violence against Tamils, which bitterly divided us. There would have been no civil war without incitement from the monks.

When we finally deplaned in Colombo, I was a bit apprehensive. The air was oppressively hot and thick. In the terminal, I noticed that everyone looked relaxed—including the Sri Lankan soldiers and police I once feared. I hadn't heard people speaking in Sinhalese since I left. I recalled the guards yelling commands at me in prison, which made me nervous. But we were able to get through security without a fuss. It seemed to me there had been more security when I left the country in 1988 than when I came back in 2002. Everyone was tired of the long war, perhaps. I was relieved to have cleared all the security without any hassle.

We went to the Oberoi Hotel (now known as Colombo Plaza Hotel). It was the hotel where my Appā took me for a celebratory dinner after I was granted an interview with the High Commission of Canada. When I was a young boy, I wanted to stay at this luxury hotel that was frequented by many well-to-do foreigners. Now I could afford it.

As we checked in, I could see the restaurant where Appā and I had dinner together, laughing and talking about silly stuff. It absolutely broke my heart. My knees buckled. All over the lobby of the hotel, people were cheerful and having a blast, and there I was filled with sorrow. The hotel walls had been painted recently, I could see that, but the windows sagged with age. Petals of fresh flowers were scattered throughout the building, each with its own story to tell. It was a great metaphor for how I felt at that very moment. I was the newly painted wall from Canada with the old sagging window called Sri Lanka, with a story to tell. Snap out of it, Roy. Don't be a victim, I told myself. Be like Appā, be a hard-headed person.

My Appā was a strong man, and his shoulder was there for me to cry on in my weakest times; he had words of wisdom for me during my darkest hour. My Appā had raised me to model him: stay strong, and not be a victim. People could say that the perfect father does not exist. I do not know if that is true. What I surely know is that my Appā was perfect for me. Could I be a great father like Appā was? Should we try for a child despite my potential infertility? Sue wasn't in a rush to have children either. For now, I needed to protect my wife and myself, help my people, and then get the hell out of Sri Lanka, so I could live my dad's dreams. I snapped out of it faster than I'd gotten lost in rumination.

Over the next few days, we visited a few relatives, but I was most looking forward to seeing my Sinhalese surrogate mother, Aunty Swarṇā Fernando. She was going to meet Sue for the first time. I would describe her to Sue all night, like a boy would talk about his own mother before his girlfriend met her. We went to my Daya Road home where I had grown up. A stray dog barked in the distance as the sun dropped from the horizon. I heard the dull revving of tuk-tuks mixed in with the usual variety of horns. It was exactly how I remembered it. Nothing had changed.

We got to the front gate of the Fernando home—forever my place of safety and coziness. It was shaded by a lush Jambu (*rose apple*) tree dusted with many ripe fruits in an attractive rich red colour. I remember climbing the tree with Aravinda, the youngest of the Fernando boys, to fetch a few fruits to eat. The home was white with metal grill windows, designed and painted to match the front gate. It was the same home, but it looked very, very different.

Aunty looked like herself, with her small frame, only older. Her hair had grown long and was starting to grey. She was happy to see us, but she looked defeated by life. She had lost her son Milroy to an LTTE ambush, her husband Dudley, and then young Suresh and Aravinda (who had been a year younger than me) to natural causes. How was this woman still standing? She had lost three of her six boys plus her husband. She was the toughest woman I knew.

She gave me a hug and a warm kiss, no different than when she first saw me after my release from prison. But this time, I wasn't a scared, smelly, skinny, child prisoner. Instead, I was a buff, confident, free man. "Putha, you look nice."

"Thank you, Aunty." I gave her a hug like I would my own mother. After all, she was my Sinhalese mom!

I introduced Sue to her, and they got along right away. How could Sue not like her? It is impossible not to like Aunty. They were laughing and joking like old friends. To this day, I'm glad I took pictures of them together; I still have them.

"Putha, why haven't you had any kids yet, after all these years?" she asked. I knew she would. She loved kids. It was a question my own mother asked me frequently, to my annoyance. But I couldn't tell Aunty that the torture her people had inflicted on me had likely made it impossible to have children.

I reflected on how the Fernandos had always been there for the Tamils at our darkest hour. Aunty was an incredible cook and had made an amazing spread for us. I missed Sri Lankan food so much, especially her food. But strangely I didn't miss Sri Lanka. Her eldest living son, Dilroy, and one of the twins, Sanjeeva, joined us with their family for dinner. Sanjaya, the Air Force man, couldn't make it. I was always conflicted by all this, but I was happy again to be with the Fernandos.

I was on a trip to reconnect with my Appā, and so I had tracked down the first love of his life. My Am'mā had mentioned her to me on a few occasions. She told me Appā was madly in love with her until he met Am'mā. I don't know why he changed his mind. Am'mā didn't know either. She came across an old love letter from his ex-girlfriend in his drawer and that's how she came to know about this other lady. Am'mā told me that she used to come to our place after I was born to carry me around and play with me for hours. Am'mā liked her and felt some sympathy for her and was not jealous at all. Had I told Am'mā that I was going to visit her, she would not have minded. But I didn't want to tell her. I don't know why.

Am'mā had told me when Appā was a bachelor, he had rented a house on Ratnakara Place in the town of Dehiwala. I knew the address, and I also knew this lady had been Appā's neighbour once. I knew how she looked, too, as Am'mā showed me a picture of her from her younger days. I had no idea if she still lived there. Though it might have been an exercise in futility, it was worth a try.

As our taxi pulled in front of her address, I saw a mature lady who resembled the younger woman in the picture I once saw. She looked at Sue and me with curiosity and a bit of concern to see two strangers at her front gate.

"I'm the youngest Ratṉavēl boy."

"Are you really?" said the lady with excitement as she opened the gate. She gave me a big smile and then a big motherly hug, as she sobbed. I could see she was also grieving my father's passing, like my mother was. It made me extremely sad. I was also mad at Appā for betraying her. I had no idea what had happened for him to drop her like that. So unfair. It was unfair to Am'mā too. He was certainly a man with many flaws. But we still loved him dearly.

I just wanted to know more about him. Her name was the same as my mom's: Indra. Damn the old man planned everything perfectly, I thought. Years after Appā ended the relationship, she was briefly married and never had kids of her own. Now I understood why she was so loving toward me, touching my cheeks with her open palms as she spoke. Maybe she saw me as the boy that she might've had if Appā married her. She was an aging single woman with a broken heart. I felt distraught.

But she was magnanimous and spoke a lot about Appā and his character positively. She was never disparaging, despite the abrupt way Appā had ended their relationship. These people lived lives I could never fathom. And they made the best of it and never blamed others around them.

We had a good chat and stayed with her for a few hours. I tried to say goodbye a few times, but she wouldn't let my hands go. We wanted to avoid Colombo's unannounced blackouts for safety reasons, as the country reeled from the financial effects of the war. After a few attempts, it was time for us to go.

Sue broke the eerie silence in the taxi. "I can't believe your dad did this to her and to your mom." She wasn't happy.

"I can't believe it either," I replied. I really couldn't. I never spoke to or saw Indra after that visit. I still think about calling her, but I could never get up the courage to do it.

We left for the North the next day. I wanted to go to Point Pedro and see where Appā was killed. Sue's cousin drove us there in a van with no air conditioner. I complained about the unbearable heat the whole time. I had a bucket of water with a towel to keep me cool. I was literally melting. Sue seemed fine, but I was a whiner.

People who had been to the North had warned me to expect to be horrified. But I was not prepared for the hardship, suffering, and destruction. Despite all I had been through in my life, I was still shocked by the proof of man's bottomless inhumanity.

Every tall coconut tree leading up to the region of Vanni was decapitated by the artillery shells. In the town of Kiḷinochchi, I saw that the buildings were crumbling and sinking. All of them were decorated with cracks and bullet holes. The roads were hardly paved and covered with loose sand on top, which was kicked up by every vehicle. Dirt hung in the air stubbornly, which reduced the visibility and made it hard to breathe. I covered my face with a handkerchief to get some relief. I was still able to see abandoned military vehicles in a field despite the cloud of thick dust. Our clothes were soon dirty as if we had done hard labour on a farm.

I could see despair and desperation in the glazed looks of the locals we passed by. The land was littered with land mines, which had the population traumatized, disabled, and still feeling the effects of war. But they still managed to smile widely at us. Maybe life would one day be normal again, and there was hope in this world. When we visited amputees, I was overcome by a river of emotion. I was living in comfort and supporting this endeavour to spill more blood and devastation. Haven't they suffered enough? I felt guilty and conflicted. What a waste of human lives. War-ravaged broken people and broken dreams, and for what? Centuries-old rich culture and land had been savaged in mere moments.

The true devastation of war is not the loss of buildings or wealth. It is the senseless annihilation of hope. What I saw on my trip was an entire generation of people, especially children, who had been completely disillusioned. They had begun to believe that fear, the daily fight for survival, and devastation were permanent fixtures of their world. Looking around at the faces of innocence, it occurred to me that during this phase of the war, many had become convinced that life no longer mattered; anxiety and fear were the order of the day. And it is obvious now, but those lessons have since been unlearned at great cost.

Every life in the North had a story and there are not enough words to describe each one of them. But it was clear to anyone who had been there that they needed help. From what I could see, my people had done a marvellous job with limited resources. Most of the kids were fed well and they were clean. They had great manners. It seemed they had been taught to be respectful, forward, not subservient. They were proud and appreciative of any help whilst maintaining their dignity, and they had been taught not to beg.

Almost all the schools in the North needed to be rebuilt, and the areas surrounding the schoolyards were littered with land mines. It was ironic that almost all the Hindu temples and churches were in great condition thanks to money from the Tamil diaspora. Many Tamils living abroad are quick to write a cheque to fund a new temple, and quick to give a long list of excuses when asked to help needy children. Have we as a people lost our minds? Since when is a kid's life less important than a concrete idol or a wooden cross? My intent here is not to take a shot at any religion but to shake the conscience of the self-righteous religious people to remind them of the concept of charity, which is prevalent in all religious teachings.

Due to poverty, some families had turned their children over to orphanages, desperately hoping that they would provide the necessary food and shelter. Despite all these difficulties, what was striking about the situation was the level of engagement by many ordinary Tamils, who were enthusiastic about participating in the rebuilding of their towns, villages, and lives. One woman I met said, "We would appreciate any support. We have all suffered the pain together and now it is time to rebuild our lives." In spite of all the problems, they were cautiously optimistic. The devastation of the past had changed their attitudes. People had every reason to pin their hopes to any peaceful political development.

The scars left by war were most painful for me as we approached my hometown. As we entered Point Pedro, I realized how narrow the streets were. Growing up there, they had seemed huge to me. Now I had an entirely different perspective. The road was full of potholes, which made vehicle travel very difficult.

The signs of war were inscribed on any building left standing. Somehow, the buildings looked older than the town itself. The town looked as though it had its soul beaten out of it, just like those who once inhabited it. I saw Ocean Road where Appā and I used to ride our bikes together to the fish market. Men and women were drying fish by the shore. The smell triggered memories of Am'mā's delicious fish curry and our last dinner together as a happy family. I came upon Hartley College and the road to the army camp where I was taken on a death march. It sent a shiver down my spine.

I saw the Point Pedro lighthouse on the horizon. It, too, had taken its share of punishment from the war. Strange pleasure and profound sadness came about me at the sight of that landmark. We used to run up its stairs to see who would reach the top first. Now it stood there alone as the waves crashed into the rocks below. It was cordoned off by a military defence line. Once its light gave hope to the fishermen of Point Pedro. They were now banned from fishing for security reasons, which deprived them from making a living. Everything seemed still as the sky began to darken.

But none of that mattered beside the landmark that drew me. I hoped to make peace with my past. I had to see where Appā died.

We no longer owned my childhood home. After Appā's death, Am'mā had been forced to sell it. I hoped the new owner would allow me to go inside. What if he didn't? I was worried about that.

The sky was brooding as we pulled up to my former home. Even the clouds seemed morose. But it wasn't sadness that threatened to burst out of me. I was angry, and I getting angrier by the minute. I was angry at the way Appā was killed. Angry at what had happened to me and our family. I didn't know who to direct the anger at. I was angry about that too.

That giant jackfruit tree was still in front of the home. I remembered climbing it all the time. I would sit there for hours after escaping Am'mā's attempts to beat me with the wooden spoon. Am'mā did that to me often. I was an irrepressibly mischievous kid who got into a lot of trouble. I had cracked my head open three times falling from the roof and tall trees. That jackfruit tree made me smile.

It was a very strange feeling to need permission to enter this home. Sue's cousin leaned on the horn. The new owner came out. He wasn't expecting us. I politely introduced myself and informed him of my mission. He was understanding and invited me in.

Am'mā had told me exactly where Appā had been shot and where his body lay dead when she found him. I immediately headed to that exact spot. Sue followed.

My father was a wonderful man, who represented strength and love in our family. I was only blessed with his presence when he visited Point Pedro. I didn't see him as often as I wanted due to him being a "commuter father." That still hurt. It was another reason I didn't want to have a child. I wanted to be a father who was always around, and I couldn't do that as a travelling salesman.

Though I would never actually see my Appā again, in my heart, he was always walking with me as I travelled the roads of British Columbia on business trips. He had shaped my life tremendously and still does. My dad knows. He knows my internal dialogue with him. If I ever had a kid, I would pass on all the valuable lessons I learned from my Appā. My thoughts were suddenly so full of sharp and painful edges, as I stood over the spot where Am'mā had found his body near the hallway between the kitchen and my former bedroom.

"I'd like to give you some time alone," Sue said softly as she gave me a hug. "Hang in there."

While I was sombre, I wasn't overcome with overwhelming emotion of any kind. It was just like when I'd heard the news about his death in my uncle's living room in Toronto: I felt blank and numb.

As I stood over that spot, I wasn't able to cry. I couldn't feel anything at all. Screw these assholes, I thought, they won't make me cry. My grief over his untimely death remained raw and intense, never diminishing as the years passed. Even after all these years, I feel the same way—hollowed out. "Time for me to go, Appā," I said, as I knelt down on the floor where his lifeless body once was, and I kissed the floor where he had lain.

I thanked the kind new owner of the house and said goodbye to him. I lit up a cigarette as an homage to the old man as I exited the house.

Sue was waiting for me in the garden. "How are you feeling?" she asked.

"Amazing. Now let's get the fuck out of this foolish country. We have a life to rebuild, Suzy!"

That wasn't the response she expected.

"The only way to pay tribute to Appā is for me to live life well. Not be saddened and be defeated by this tragedy. Not be a victim. But a victor. I won't let these assholes destroy me. That's what Appā would have wanted for me." I felt an overwhelming calm. It was strange.

A few days later, we left Sri Lanka. I wasn't sure I would ever return.

Back in the day, I was a decent cricket player. I wasn't a tactician, mind you, but a player who took chances and whacked the ball hard to intimidate the other team. Most of the time it didn't work; my recklessness would result in me striking out. But once in a while, the approach worked spectacularly well. I was a hitter, a middle-order batsman. I remember a few games where we were on the verge of losing badly and I would be sent in to change the course of the game. I was successful but not reliably so. I was very tough mentally. And I was reckless.

As the Tamil saying goes, "When the water is above nose level, it doesn't matter if it is by an inch or a foot." I had been completely wiped out by my aggressive financial manoeuvres. I had been struck out by the stock market. My reckless swinging hadn't helped. Now it didn't matter how deep our debt was. Assets were gone and the liability remained. Servicing the debt was a challenge. We had a negative net worth; we were broke. Our world had changed. Strangely, after losing everything, we were much happier as a couple—though I missed my Opus One.

True growth was really up to me, regardless of what was going on around me.

I had to be willing to adjust and adapt to changing conditions. My next step was to decide on what actions would help me attain better outcomes. Implementing those actions and continually assessing my results would keep me accountable to myself and move me beyond the blame game. "Making good decisions involves beginning with a commitment to make a decision. That's the hard part," Bill said to me once. No one could govern this for me; I had to do it myself. I was not afraid of change. I was afraid of not changing. I knew that. I had learned my lesson. It was an expensive one.

All motivation is self-motivation. I didn't want this setback to dictate my future. I wanted to make a conscious decision—to stretch beyond the present situation I found myself in to create the future I desired. I could overcome whatever life presented me by believing there was a solution and directing my energies to pursuing it. I had done that before; I had gotten myself out of prison by sending a message to Uncle Fernando. Regardless of whether it was conscious or unconscious, success or failure was my choice.

American baseball Hall of Famer Reggie Jackson struck out 2,600 times in his career. The most in the history of baseball. People only remember the home runs; you don't hear about the strikeouts. I had struck out big. Now I needed a home run. I was the sole architect of my life and career. I, and I alone, was the only one who could create, construct, and care for my life and career. No one could cheat me out of my ultimate success but myself—not even the stock market.

Failure is part of living a full life. It is better to risk and fail sometimes than to take no risks at all and fail for sure. I had failed spectacularly. But I still wanted to win. I knew I would. It was time to bet on myself again. I wanted to make the most of my next opportunity.

CI was also rebuilding its business after the tech wreck. On May 22, 2002, CI announced that it had entered into an agreement with one of Canada's premier insurance companies, Sun Life Financial, through an asset-ownership swap. In return for a 30 percent stake in CI, the insurance giant would sell its two mutual fund subsidiaries to CI, while becoming its largest shareholder. This deal would make CI the sixth-largest Canadian mutual fund player, with thirty-two billion dollars in assets and access to over four thousand financial advisors. This business is all about scale and distribution. This deal would give CI both. It was a brilliant strategic move by our CEO, Bill Holland. I was excited, as the market responded positively to this news. Our stock was on the rise again.

Through this deal, our staff count went up in Vancouver. One such person who joined us was Sean Hirtle. When we first met, I immediately knew he was an intelligent guy with a wicked sense of humour. I adore people with a sharp sense of humour. He had a lambent personality. We struck up an instant friendship. We would make each other laugh hysterically to the point that it was becoming very disruptive in the office. We both covered the same regions but different clients. Sue would roll her eyes when we got going with our antics. Through our friendship, I learned that humour and kindness transcend colour, creed, and culture.

My white friends had nicknamed me "Rat" from the first three letters of my last name, Ratṉavēl. I used to tell them that it was a good thing I was not in the mafia, because I'd be killed. I would be wearing cement shoes. You never want to be a rat in a mob. But it was a term of endearment. Close friends called me that and still do. It showed, at least to me, the strength of the relationship we had. In that sense, Sean became the white Rat and I was the brown Rat. Sean and I were inseparable. We were working hard and playing harder. He had a very good sense for business as well.

We started a contest at the office: a wall of autographs for B- or C-list celebrities. Getting an autograph from Al Pacino wouldn't qualify, but George Hamilton—who played B.J. Harrison in *The Godfather: Part III*—would score big. As travelling sales guys, we were on the hunt. A few other guys joined in as well. I was dining at the Vancouver Morton's with a client of mine from Merrill Lynch and saw Judge Reinhold—Detective Billy Rosewood from *Beverly Hills Cop*—dining with someone. I got his autograph. He was more than happy to oblige. It was a big win for me.

One time I saw Ed Jovanovski, former Vancouver Canucks hockey player, at Cioppino's—an absolutely fabulous joint in Yaletown. I was there with Sue celebrating us buying a sub-penthouse condo at Quaywest I, overlooking the False Creek marina, a prime waterfront location by Vancouver's famous seawall. Our first home ownership.

It had a panoramic unobstructed water and city view, an expansive 180-degree view from Mount Baker to English Bay. Without question, our unit had the best floor plan in the building. We were very proud of our purchase. This restaurant was walking distance from our new home. I chased Ed into the washroom and saw him at the urinal. After he was done, I asked for an autograph. He replied, "Sure, man. Can I at least wash my hands?" It was hilarious.

Sean, of course, tried to outdo me. During his stay at the Banff Springs hotel, he tried to lift Chevy Chase's chair from a movie set. That chair would have been great in our office. But two security guards were onto him. After a long foot chase, they busted him. Good thing he was a Fairmont President's Club member. As the guards tackled him to the ground, he showed his membership card and said, "I'm a Fairmont club member! I'm a Fairmont club member!" They spared him.

Sue and I were happy to own our own place. I felt proud. In a short while, we were able to fix up our debt issue, thanks to the rising CI stock price and good markets. Options were back in the money.

One day, I had been walking around defeated on West Georgia Street and saw Kent, a veteran investor, smoking outside of his building.

"How are you doing, kid?" he greeted me.

"Like shit." I didn't hold back as I lit up a cigarette to join him. I proceeded to tell him, between drags, about my investment woes.

After patiently listening to me, he said, "No matter what kind of market it is, there is always something to invest in." Then he made a convincing case for why he thought the global resource and energy sector was about to take off. Some of the money managers at CI had similar views. I didn't need any more convincing. CI also moved money into this space to get back in the game, which helped to regain our reputation among our clients.

I had decided not to repeat my mistakes of the past with regards to investments. I had built back in a steadfast way and vowed not to go back to below zero again. But the price we had paid for the condo was troubling me. I thought our mortgage was beyond our means. I had called Peter, my head of sales who had given me this job, for advice before I closed the deal. He said, "Always buy a place *slightly* more than you can afford and, believe me, you will always find a way to pay for it." Best real estate advice I ever received. I believe it has to do with being uncomfortable. Complacency is bad. It leads to failure. This financial position kept me honest, somewhat paranoid, and working hard.

Being with Sue in that condo was amazing. We had so many stormy arguments, but I realized that love and discord could coexist. We were building a life, a proper life, as I'd always wanted. We threw our first Christmas party for my work colleagues, which grew into a legendary year-end party that everyone looked forward to each year.

For the first party, Sean brought a bottle of Stolichnaya vodka and a bag of sugar. Vodka for me, and sugar for Sue because she was "so sweet," he said. I thought he just didn't know what to get her or it was a last-minute decision. That night, he broke a few eggs over the kitchen floor tiles while clowning around and the egg yolk stained the grout yellow. He was forever banned from the kitchen by Sue. I was killing myself laughing. But Sue loved him.

Meanwhile, I also knew I needed continued professional intervention and started seeing a new psychologist. Just like the first one, I didn't find him to be particularly helpful. He didn't seem to really understand my issues, nor could I explain them well. I always seemed to keep my deepest, darkest thoughts to myself. In some ways, I can't blame my therapist as I had set him up for failure. But it did help me to slowly open up to Sue.

While rebuilding our finances, we were also working on our marriage by minimizing the arguments. Those were mostly caused by me and correlated with Am'mā's illness. When it flared up, it made me angry at everything and I would take it out on everyone around me. I was becoming a lot better at dealing with this. But the rage was always lurking. I needed to learn not to take out my trauma on others. I wanted to become a better person.

A few years after our trip to Sri Lanka, I had started thinking about becoming a father. I never shared these thoughts with Sue because I wasn't sure of how serious I was. I knew I had a fiery temper that could go off just like that. That would scare a kid. Heck, it scared adults. I needed to tame this demon. For most of my life, I knew I would not have been a good father; I was too self-involved and too messed up. I wasn't up to that kind of challenge.

I was never a perfect human, nor am I currently, but my greatest strength has always been knowing my blind spots—my own imperfections. I was always self-aware. My biggest issue was that I needed to be in control, and no one could ever tell me what to do. I suspected it was a reflexive reaction to my prison experience. I knew full well that a child could change all this.

I approached Sue with my change of heart in the kid department. We made a decision: we were going to try for a year, and if it didn't happen then, we would never try again. One day, I was in the Kelowna Grand lobby waiting for my cab to pick me up and take me to a business dinner. My phone rang. It was Sue. (By 2004, Kelowna had cell service.) "I'm pregnant," she declared enthusiastically. I was over the moon. Apparently, the Sri Lankan army had left me intact. Those rods in the nuts had nothing on this virile stud.

The first person I called after hanging up with Sue was Sean. "Hirtle, Sue is pregnant," I said.

"Rat, I didn't do it," he replied. What an ass! He was thrilled for me though. "You will make an amazing dad, Rat." He was convinced.

"Let's see," was all I could muster. I wasn't so sure.

At dinner, I wasn't able to contain myself. I shared the news with the dozen clients I was dining with. They were all white and from the

Interior and had never before met a Tamil in their life. Racists? Definitely not. Decent humans? Profoundly yes! These were some of the best people I had ever met. Most of them were great clients and, more importantly, great friends. I'm still in touch with many of them.

Sue didn't have much in the way of morning sickness. She went to work with no problem, like a champ. Absolutely no drama or mood swings. I had all that. Well, someone had to take one for the team, right? But she craved dim sum a lot. We would go to Sun Sui Wah at Main Street and 22nd Avenue every Saturday. One Friday she called me and said she would like to go for dim sum. I was in town that day and had no lunch appointment.

As we were waiting for our food at the restaurant, my BlackBerry buzzed. I looked to see if it was urgent. It was an email from Bill to inform the entire company of Mr. McRae's passing. He had died on Wednesday, July 21, 2004, at the age of eighty-nine. He had been very kind to me and helped me immensely. He came to our wedding, and here we were, years later, about to be parents. Regretfully I couldn't go to the funeral. But his kind gestures and infectious enthusiasm will never be forgotten.

That Christmas season, Sue still managed to throw an amazing party for my friends and colleagues—while heavily pregnant. It coincided with my thirty-fifth birthday—Saturday, December 4, 2004. That night, after everyone left and Sue had gone to bed, Sean and I had a few drinks and smokes on the balcony overlooking the marina.

"Hirtle, from this day forward, I will never smoke again."

"Rat, don't be silly. Be realistic." He refuted my bold claim with his usual charming laugh.

I hated my Appā smoking around me. I had made a promise to myself that if I ever had kids, I would never smoke. So that was that! I never smoked a cigarette again from that day onwards. Self-discipline is paramount to me. Fifteen years of habit ended abruptly on that balcony. Never again!

Sue came out of the room at three in the morning to break us up and send Sean home. She was a bit peeved that we were carrying on that late. But it was not new to her. In the lady's defence, she needed some sleep. She didn't want to hear two drunken jerks repeating the same jokes.

Christmas Day came and went. The next morning, we woke up to the terrible news of the Boxing Day tsunami caused by the earthquake in the Indian Ocean. The deadliest in recorded history, it took 230,000 lives in the Asian continent in a matter of hours with its mind-boggling destruction. It devastated Sri Lanka and caused 35,000 deaths on the island. It especially devastated the Tamil-dominated northeast region, which was already devastated by war. Anti-personnel mines, left after the prolonged civil war, were feared to have been washed up and spread by the surge of water. More bad news for Tamils. It put a damper on the excitement of the baby's upcoming arrival. Sue and I were worried about our friends and family. We were involved in emergency relief efforts. The fragile truce between Sri Lanka and the Tamil Tigers held in large part because of this devastation.

Sue's mom was in town from Toronto for the birth. She was very helpful to have around. I needed all the help I could get in this department. We took the Christmas decorations down early in anticipation of the new arrival. Usually that's a January 1 ritual in our household.

Labour pain started late on January 2. It was go time! The moment that we had been waiting for, for nine months, had finally arrived. After a few hours of pain and suffering, Sue gave birth to our boy. I always thought it would be a girl and perhaps, just perhaps, we'd name her Kannam'mā. Like Petrarch's Laura, Dante's Beatrice, and the "Dark Lady" of Shakespeare's sonnets, Kannam'mā was the "Brown lady" in the work of classical Tamil poet Pārathi. Am'mā told me that Appā loved Pārathi's poetry so much that he wanted to give the name Kannam'mā to his daughter, but that name belonged to the 1860s, not the late 1960s. Am'mā fought with him on his choice of name for her future child. So, naturally she was thrilled when I was born and the point became moot. Appā would have been happy to have a grand-daughter named in honour of his beloved poet. But I knew Sue would have killed me. If it was a girl, we had decided to name her Maya, a name connected to the Hindu goddess Lakshmi.

It was a boy! When the birthing nurse brought him to Sue and put him on her chest, I drew my face close to give them both a kiss on their heads. I couldn't help but smile. I almost died twice in my life. Survived imprisonment. Survived torture. Survived a war. And now I'd become a father on January 3, 2005. Wow! I had never thought this was in the cards for me when I was ducking bombs in Point Pedro.

I stood there in amazement. A rush of excitement surged through-out my whole body; I had never felt like that before in my life. I just stared at him. He looked so peaceful. His little eyes were closed, and he had bushy eyelashes that looked just perfect. He had a petite nose that was like a little button, and his rosy cheeks looked like a fresh plum off the tree. I loved looking at him. He gave me purpose. For a moment, the world seemed to stop and hold its place in time for all three of us, for that perfect moment at B.C. Women's Hospital.

While Sue slept, I carried this precious little boy around the hospi-tal hallway like he was a trophy. My hands quivered when I touched his little face and felt the softness of his cheeks. I ran my fingertips very gently across his smooth face, and right away, I fell in love with my boy. Now I had to live for more than just Appā.

We named our boy Aaron. It was Sue's choice. I liked it too. Aaron, while a biblical name, is also a Tamil name. In Tamil, it means *king*. Lord Shiva, the chief Hindu god, was also called Aaron. It was a cul-turally neutral name, we thought. But even today, we jokingly tell him that we were lazy parents and picked the very first name on the baby names for boys book and went back to heavy drinking.

My mother-in-law relieved me at the hospital from my night shift. On my way home, I stopped at the Urban Fare in Yaletown to pick up a few newspapers so that I could show the headlines of the day to Aaron in the future. All the papers had grim headlines about the death and destruction caused by the tsunami. One had a picture of a hand coming out of the sand and reaching to the sky. So many lives were lost, but Sue and I brought a new one into the world. The condo was quiet. I got there around eight o'clock in the morning. I was on a natural high of being a father for the first time. Then I saw myself in the mirror in the washroom and broke down. I broke down like never before.

I cried for everyone and for everything that happened. For not crying when I heard about my Appā's demise. For not crying when I was in the room where Appā was killed. For always bottling it up. For knowing I was now a father who needed to care for another human who depended on me. I was paralyzed by the surge of all those emotions. The assholes finally may have had me. Sixteen years of bottled-up emotion spewed out in six minutes. After that, I felt as if my chest had been relieved of all the heaviness.

Aaron the King was my focus now. I needed to find a way to be a good father.

All I wanted was for him to not have to make the choices I had to make. And for him to not go around being fearful that somehow some people would come after him because of his race. I just didn't want him to have that fear in his heart.

~~IIII~~ IIII

THE LEADER

Winter in the Canadian Prairies can be very harsh. The warmth of the people is palpable, especially in the wintertime when all else is so cold. Some of the nicest people I have met in my life. I had fallen in love with Western Canada. I wanted to stay here forever. I loved the Prairie perogies too.

I was staying the night in Regina when a snowstorm rolled in. After my business dinner, I had only a short walk from the Diplomat Steakhouse to the hotel, but the bone-chilling temperature of -40 degrees Celsius with the wind chill made it quite unbearable. It reminded me of my first snowstorm experience in Toronto, walking from the factory to the bus stop in my BiWay jacket. I was dressed much better now. When I got to my hotel room, I never wanted to leave. But I had to be in Saskatoon the next morning for a series of meetings.

After an early morning workout in the hotel gym and a quick breakfast in the lobby restaurant, I got into my very cold rental car. I panicked a little when the engine struggled to start. Stalling car engines after a very cold night in the open parking lot was an all too common occurrence in this part of the world. But it finally coughed to life and I headed onto the highway to Saskatoon.

Strong heavy winds attempted to lift the car off the ground. The white powder tossed about made it difficult for me to see the road. Many horrible crashes had happened on this highway of death. I was a newly minted dad, and I wanted to make sure I saw my son grow up. I knew how painful it was to lose a father at a young age. As new parents, Sue and I were muddling through this terrain rather confidently, given the fact that neither of us had any prior experience caring for an infant.

Aaron was a year old by now. So far, thankfully, there had been no midnight visits to the emergency room. He was a healthy boy with a good appetite for food and sleep. He had started attending daycare. Sue was working again at a well-known real estate investment management company. A few weeks earlier, I had said to Sue that with both of us making good money and with all our investments up, we should probably buy a house. Aaron was already walking and would be running soon. We had discussed selling our condo and upgrading to a larger home. We wanted to own some dirt.

The drive to Saskatoon from Regina was about three hours in normal weather conditions. These were not normal conditions. Icy roads with billowing snow made the journey harder and slower, as gusts of wind shook my car. Good thing I had an early start, I complimented myself for thinking ahead.

The billowing snow was becoming intense and I could hear the howling prairie winter wind. I wanted my vision to be focused on the road ahead, despite all the big plans bouncing around in my head. I could feel the tires skating on the icy road, but I kept the car as steady as I could. The snow lashed against the windshield of my rental as I crawled along the two-lane highway, well below the speed limit. I could barely see the road.

I was in the right lane the entire time to be safe, and to steer clear of any oncoming vehicles.

I wasn't even halfway into my journey when my stomach clenched. I held in my breath as I saw a stationary farm vehicle waiting to turn right about forty feet in front of me. I reflexively slammed the brake and steered left, giving challenge to Newton's second law of motion.

The sound of the car's screeching brakes and tires skidding on the icy road broke the precious silence that had been hanging over my thoughts.

I fishtailed into oncoming traffic and barely missed a transport truck, flipping my car upside down onto the snowy field. A montage of images of Sue and Aaron flashed across my mind. I was somewhere between Regina and Saskatoon upside down in a rental car. I knew I wasn't hurt, because I could think clearly, but I was quite shaken. The crash only strengthened my resolve to find more reason to live. All my life I had been reckless. Now, as a father, I wasn't ready to take those kinds of risks.

My immediate problem was how to get out of the car. As I pondered my predicament, I saw a pair of workboots appear in the snow by my upside-down widow.

"You okay, fella?" said a man in overalls.

He helped me crawl out of my car. He had seen the whole thing.

"I'm fine," I said. But I was shaken. He took me to his truck. I hopped in the old F-150. Inside smelled like horses. I thought he might be a farmer. The back of the truck was full of horseshoe stuff and empty horseshoe boxes piled to the brim. The passenger seat had a few empty pop cans and coffee cups. He cleaned it hurriedly and poured me a hot cup of black coffee in a new Styrofoam cup. "I'll drive you to the nearest establishment and you can figure it out from there, hopefully," the man said.

"Thank you," I replied shakily.

I closed the door but felt the prairie chill seep through the cracks of the window. The truck fell silent, and I suddenly felt alone. Alone for one more night in a hotel? I said to myself. On the road. Alone. Empty. Shouldn't I be happy? This was what I'd always wanted, to be like Bill, a travelling salesman on the hunt for a life of luxury and glamour. But for some reason, I felt empty. Why was I feeling like this? I looked in the side mirror and saw my reflection. A ghostly figure stared back at me. The longer I looked at who I really was and all my imperfections, the more doubts began to flow through my mind. I felt powerless and scared, like the teenager in prison I once was. I was so lost in my thoughts and shaken that I never even asked for the man's name or his profession. A farrier perhaps? Skilled craftsperson capable of shoeing all types of equine feet?

At a gas station, I got a cab and was driven the rest of the way. I called a tow truck company to grab my rental car out of the snow. I missed some of my meetings that day. By the next day, I was happy to be home in Vancouver with my family. That night, we all slept in one bed with Aaron in the middle. I loved it. A few weeks after that, we put the condo up for sale.

No one wakes up thinking, I'm going to make bad decisions today. Yet I made them. When your car is in a snowy ditch, and you're hanging upside down by your seat belt, knowing you could have lost everything you've devoted your life to, and failed the people who count on you, there is no point blaming the icy roads or the farmer moving equipment in a blizzard. I was the guy who got in the car, and I was the guy hanging upside down. The only way any of us can learn from our bad decisions is to make sure we are perfectly clear with ourselves: we are responsible.

The trip that brought me to that ditch in Saskatchewan was the result of a promotion. I was the new senior vice-president and head of Western Canada—at the age of thirty-six. Some people in the company had thought I was unlikely to succeed. Now, I was in a leadership role and in charge of everything between Winnipeg, Manitoba, and Victoria, British Columbia. That trip was so I could introduce myself to CI's client base. But the way I saw it, the people I really needed to get to know in a new way were on my team. Going from a colleague to a boss was the hardest transition I ever had to make. Something I wasn't prepared for. As the saying goes, "Life isn't about finding yourself. Life is about creating yourself." I wanted to create a leader out of me.

My ability to make good decisions came from experience—and from my experience of making bad decisions. I wanted to gain confidence, learn to communicate with my team better, and construct a leadership path to success. I knew there would be obstacles. There would be people who doubted me. And I would make mistakes.

Most people accepted my leadership, but some key members of the team did not. I had no doubt that I was capable of the job. I always thought that I was one of the most misunderstood people. Maybe I deserved that with my past behaviour. I had been described as the most polarizing person in the company. Because people never forgive. I still get that after all these years of trying to disprove that reputation. The reality is that people hardly ever change their opinions, even when you have changed your behaviour and atoned for your sins. I really wanted to make this leadership role work, and I wanted to be the best at my craft.

I knew I would get there. After all, I came to Vancouver in 1998 without knowing how to do the job, but I was staggeringly successful at it. I was a huge portion of sales flow in B.C. I was a natural sales pro. I created unique content: useful weekly emails and my own monthly newsletters. Unlike an animal in the wild, you don't survive by blending in. Instead, you needed to stand out to survive. To be seen. To be heard. I stood out among our competition. I differentiated myself. Many financial advisors knew who I was. I had an absurd amount of self-confidence—truly. No more a lamb!

I didn't know where my confidence came from, but perhaps it was from seeing mediocre people do things. When I was in prison, I became the leader for about fifty prisoners at a very young age and led men twice my age. So, I felt I would be fine in this role. Plus, why would CI management give me the role if they didn't think I could do it?

I always reserve the right to change my mind when facts change. Many people are effective leaders when their skill sets align well with the industry environment that they are working in. The tough mindset

I had developed enabled me to remain relevant as a leader regardless of how the industry evolved. This was a great strength and not one that is easy to learn.

My new role was not focused on whether I added more to those who were self-motivated and performed at a high level. It was about those who lacked these qualities. It was about seeing potential in those who did not see it in themselves, as Bill had in me. I so badly wanted to be an advocate for others and to believe in them even more than they believed in themselves. There was a huge distinction between my previous role and my new one: before I had done things right, but as a leader, I needed to do the right things. It was no longer about my personal achievements but about enabling others to achieve. Time for me to pay it forward.

I decided to get to work. The goal I set for myself was to make the West shine in terms of sales and to create a cohesive team with the best camaraderie in the country. My good friend Sean was very helpful to his new boss in this quest. He became my consigliere. This title was apt for him, because we were both huge fans of the movie *The Godfather*. Probably the best movie ever made, in my opinion. We would quote the movie all the time to the amazement of some, and annoyance of many.

In this new leadership role, I needed to project confidence even when I didn't feel confident. I had worked with managers who were so internally focused that they were unaware of what they were pro-jecting. I, on the other hand, believed that projecting confidence propels a team by enabling others to accomplish. My responsibility as the leader was to serve my team so that the team could better serve CI's clients.

I needed to delegate tasks for others on my team to accomplish. It had been my observation that insecure managers often don't delegate as much as they should because they fear losing control—and being seen as burdening staff. I don't believe delegation is an abdication of responsibility. The best leaders often take a back seat and build talent by delegating the driving to the team, like Bill had. I also knew that sometimes I must take charge and drive change forward.

A true leader coaches for real skills and encourages team members to develop into their full potential. I was fully committed to excel in the role, to make Bill proud. He had always been an advocate for the leader in me. I was always learning from him. But I wasn't always the best student. His patience with me was remarkable.

Aaron was three now. I wanted to be at least a decent father. I had prom-ised myself that I would never be a commuter father, like my Appā. And yet here I was travelling about three weeks each month. I was clocking over one hundred flight segments per year on Air Canada. I'd had Super Elite status with Air Canada since 2000. I had flown over one million miles and made it to the "Elite for life" club. Clearly, I had broken my own promise of not becoming a commuter father. Travelling most of the time, how normal of a father could I ever hope to be? It broke my heart. But strangely enough, nothing felt better than going home and nothing felt better than leaving home. It was like asking for loneliness.

Sue was operating as a working single mom with me on the road so much. You really need a supportive spouse to be successful in the business that I'm in. I often offer young people who want to enter the business this advice: make sure your significant other is supportive; otherwise it won't work. I have missed so many birthdays and anni-versaries, but Sue was always very supportive by saying, "You don't love us any less because you aren't here. You are a great provider for our family. That is most important." I can't disagree with that senti-ment. I always disliked fake sentimentalism. I prefer real action over empty gestures.

I loved spending time with my boy whenever I was in town. Often when I returned from a trip, he would see me and then run away unsteadily from me along the hallway in a playful manner. On a few occasions, this ended in tears after he bounced off a wall. I would ask Sue to take a break and go out with her friends or for a walk. I loved spending time alone with him. I would observe him for hours. Aaron liked grapes. He would sit by the window in his high chair and look at the cars crossing on Cambie Bridge from thirty-eight floors above ground, while gorging on his grapes. I would watch him in awe. All I wished for him was that he could go out into this world with this same happiness and joy, full of love and easy laughter.

He was having the time of his life. I was, too, just looking at him, knowing that I was a dad. I never thought I would be here. Growing up in war, the odds of this scenario looked slim to none. I would often lament to myself how Aaron would never meet his granddad, my Appā. My old man would've loved him and taught him English and Tamil literature properly. A certain melancholy settled over me. In the midst of my raw thoughts about Appā, Aaron flashed me a sneaky smile mid-bite, as though he knew I was sad. The smile seemed to say, "Be happy, Dad. All is well now." And then it was.

This boy is my legacy and I am my Appā's, and I know it will always be that way. Sometimes when it was just us alone together, I would recall the lyrics from the song "Mayakkamā kalakkamā" by Appā's favourite Tamil lyricist Kaṇṇathāsaṉ: *"Life has a thousand struggles; there is pain at every door. Whatever the sufferings are, if you stand there defeated, the problems won't run away. But if you have the heart to endure it all, there will be peace to the end."* Looking at Aaron sleeping peacefully in my arms, away from the horrors of war and chaos, gave me resolve to snap out of it, to cherish life, and to live for the sake of this little one. "Yeah, it is still a nice life," I muttered.

I wanted him to spend part of his summers with his grandparents, my in-laws. He never had the pleasure of knowing his paternal grandpa, so I felt this was important. He could visit my Am'mā too. She was happy to see him, but her condition was deteriorating further. This was always an anvil of anxiety for me. The threat of her having an all-out meltdown hung over me like the sword of Damocles.

She was my constant worry; I did what I could by setting her up in luxury. I would send her to Denmark to visit my brother and her two granddaughters. I visited my brother in 1992 and with Am'mā in 2003. I also sent her to the U.K. and Australia to meet our relatives. But over time, her condition was becoming not only unpredictable but also unmanageable. It was heart-wrenching.

Her paranoia only got worse. She would often call me and say, "I hear the voice of this unknown man. I think he is trying to harm me." All of a sudden, those calls got even darker. She would say, "He grabbed my neck and told me if you won't kill yourself, I will." I was worried that she was going to harm herself. Suicidal ideation also runs in the family. I decided to get the best care I could for her. I flew to Toronto and took her to Scarborough Grace Hospital. That hospital had the area's only Tamil psychiatrist at that time. Language had been an ongoing issue in her care: she couldn't connect with a doctor who was unable to speak Tamil. I got her admitted. She needed supervision, and I couldn't stay there forever. I was under pressure and didn't know what to do. In situations like this, I always consult Sue. She said, "Come back and focus on the business. I will fly to Toronto to look after your mom as long as she needs me." My mother had not always been kind to my wife, yet Sue put all that behind her in Am'mā's time of need. That's character. I can't ever repay Sue for what she sacrificed. She had stopped working to care for our only son. She left behind her thriving career for our family and me. I really couldn't screw up.

Ultimately, I knew that I couldn't control outside events, only the view I took of them. The frequent thought I hold shapes my destiny. Setbacks in my life would be the best teacher; I knew that. I couldn't let the situation with my mother distract me from my work, as too much was at stake.

Only months later, on May 24, 2008, we received the news that Sue's dad passed away suddenly. I had a good relationship with the man. He wasn't the warm and fuzzy type, but he was thoughtful. He took a risk on me by blessing our marriage while I was still trying to find my way in the world. He entrusted me with his only child because he wanted her happiness, not status. Just like Appā, he was ahead of his time. I respected him for that. On the way to India, he visited us with Sue's mom after we had moved into the new home. He couldn't have been prouder to see our home and hear of my new role at CI. And most importantly, to see Sue and me as a happy couple. That's everything that he wanted for his daughter after hearing our old quarrels in his basement during the early stages of our marriage.

When Aaron would visit Toronto, he gave so much joy to my in-laws, especially to my father-in-law. Aaron's feet never touched the ground, as he was carried by his grandfather everywhere. He nicknamed him Champion. I was happy for them both as they truly enjoyed each other's company. My mother-in-law, a talented cook, would make amazing food for Aaron. Sue would have to put Aaron on a diet after every summer stint in Toronto, as he would return pudgy. It was also good for Aaron to have access to the Tamil community and language. Vancouver had scant opportunities for that.

For my father-in-law's seventieth birthday, Sue decided to take Aaron to surprise him. That was his milestone birthday gift. When he opened the door that morning, he was absolutely surprised and overjoyed. The best gift he could have hoped for. He called me that day and thanked me as well. I had never heard him that happy. I was truly happy we could make that happen for him. Sue left Aaron behind with her parents and flew back a few days later. He would send daily pictures of them together doing fun activities. It reminded me of fond memories of my own grandfather. It felt good.

The day we heard the news, we had a few guests coming over for a barbeque. Sue had made all the necessary preparations. I was marinating a nice coho salmon. I heard our home phone ring and then Sue speaking to someone. I didn't think much of it.

Then I could hear Sue's footsteps coming down the stairs. She looked shaken.

"Is everything okay?" I asked.

"No, Dada was taken to the emergency in an ambulance." She was calm, but her dark-brown eyes revealed a deeply concerned woman.

I hugged her and said, "Don't worry, he will be fine."

"No, I don't think so," she said with certainty.

That took me aback. "Do not say that, Sue," I said.

He'd had a stroke a few years ago. He fought through it and started walking fine again. He was even refereeing Tamil men's volleyball games. He was very involved with Canadian politics and the Tamil freedom struggle in Sri Lanka. He knew David Collenette well, who served as minister of national defence in the mid-1990s during Jean Chrétien's time as prime minister; Collenette attended our wedding as well. My father-in-law was also playing in Ontario bridge tournaments. Even that day, he came back from a bridge tournament after placing third in all of Ontario. We later learned he had been playing with Aaron on his bed and then pushed him away and asked his wife, my mother-in-law, to call the ambulance.

I sat on the sofa in the family room nervously. Earlier, I had opened the French doors to the garden to enjoy the summer-like breeze. As I sat there, a small bird flew right into the room, startling me. I tried to chase the bird away. The phone rang again, and my heart beat faster; I knew this would be a call from Toronto to update us on my father-in-law's condition. I ran upstairs, ignoring the bird for the moment. Sue was on the phone and it didn't sound good. She hung up and said, "Dada passed away," in an eerily calm voice. She didn't cry when she heard the news, just as I hadn't when I heard of my Appā's death. I gave her a hug and we started packing our bags. We showed up at Vancouver airport in time to catch the last red-eye flight to Toronto.

Perhaps that bird that flew into our home was my father-in-law paying us a final visit? Hindus believe there is life after death. But I am sure this bird was alive before he drew his last breath.

Our cab pulled up to my in-laws' house in Markham. Sue hopped out of the car, as I settled payment with the driver. I could see Aaron shrieking, laughing, and running in the front yard with kids around his age. He was completely oblivious to the news that the man who nick-named him Champion was no longer. I felt immense sadness for my boy. Both of his grandfathers were now gone. He was only three. Before going inside, I picked him up and gave him a big squeeze. He gave me a wet kiss on my cheek and carried on playing.

The same day, we went to the morgue to view the body. When Sue saw her father's body, she came unhinged. He had a smile on his face. He looked pleasant while frozen in time. Sue was wailing. I wanted her to cry and cry it all out. Not to bottle it in, as I had. It's never healthy to do that.

I stood next to Sue with my arm around her shoulders. After a few minutes, she kissed him on his forehead. She looked to me. "This was a good end for Dada. I couldn't see him wasting away in a nursing home or in a wheelchair," she said. I agreed. He was way too proud to be helped by others.

Friends and family flew in from all over the world. The funeral was cathartic for me and for Sue's cousin Prad, who flew in from London. His father, Sue's uncle, had been killed by anti-Tamil mobs during the 1983 riots when he was about five years old. This was the closest we would both come to our own fathers' funerals. We hugged it out while tearing up. Sue consoled us and said, "I thought you two were here to console me." She was right.

Apart from the personal loss our family experienced in this era, 2007 and 2008 saw a major global financial crisis, which tested my leadership abilities at CI.

It was the perfect time for me to act with integrity and ethics—and to display a real sense of purpose to get the team through this crisis. I was slowly starting to inspire my team in my own way. Inspiring leadership is about leading by example with great generosity of team spirit. A true leader is not divisive, mean-spirited, self-promoting, or other-blaming. A true leader brings out the best in others and becomes an advocate for the team. They give credit where it is due—and accept responsibility without deflection. A pragmatic leader is inspirational even when times are bleak and demonstrates a realistically positive view of the future.

In early 2007, I attended a meeting in New York where a few CI portfolio managers were presenting their thoughts on the global macro-economic outlook. All day long, the mood was upbeat. Everyone thought the good times would just keep rolling. I was planning the evening's entertainment when the final speaker took the mic at four in the afternoon.

His opening sentence got my attention: "Let me begin by saying the world is a mess." I figured he should know. The speaker was Nandu Narayanan, an Indian Tamil who ran a hedge fund called Trident. He was generating huge returns by short-selling subprime mortgage lenders. That was well before the adjective *subprime* became an international obsession. Narayanan was making a killing because he saw the crisis on the horizon. As we sat there, he painted a grim outlook for the market. In fact, he made a convincing argument for the imminent bankruptcy of Lehman Brothers and the collapse of the global financial system.

I took his bearish market outlook seriously. I had built back from my own personal dot-com bubble collapse in 2001 and didn't want to experience those losses again. Bill, too, was increasingly worried. His instinct was always to go against the crowd. If the crowd was saying leverage up and go long, that was a red flag for Bill. "A market sell-off may be imminent," I remember him saying.

Some of our money managers were also raising cash in their port-folios. But no one ever knows for sure. What I did know for sure is that the market will do its best to screw up as many people as possible. So, I decided not to look at the world and make my financial decision, but to make my financial decision and then look at the world. The decision I made was to liquidate most of my holdings and use the proceeds to buy into CI Global Opportunities Fund, a hedge fund run by none other than Nandu Narayanan.

A few days later, I called my broker and asked him to execute this trade by delivering my account and selling off any risky positions. But I still didn't sell my CI stock. Unlike in 2001, this go-around the com-pany had exposure to broader, conservative investment mandates and few concentrated positions. When the sell-off started, it minimized the impact on both my personal finances and CI's business. We fared much better than most of our competition. Although a lot of mutual funds had limited exposure to subprime loans, they were negatively impacted by a widened panic sell-off at all levels of the capital markets, as trig-gered by subprime unrest. It was collateral damage. CI performed relatively well—meaning we lost less. Our business was always about outrunning the competition.

The CI Global Opportunities hedge fund in Canadian-dollar terms went up 109.4 percent in 2007 and 23.4 percent in 2008, while the MSCI World Index was down 7.1 percent and 25.4 percent respectively.

Still, Sue and I decided to cut back on our spending to increase the "Ratṇavēl Reserve." Our property was too big with too many trees for me to tend to. Plus I had no such skills and no time. I was leading a team. (I've never been handy either. My toolbox just had a chequebook inside it.) So we had a gardener. But I could rake leaves. And the property was covered in leaves, right around Canadian Thanksgiving. We were the only people of colour in our neighbourhood. Any others of colour in our hood would be those who tended the gardens, like my gardener. But, given the credit crisis, I wanted to save a few hundred dollars and decided to rake the leaves myself, much to my gardener's dismay.

It was a cold but beautiful sunny Saturday morning. I got myself a cup of coffee and started raking the leaves. I was enjoying the work. It felt like I was adding some tangible value to our household. I used to clean large Hindu temple grounds with my granddad, so this was nothing. I should do this more often, I was thinking. Given all the stress with the business at the moment, this feels more dignified and meaningful. This is definitely stress-relieving.

Just then, my thoughts were interrupted by the sound of tires screeching to a stop. A new souped-up and shiny silver Porsche Cayenne GTS with bright-red calipers had stopped, and an affluent-looking driver lowered her window. Our home was located at a three-way junction; people were often confused when they arrived at it.

"Excuse me, do you speak English?" she asked.

"Yes, ma'am. Are you lost?"

"No, but are you available for tomorrow?"

Wait a second, for what? I wasn't sure. I'm no gigolo. Although given the cash crunch brought on by the credit crisis, why not a side hustle to make some extra cash?

I smiled at her and said, "Available for what?"

"To clean the yard," she replied.

I thought for a second and then I calmly replied, "Well, the lady inside this house," as I pointed to my home, "keeps my schedule. I'd first need to check with her." Turns out it is true what they say about the Porsche Cayenne GTS: it can reach 100 kilometres per hour in under five seconds. Later I recounted the incident to Sue while I decanted her some wine. We had a good laugh. But we weren't mocking the woman. I make mistakes like that myself, and sometimes in more public ways.

One hot sunny Friday, Sean and I and a few others were trolling patios after a long, tough week and ended up at one of the premier spots in the city. We had had a couple of rounds when I looked over at the next table and recognized a well-known B.C. politician and fellow brown dude. I couldn't resist saying hello, even though he was quietly chatting with another man.

"Hello, Ujjal, great to see you," I half-shouted to the next table. The man looked confused. The look on his face clearly told me he had no idea who Ujjal was.

Immediately I knew I'd screwed up. It wasn't Ujjal Dosanjh, a man of Indian descent who served as the thirty-third premier of British Columbia of Canada briefly in 2000.

"I am not Ujjal," he explained with a smile. "I am Wally." It was Wally Oppal, the sitting attorney general in B.C.

As I said, I'd had a couple of rounds, so I wasn't inclined to let the conversation end there. "Oh well. You guys all look the same to me."

The place went quiet. People were unsure of what my snappy remark meant, especially Wally. "You mean us brown folks?" he asked, the smile gone from his face.

"No," I said. "You politicians."

I was quick on my feet. Wally erupted in thunderous laughter along with Sean and everyone else at our tables who heard the retort. I probably laughed the hardest. Wally came over and shook my hand, and we proceeded to have a drink together. He was such a gentleman. Years later I ran into him again, and we spoke about the incident and had another chuckle. In any case, I have to cut the lady in the Porsche some slack.

For the past few years, both the Sri Lankan government and the Tamil Tigers had repeatedly violated the cease-fire agreement. The conflict had been reignited in August 2005, with the assassination of Sri Lanka's foreign minister, Lakshman Kadirgamar. On January 6, 2008, I got an email from a friend of mine that my former Hartley College schoolmate

Ravishankar—*nom de guerre* Colonel Charles, the guy who orches-
trated the destruction of all the bombers at Colombo's air base—had
been killed the day before by a mine placed by the Sri Lankan Army's
Deep Penetration Unit. Whenever I heard news like this, I always felt
guilty beyond words. Here I was living in a nice home in a safe, free
country as a husband and father. Some of my friends were sacrificing
their lives to provide those privileges to the Tamils in Sri Lanka.
Meanwhile, I was debating which colour to paint our new home.

But I was a father and I had responsibilities. Should I have returned
to Sri Lanka to take up arms? I wasn't convinced that armed resistance
was even helpful in the post-9/11 world. And yet maybe hopeless
struggle was better than no struggle at all. But how can robbing one's
own family of hope be the right thing to do? There seemed to be no
way to reconcile the two worlds I inhabited. I was always conflicted.

There seemed no way to do something, and doing nothing wasn't
an option either. The world was witnessing Sri Lanka's resolute drift
back toward apocalyptic carnage. As someone who had suffered at the
hands of Sri Lanka, I knew what that meant for those on the ground.
Did I sympathize with Ravishankar's cause? Of course. Did I believe
Sri Lanka had the right to exist and to defend itself? Only a fool would
expect the government to accept Tamil demands without a fight, just
as only a fool would expect the Tamils to submit to government oppression without a fight. But a special responsibility for restraint to ensure
future reconciliation lay with the government. They had the preponder-
ance of force and the weight of international support behind them. And
I was seeing—yet again—Sri Lanka's arrogance and misguided
approach to dealing with Tamil grievances.

Sri Lanka was not allowing foreign correspondents to enter the
North to report on the war. What was it that Sri Lanka didn't want the
world to know? What was happening in the Tamil area was a humanitarian and moral tragedy. Even if one asserted that the Tamil Tigers
were largely to blame and were the authors of their own people's

misfortune, the plight of the Tamils and the egregious transgressions of Sri Lanka simply could not be ignored.

When I had returned to Vancouver from Sri Lanka years before, I decided I wanted to fully back the Tamil liberation struggle, whatever the personal cost. I didn't quite know what that meant, but I knew that I couldn't live my life only for myself and my immediate family. I wasn't naive about the Tamil Tigers. I knew they were part of the problem. Violence creates violence. Sri Lankan violence had created the Tamil Tigers, but the Tamil Tigers' violence could only deepen the spiral. All I could do was use my voice to amplify those I'd heard in the shattered towns and villages of my homeland. And not only their voices. I knew I spoke for the brave and humane Sinhalese like Colonel Dudley Fernando. I could not defend against tanks and bombers, but maybe I could help prevent the poisonous nonsense of government-sponsored hate from metastasizing in the marketplace of ideas.

Even though I lived in Vancouver, my name was familiar to many in the Toronto Tamil community because of what I had written about our freedom struggle. I have also attended a few community events when in Toronto on business. As the war reached its peak in Sri Lanka, I received a call from a community leader asking me to join the Canadian Tamil Congress (CTC), a non-profit organization. I agreed and was appointed the vice-president. I thought this position would help me to spread the message to the public and to serve my people who were facing an existential threat. Their struggles, my nightmares.

Meanwhile, the mainstream media and some politicians were whipping up hysteria against Tamils who were speaking against Sri Lanka, suggesting that anyone who did so was a Tamil Tiger sympathizer and supporter of terrorism. Michael Ignatieff was the leader of the Liberal Party of Canada and took an active part in drafting the report that came to be known as *The Responsibility to Protect* (R2P), published in 2001. He rejected the Tamil community's plea at the Parliament Hill and callously refused to meet the grieving families. It was a devastating

blow to Canada's Tamil diaspora, who had spent several months holding demonstrations, hunger strikes, and rallies to raise awareness of
the bloodshed in their homeland while demanding that the Canadian
government intervene. Why do Tamils not deserve to be protected?
Does one race have a monopoly on pain? Were the Tamils incapable
of feeling pain? Listening to and reading all the rhetoric about Tamils
would make you think so. March 2009 marked the moment when I
took a public stand against such xenophobic attitudes.

On March 17, 2009, after a long day in Calgary, I was flying back
to Vancouver. The flight attendant was distributing newspapers to the
passengers in the cabin. I asked for the *National Post*. I was an avid
reader of that paper. As the plane took off, I started browsing through
the paper and came across Jonathan Kay's unflattering editorial regarding the Tamil freedom struggle.

I was saddened and upset by that piece. I was bothered by it the
entire flight. As soon as I arrived home, I went straight to my computer
and started writing a rebuttal email to Jonathan Kay with the subject
line "This is not hate mail." I wasn't rude, threatening, or bashing. I'm
sure journalists often receive vile rants directed at them. I felt calmer
after sending the email. I went to bed. When I woke up, I saw a reply
from Jonathan. I was very surprised. He said, "If you feel strongly
about this, I will give you space on *National Post* for you to write an
op-ed to tell your side of the story." An offer I happily embraced.

My first op-ed was published in the *National Post* on March 20,
2009, under the simple headline "Why Canada's Tamils Are Upset."
In this 599-word piece, I shared my personal story and wrote that I
hoped that Canadians will spare Tamils still living in Sri Lanka a
thought and urge our government to raise its voice against an ongoing
tragedy. I struck a chord with readers. I received many emails of support. A reader named Sarah sent me the following note: "I wanted to
write to let you know that I FINALLY understand from your editorial why
the protests have been happening—something the regular news

coverage hasn't managed to do in either of the past two protests—
instill understanding. Thank you for your clarity and for sharing your
experience and for educating me." I also received a lot of hate mail
from Sri Lankan supporters and operatives working in Canada.

A few days later, Al Jazeera, Radio Australia, and many other media
outlets from around the globe were calling me for interviews. Between
leading a team at CI, writing op-eds, and doing interviews, I hardly
had time to sleep. But my people in Sri Lanka had not slept in months.

Later that month, I flew to London and spoke at the Parliament in
front of many lawmakers. The event was sponsored by a leading Tamil
organization in the U.K. Here, in part, is the speech I made:

The freedom I enjoy in the West is precious to me. I want to state
this at the outset, because I grew up in a country where freedom
is a rare commodity, and the slaughter of innocents is all too
common. I escaped state terror as an eighteen-year-old boy, and
today I stand in front of you as a forty-year-old man and father
of a four-year-old. Ladies and gentlemen, as a survivor of Sri
Lanka's tyranny, I have come here today to express my thoughts
in the hopes of ending this ongoing human catastrophe that has
engulfed my people. Even if I fail at my intended goal, at least I
can one day look my son in his eyes and say that your father did
everything he could to stop his cousins from being wiped off the
face of this planet.

Many of us have come together from all corners of the world
to London—the land of liberal democracy, with heavy hearts and
high hopes. Heavy hearts—because, while the world is silent,
Tamils like us around the world are watching a brutal, shameful,
despicable, and totally unnecessary takedown of our innocent
kith and kin. It's a disgusting spectacle, especially when we hear
Sri Lanka say that by doing so it is defending democracy. High
hopes—because we see such esteemed and noble dignitaries,

diplomats, politicians of different backgrounds with different
political ideologies, who have willingly come here to bring an
end to this ongoing, heart-wrenching, horrific human tragedy.

I concluded my thirteen-minute address by stating, "If Sri Lanka
wins, it will be a stupendous victory for state terrorism—not for
democracy." People clapped, perhaps to be polite. I wasn't hopeful
that anything would come of it. The world had decided to get rid of
the LTTE. And the LTTE had signed its own death warrant. In my
mind, the struggle had been lost since 9/11. Innocent people were
caught in the middle and being killed by both actors of aggression. I
met Reverend Jesse Jackson that night at a dinner event. He shook my
hand and said, "We are with the Tamils." I didn't pin any hope on that
either. On April 2, I reached out to the office of Archbishop Desmond
Tutu as a last-ditch attempt, hoping that he may have been able to
change the opinion of the world.

Tamils protested all over the world and all across Canada to save
their families. There were many peace marches, hunger strikes, and
vigils held. I let my pen do the talking. I felt more education was
needed for the Canadian public to understand this contentious issue.
Jonathan Kay was receptive to that idea. I subsequently produced one
more op-ed for the *National Post* on May 4, 2009, called "Understanding
Sri Lanka's Tamils." Sue organized the ground game in Vancouver.
We were doing this between working and looking after a four-year-
old—with no family in Vancouver to help us. We were keeping long
hours and quickly becoming exhausted.

My public denouncement of Sri Lanka caught the attention of the
thin-skinned criminals of Colombo. We were getting threatening phone
calls from anonymous men. The long arm of the Sri Lankan terror
apparatus had reached my quiet neighbourhood. One of our cars was
smashed by a baseball bat. The Vancouver police checked up on us
from time to time, which we are still thankful for. A few years after

that, I was put on a list of persons banned from entering Sri Lanka. It was a badge of honour.

After how long should a particular people's indigenous placement on the Earth become official and should they have unquestionable, inalienable rights? Fifteen years? 150 years? 1,500 years? On purely ethical and moral grounds, the West should help to stop this cleansing of Tamils from their traditional and ancestral lands, support the Tamil struggle for self-determination, and speak up against Sri Lankan tyranny. This was my position—and I believed it was consistent with humane ideals. Despite LTTE's shortcomings and misdeeds, I still supported the Tamil freedom struggle. How could I support Sri Lanka?

On May 10, 2009, out of desperation and in a watershed moment, about two thousand Tamils blocked the Gardiner Expressway in Toronto. But it didn't make a difference. It only further inflamed anti-Tamil sentiments.

The guns fell silent on May 18, 2009, with the defeat of the Tamil Tigers—the decades-long conflict came to a bloody end in the Sri Lankan breadbasket region of Vānni, nestled between fertile land and brilliant blue Indian Ocean in the besieged and blood-soaked village of Muḷḷivāykkāl, where the rain of death from Sri Lankan shells, mortars, and machine guns killed scores of Tamils. Thousands of the dead were children, and most of them died before they even knew that they were Tamils. Many died in bunkers or were burned alive or bombed in open spaces.

I woke up in Hotel Saskatchewan in Regina on that day. I was mentally and physically exhausted. I had no desire to meet with anyone; I just wanted to stay in the room and not talk to anyone. I wanted to crawl back into bed and wake up to a different kind of dawn. A dawn of freedom for my people. The unthinkable had happened. I was absolutely devastated by seeing the horrible footage that was coming from

Sri Lanka—the scorched-earth policies in Tamil areas, the use of Tamils as human shields. To kill the innocent on such a vast scale was horrifying; to deny the horror is simply inhuman. We know the kind of people who deny the Holocaust. What interest anyone has in denying the suffering of Tamils remains to be discovered.

I had to force myself to get ready and meet my direct report and a few clients in the lobby for breakfast. I got ready and waited for the elevator. In the hallway next to the elevator bank, I saw a stack of newspapers. The headline read "Sri Lankan Civil War: Tamil Tigers Are Defeated by the Sri Lankan Government, Ending Almost 26 Years of War." The war ended but the suffering of Tamils continued. This prompted me to write a third and final op-ed on the matter. On July 17, 2009, *National Post* published my final column called "The Silent Suffering of Sri Lanka's Tamils." By now, Jonathan and I had formed a friendship. A decade later, we remain friends. We had our differences and disagreements regarding the Tamil issue, but we maintained a civil and respectful discourse. If only Tamils and Sinhalese could do this, perhaps the country will find lasting peace and harmony.

The day after the war ended, on May 19, 2009, I finally received a reply from the international aide to the Archbishop Emeritus Desmond Tutu, which read, "On behalf of the Archbishop, I wish to thank you for the invitation extended to attend the World Tamil Peace Forum. Due to confirmed commitments, the archbishop will not be attending the event and sends his regrets."

Elie Wiesel, a Holocaust survivor and friend of the Tamils, released a statement on June 30, 2009: "Wherever minorities are being persecuted, we must raise our voices to protest. According to reliable sources, the Tamil people are being disenfranchised and victimized by the Sri Lankan authorities. This injustice must stop. The Tamil people must be allowed to live in peace and flourish in their homeland." I was so thankful for that.

But the reality on the ground was grim. Even in the aftermath of the war, many Tamils were kept in internment camps, long after the threat of military insurgency was over; there, they endured unspeakable human rights abuses by their own government. Many thousands died, and many more are still unaccounted for. Those who surrendered, including kids, were shot at point-blank range. I still maintain that war crimes charges on both sides are needed for reconciliation to happen.

It wasn't long before the fallout from Sri Lanka's descent into horror arrived in Canada. Once again, my two worlds converged. War found me in my new homeland.

I was already spent from all of the attention I had devoted to the cause of Sri Lankan justice when the MV *Sun Sea* showed up in Victoria, B.C., packed with Tamil refugees. That was August 2010. Not only was I tired, the person I reported to was tired of seeing me in the papers. He wanted me to get back to work.

But could I do nothing to help those who only wanted what I had been lucky enough to receive—freedom from violence and an opportunity to make the most of life? No one who believes in what Canada stands for truly believes that we should do nothing. When public opinion turned against the refugees, even those who were sympathetic felt that no one should be able to jump the queue. After all, people all over the world were waiting to get into Canada. Why should the Tamils be allowed to just show up?

Because they had no option. That was my answer. They were literally fleeing for their lives. They couldn't go to Colombo to apply for a visa. Tamils were not welcome in Colombo. No one can stand in line to do paperwork when their lives are in danger. They can't.

Sue organized a press conference at the Four Seasons on behalf of the Canadian Tamil Congress, making the case that all the refugees were asking for was a fair hearing. They didn't want to jump the queue and weren't asking for any special treatment.

The press conference did not go well. I had promised my boss I would keep my name and face out of the papers, and I stood there biting my tongue while the back and forth with the media got bogged down in statistics and abstractions. The oxygen was draining out of the conference room. Finally, I couldn't take it any longer.

"I was in their shoes years ago. I just want these people to get the same chance I got."

All the cameras panned to me. The lights were shining in my eyes. My promise to my boss had been broken. My face was on the cover of the paper the next day. But it was worth it. A few days later, I was talking to a client in Smithers, B.C., a small town northwest of Prince George. If you want to find an actual Canadian lumberjack, Smithers would not be a bad place to look. The people there are great, but you might not expect them to take a keen interest in human rights issues stemming from ethnic conflicts on the other side of the planet. And yet when I talked to my client, that was what was on his mind. When he read what I said that day, he told me, he realized that he hadn't been getting the whole story from the media. That convinced me I had been right to pipe up, even if it meant my boss (quite reasonably) wanted me to get back to work. That is what it means to live in two worlds.

The scale of the humanitarian tragedy in Sri Lanka was hard for me to fathom, looking on from so many miles away. Meanwhile, Sri Lanka's Sinhala majority celebrated the war's end with fireworks and parties as if they'd just won a cricket championship—hardly a sign that accommodation and reconciliation toward Tamils was in the offing. Uncle Fernando would have been appalled by their behaviour. The world consoles itself by talking of common human feeling, but as Tamils found out in May 2009, there are times in history when there is no such thing.

For many Tamils like me, this tragedy is a living flame from which we continue to draw sustenance and strength, as we build our lives successfully outside of Sri Lanka. In this light, the year of infamy—the 2009 massacre—will never be a mere historical footnote for Tamils. This and many other monstrous barbarities against Sri Lanka's Tamils still resonate within the hearts of many diasporic Tamils, including my own. We need to be victors for them not by bowing our heads as victims. Just as I have lived for Appā.

In an irony that can give hope only to those with the courage to remember, the violence of the Sri Lankan government helped define the Tamil homeland. Where are the boundaries of Tamil Eelam? That question was once asked by an Englishman connected with the British Refugee Council to the senior commander of the LTTE, Colonel Kiṭṭu. He answered it perfectly: "Take a map of the island. Take a paintbrush and paint all the areas where Sri Lanka has bombed and launched artillery attacks during these past several years. When you have finished, the painted area that you see—that is Tamil Eelam."

For me, an era may have ended in May 2009, but the significance of the freedom struggle—and the many thousand lives sacrificed, including my Appā's—would never be forgotten. If any good were to come from this ugly chapter in the cursed history of Tamils, it would be a celebration of the notion that Sri Lanka's anti-Tamil policies will never ultimately triumph over the indomitable spirit of the Tamil people. Tamils should celebrate this interminable triumph in the midst of this tragedy. Many Tamils like me are living this today. The Tamil diaspora has an important role to play in making sure we remember.

Sri Lankan Tamils deserve to be heard by the international community, as the pendulum of oppression has clearly moved against them. I hope the world won't wait until the Museum for Human Rights curates a history of the persecution of those who are left behind to tell their story. The proud flags of true democratic nations must not wave alongside those countries whose leaders lust to spill blood in a barbaric frenzy of ethnic fanaticism. In the absence of overwhelming and fundamental political change, true equality and dignity for Tamils in Sri Lanka will never be possible.

I was completely dejected and exhausted. I was at the edge of physical collapse like a marathon runner tottering toward the tape. My leadership was suffering as a result. I just wasn't around. I had to get back to work with focus. I needed to regain some lost ground.

A small movement within my direct reports had grown to topple me, which included a few key members and junior staff. I had bled in the shark's tank, and they saw an opportunity. Not only that, the person I was reporting to went from a long-term friend to a foe due to one major contentious issue. He was self-centred and lacked sympathy for others. Despite all the battles we had fought together, I knew his knife was out. He was calling all my reports to bury me. I knew my pal Sean and a few others came to my defence. Bill called me to see how I was doing, but he never asked about work. He knew I was in a dark place.

I feared my termination was imminent. I had a new kind of war ahead of me.

Soon I found myself in the middle of corporate war. There was intense competition that was occurring in the industry and at CI, and it was hard not to notice. I was being ignored when the big strategic decisions were made and not being invited to important conferences. I found myself no longer at the table and I felt marginalized. I was three hours behind the head office by living in Vancouver and felt left out. I came to know about important things when I woke up and read emails, after the fact. There was a joint effort by a few senior leaders in the company to undermine me and give me less exposure. Some of them detested my strong relationship with Bill. If I were a lesser person, I would've blamed it on racism. Instead, to quote former Intel chairman Andrew Grove, it was ABC: arrogance, bureaucracy, and complacency. Success breeds failure. We had been successful as a firm for far too long and it showed.

I fundamentally disagreed with the person I now reported to on the direction of our maturing industry. Canada's largest banks were dominating our industry, while independent firms like CI were being squeezed out. Meanwhile, we were preaching to the converted. I felt that we needed to invest in new growth opportunities. A new robust, sophisticated product lineup could focus on a new set of financial advisors and modernize our business to stay in lockstep with the rapidly changing times. We could be relevant again.

The status quo wasn't an option and it was indefensible. The retail investment business was increasingly being institutionalized. And we didn't have the right product or pricing. I also adamantly believed that we needed to diversify our financial advisor base as CI assets were concentrated in fewer hands. But my position was ignored, roadblocked, and, in some cases, ridiculed. Managers, instead of owners, were making important decisions. I was an owner and had a sizable amount of my own net worth tied to CI stock. I would always make decisions that were based on what was best for CI. I was getting more and more annoyed by this clique.

I did not like to be held hostage by the mood swings of the person I was reporting to—especially when I had done my best to bend over backwards to help him in the past and, more importantly, to protect him. It was amazing how quickly he forgot. His irritating manners were becoming the main source of my strife. My loyalty to CI was limitless, but my patience wasn't. I was on a collision course. It has been said that leaders who don't listen will eventually be surrounded by people who have nothing to say. I was seeing this play out. He was surrounded by short-term, finite thinkers who had nothing to say.

But I know this business is a long game. I needed patience. Not one of my strongest suits. After my prison experience, I do not tacitly relinquish responsibility for my welfare to someone else. If I had done that then, I might not be alive today. I had sent a message to Uncle Fernando and taken matters into my own hands. Here again, I found myself at the crossroads of corporate life and corporate death. If I did not take matters into my own hands in this situation, I knew I would be the last to know of the potential changes that would impact my corporate life. I survived a civil war. Whether I would survive a corporate war was yet to be determined. But I knew that I needed to be the head of distribution, and living in Toronto, to have a say in CI's destiny as well as my own.

So far, no one has ever *expected* me to win. As someone who has been consistently underestimated his whole life, I learned how to use this to my advantage.

It woke up the Point Pedro boy!

THE REBUILD

Over the years I've noticed that companies and countries take shape in similar ways. The best ones are built around an idea and a culture. They're populated by people busting their butts not just for themselves but for the greater good—and the ones that outperform others are often the ones that attract and nurture those with a combination of ambition and altruism. We don't usually think these things go together, but in my experience they do. I've seen it with my own eyes. People think the world of business is dominated by selfish, greedy assholes. And sure, they exist. But from what I've seen, those aren't the people who define our culture. They tend to be parasites on the margins.

That only makes sense. People who think only about themselves miss a *lot.*

Remember that I had to figure out how Canada works pretty much from scratch when I got here. I'm not going to say I got it all right, even to this day. But I will say that an outsider's perspective brings with it a clarity you will never have if you were born an insider. Insiders can take for granted all the little and big things that come together to make a functioning society and economy. When you are an outsider, you are always looking for clues. You have to keep your eyes open.

I had to figure out this cold, exotic place called Canada, and I also had to get my bearings in a new company and a new industry. Mutual funds were a relatively new product when I showed up in the mailroom. I had to figure out the subtle social rules and the unspoken norms that define any culture. The place where these rules applied just happened to be covered in snow and slush half the year.

One person who helped me orient myself back in those days, when I commuted from Scarborough to my job downtown, was a gentleman named Del Budd. He was full of life and enthusiasm, and his smile was electric. Whenever he was around, his presence made me happy; Del had that kind of impact on others. He would walk into the mailroom and greet me with big smile, say "Hello, kid," and then pull a sample marketing package for me to assemble. "Make me three hundred of those, please."

"Okay, Mr. Budd," and I would get to work. He would return a few hours later to pick them up and say, "See you in a month, kid," as he headed to cities in southwestern Ontario to make investment pitches. Sometimes I would help him carry the box to his car.

Looking at this cheerful, well-dressed man, you would never guess he had seen the worst of humanity. He and Mr. McRae both fought in the Second World War as pilots in the Royal Canadian Air Force. Mr. Budd flew 161 missions between India and Burma, supporting the British Fourteenth Army, when he was just twenty years old. Though Mr. Budd was fired at and witnessed the horrible things humans do to each other, he always maintained a happy disposition. Little things like death and destruction didn't get him down.

As I've said, Mr. McRae was an inspiration to me. His generosity helped me get through university, sure. But what kept me going was not money. It was gratitude for including me in a culture in which we all helped each other, and we all valued hard work and sacrifice. Talking to Mr. Budd in the mailroom, I learned that not only had this man seen horrors much like those I had seen but also he had put his life on the line to try to rid the world of those horrors. Mr. Budd had the same influence on me as Mr. McRae did. You stand a little straighter after you talk to people like that.

That's what I mean when I say that companies and countries take shape the same way. Leaders like Mr. McRae and Mr. Budd shape them. I have been grateful for those leaders since I got to Canada. Were they saints? Probably not. No one is. But that question misses the point. Who are we to judge them? Before we judge those who shaped the world we inhabit—and who shaped us—we should first acknowledge what we owe them.

That is a long way of saying that no one succeeds on their own. No one. Certainly not me. I couldn't even buy furniture when my mother arrived in Canada. My colleague Ray Chang took care of that for me, without even being asked. Like so many people within the company, he nudged me along the path to the top. And, of course, I was not the only person he helped over the years. Not that anyone knew exactly what he did for others, because he never told anyone.

I will always owe Ray, just as Ray was no doubt shaped by those who came before him.

I had to think about these things early on Sunday, July 27, 2014. I was at the gym when my phone started buzzing. It was a call from Lorraine. Due to club rules, I couldn't answer the phone. So, I went outside to call her back.

"Is everything okay?" I asked. Lorraine wouldn't call on a Sunday morning without a reason.

She was distraught. "I'm sorry to tell you," she said. "Ray has passed away."

I was as crushed as she was. I had just seen Ray in June, only a few weeks ago at our twentieth anniversary celebration of CI going public. He had some health issues, but he looked healthy and was on the mend. I'd had a lovely chat with him, remembering old stories and enjoying a good laugh. "What? He is gone?!"

"Yes. I will send you the funeral details when I get them," she said. She hung up in a hurry. I was absolutely saddened by the news. I hadn't been able to attend Mr. McRae's funeral, but no matter what, I wasn't going to miss this one. A day later, I had changed my scheduled trip to Chicago so that I could attend Ray's funeral in Toronto.

On August 8, I paid my respects to Ray. As I stood there looking at the lifeless body of a man who was once so full of life, I remember thinking of all the lessons I had learned from this kind human. "Three things: you must have a product. Then you must know how to market it, and you must know how to collect. It's not a sale if you don't collect," he would tell us all as he enjoyed a few puffs of his cigarette. He gave great life advice: "Strive to be the best, but keep an open mind. Question even the obvious because critical thinking will keep you relevant."

I spoke to Ray's family, told them about all the ways Ray had helped me to become who I am today. Then I sat outside with a heavy heart. I could never thank him enough for everything he had done for me. As I was reflecting on this, I saw Bill arrive. He saw me sitting there and came over.

"How are you doing?" he asked with care.

"I am managing, Bill."

"I hear you. Same here." He looked sad. I had never seen Bill like this in all the time I had known him. "I want to go pay my respects to Ray. Will you come with me?"

"Sure, Bill."

I could see Bill was shaken. I could understand. They had been business partners for more than two decades. And they deeply respected each other. "Tell me about everything Ray did for you, because I will be doing the eulogy tomorrow," said Bill. He had to ask me to find out because Ray was known as the "covert philanthropist."

When he did something good for others, he quietly helped and left his camera at home. When he generously donated to Ryerson (now Toronto Metropolitan) University, he refused to have his name on the building. After much cajoling by the president of the university, he finally agreed. Now the building bears his name: the G. Raymond

Chang School of Continuing Education. Ray's trademark modesty and generosity were legendary. Bill made a fitting tribute to a life purposefully lived.

He mentioned the many ways that Ray helped me. "What Ray did for Roy stands out as his true legacy. I see proof of Ray's kindness all the time when Roy offers his support to young people," said Bill to a fully packed St. Patrick's Roman Catholic Church audience. "His help turned Roy into a ridiculously successful, educated, and proud Canadian who is still at CI to this day."

Bill continued, "What set Ray apart from anybody I have ever known was that he was genuinely nice, and the generous things he did for people he came into contact with that nobody would ever know. In a world with so many rich and famous people, Ray lived his life being generous and anonymous. Giving his time and money was not a conscious choice at all. It was in fact his duty that was fulfilled with grace, dignity, and humility. He never really felt comfortable asking other people to do what for him was just a duty."

Bill could not have said it better. Ray was appointed to the Order of Canada the same month he passed away. What a tremendous loss to Canada and humanity.

I had been lucky to know such a man and to have benefitted from his example and his advice. I was fortunate, above all, to have glimpsed in his life an important principle—sure, we do things for ourselves, and we all want to do what is best for the next generation, but we owe a debt to those who came before us and created the world we live in with their courage and generosity.

With that principle in mind, Sean and I soon turned our thoughts to Del Budd. "Do you think Del is still around?" Sean asked me. We were a few minutes away from Kelowna on one of our road trips.

"Not sure, Hirtle," I said.

The next day at breakfast, Sean said, "I Googled Del Budd. He is in the Memory Project." This was a project to honour war veterans.

I called the Memory Project and left my contact information to be passed on to him. A few hours later he called, and we had a long chat. He remembered everything and still had the same happy disposition.

In his honour, Sean and I created the Del Budd Award of Excellence. It was Sean who initiated this. It was awarded to the salesperson who demonstrated great dedication, perseverance, and the most miles travelled to get a sale. It was our way of saying that the world needs more people like Del. The company was on board. It was obvious everyone considered the award a great honour.

A few years later I wanted Del to speak at our sales conference in front of the entire team. He was more than willing to do it. I sent a car service to his residence in Owen Sound, a couple of hours north of Toronto. When the car arrived at the hotel, I was there to greet him, and I noticed Del was sitting up front with the driver.

The driver, Nicholas, was from Lebanon. I have known him for over two decades. Sometimes when I would arrive after a very long day and many flight delays, I greeted him by saying, "It's a shitty day, Nicholas." He would reply, "It is never a shitty day when you land safely, Roy," with a beaming smile. I always liked his positive attitude. I used his service every chance I had. He had been driving for a company before, and now he had his own business. Nicholas was just like me: he came to Canada for a better life far away from trouble. Del bonded with Nicholas the entire ride. Nicholas tried to open the door for him, but Del refused and did it himself.

When he emerged out from the car, I saw a man with a full head of silver hair in a navy-blue suit, bold red tie, shiny shoes, and a bright smile that matched his white shirt. He looked sharp like a military officer, like Uncle Fernando. I put my hand out and said, "Mr. Budd, I'm not sure if you remember me. I'm Roy Ratnavēl. We met in the mailroom at Universal."

He shook my hand and said, "As they say in North Africa, I may not remember your face, but I remember your fez." What a guy! He still had that sharp wit.

I helped him settle in for the night at the hotel. He was to address the conference in the morning. He brought all his past sales memorabilia and showed it all to me with pride. I said goodnight. I slipped the night security guard a few dollars and said, "Please keep an eye on that room. The man inside is Canada's treasure." He nodded and assured me he would make sure of that.

The next morning, Del addressed the team. He hadn't lost his fast pitch at the age of ninety-three. Once a salesman, always a salesman. The room fell silent as he spoke and would erupt in laughter at his funny lines and observations. He shared war stories and life stories. He spoke for maybe twenty minutes. It was an inspirational and riveting talk. He may have gotten his training from Mr. McRae, because "he left when my team wanted him to stay."

He received a standing ovation. He was grinning ear to ear. It was so good to see him happy. His advice of the day was "you have to look at the funny side of life or you will go around moping all the time." It was a good reminder for us all. Off he went back to Owen Sound. They don't make men like him any longer. No, they don't!

I felt it was my duty to pay respect to Del. Canada is a free country because of the sacrifices that people like him made for this nation.

I had been consumed by the final stages of the war in Sri Lanka, and that had resulted in me failing as a leader: I hadn't shown empathy, interest, or care to the team that I had been entrusted to lead. With the distraction of civil war now behind me, I gave the leadership role my full effort. I went back and thought deeply about every mistake I had made. Bill was once again instrumental in coaching me through this failure. A few members of the team quit for various reasons, and I was focused on building and shaping a new team. By then, I had become a good talent spotter. But the knives were out for me in Toronto.

The thing about failure is that it is bound to happen at some point in life. You will embarrass yourself; I had. There was no doubt about it. Every person has some talent and perhaps even the training to succeed. But do you have the guts to fail? I have tried and failed—and I wanted to try again. I had to take that risk.

I built a rock-star team on my second try. When I was looking for talent, I didn't have a lot of time for advice like, "You need to hire X people; you need to hire Y people." I just went out and hired the most talented people I could find. CI's Western Canada team was very diverse in terms of gender, race, and sexual orientation. Not because I thought about diversity for its own sake, but because I care about diversity of thought. Diversity of demographics wasn't our strength; diversity of thought was. The team just happened to look like the United Nations. That was also true for CI as a whole.

I have learned one thing from leading teams: even with good intentions, planning, and the positive input of people around me, victory always came down to having a will to win. The Western team shined so brightly from 2010 to 2016. It was my crowning moment. The goal I had set for myself, to make the West shine in sales and be a cohesive team with the best camaraderie in the country, had been finally achieved.

I was proud of what I had done. The entire West was firing on all cylinders. In 1998, when I arrived there, the Western team had about two billion dollars in assets under management. In 2016, it had crossed over forty billion dollars. That was due to a combination of many factors, mergers and acquisitions, market appreciation, and solid sales momentum. Bill was quite pleased with what I had achieved. Redemption finally!

We were able to build great team camaraderie. Aside from team gatherings and legendary Christmas parties at my place, I was able to

build cohesiveness by caring intently for team members on a professional and personal level. It was like a family; people cared for each
other. I realized that sometimes acknowledgement by peers is worth
more than money.

Despite the successes, there was still an intense fire deep within
me, always burning. I wanted to reconnect to my past. Tamil music
had always made me relive the happier times while burying the horrors
of the past. Sue got me tickets to see my favourite Tamil music director Ilaiyarājā in concert in Toronto.

One of my favourite Tamil songs of all time, "Pūṅkāṟṟu Puthithāṉathu"
(*The garden air is new*), has lyrics that loosely translate to *"New life is
a struggle, which plays with two lives."* These poignant lyrics by Appā's
Kaṇṇathāsaṉ—one of the last songs he penned before his death in
1981—summed up the lives of my father and me. The first thirty
seconds of this song are Grammy-worthy. A stunning piece of compos-
ing! Ilaiyarājā is an absolute genius.

He was the first Indian musician to ever play with the prestigious
Royal Philharmonic Orchestra of London under the baton of the legendary John Scott. Ilaiyarājā's soothing music kept me sane inside the
dark bunker during the relentless aerial bombardment and shelling in
Point Pedro by Sri Lankan forces. At least for a moment, it helped me
forget about the death and destruction around me.

Those had been trying times even for an optimist. His music was
a vessel for my anxiety and profound sadness. I flew all the way from
Vancouver to see him in Toronto. I was so excited to be inside Rogers
Centre with the maestro, only a few metres and metal barriers between
us. It was a treat of epic proportions not just for me but also for the
many thousands in attendance. It was nostalgic. And I was glad that
this time there was no Mirage 2000 or MiG-27 buzzing over my head
and dropping bombs. Just music in peace.

Everything in the West was going well. My team was happy, and
things were running smoothly. I was enjoying being a leader, but I was

becoming bored as I closed in on my ten-year mark in this role. In March 2016, I flew to Fort Lauderdale to meet Bill. I joined him at the terrace bar at the Ritz. It was nice and hot that day. We ordered refreshing Hendrick's gin and tonics to cool off.

"Cheers, congratulations on a great achievement," Bill said. Finally, I had his approval. He was by then the executive chairman of the board, no longer the CEO.

"Thanks, Bill. I appreciate all that you have done for me, showing so much patience."

He smiled. He knew it was true. I was a bloody work-in-progress— but now I was a lion full of confidence.

"I would like to lead the national team, Bill."

"I think you would be tremendous at it," he said without hesitation.

First, I had to audition for the role. I was asked to come and present to the board. Of course, the person I reported to was against this idea.

"Make sure to treat this like the most important job interview you have ever had," said Bill. Point taken. He helped me prepare my presentation to the board, as I have never done it before. I went back to my wholesaler days. I stood in front of a mirror and practised my talk over and over. It reminded me of how Appā had trained me for my interview with the Canadian high commission in Colombo. My posture and words were meticulously choreographed, this time by me. I remember the lesson from my old man: "Do things to perfection." How could I forget that?

A few weeks later, I flew to Toronto and presented to the board. There was another individual in the race, endorsed by the Toronto faction. But I was ready. The fighting instinct of this Point Pedro boy was unleashed. I presented to the board. I knew I'd nailed it. At dinner that night, I was told by some of the board members that they really liked what they heard. The next day, I returned to Vancouver. Bill called me and said, "The board was very pleased by your talk. Well done." Do things to perfection. I hadn't let Appā or Bill down. I will never.

Despite the continued fierce objection by a few, in July 2016, at the age of forty-six, I was appointed head of distribution for CI Global Asset Management and executive vice-president of CI Financial. I was at the helm of retail distribution.

One could argue that I had inherited one of the toughest jobs at the firm at a turbulent time. I knew a long road was ahead of me. But this new role would make me grow even more. I was thrilled I'd made it this far. I could never have predicted this outcome when I'd been sitting scared in the dark bunker as a teenager. A long way from the mailroom to the boardroom. An even longer way from the Sri Lankan civil war.

This one was for Appā! He had made the right choice by sending me to Canada. Here I was: an executive at Canada's largest independent asset manager. I got there by demanding more out of myself and by never backing down to bullies. I never tried to please everyone. I would never have said anything honest if I had been hoping to make everyone like me. That's just not how it works.

Again, there were those who resisted this change. I had realized that's the nature of things. Humans have the endless capacity to bicker even when our very existence is under threat. I had seen this as a political prisoner as well. My many years of service to CI had been both a blessing and a curse. People often remembered me from a certain point in the past, rather than today's better version of Roy. I just had to win them over. Our industry had changed dramatically, and we needed to transform our business to win back our competitive position.

Every moment of my time in Canada has been marked by my sense that I was living in two worlds. My promotion meant seeing the personal and the professional overlap in a new and very painful way. The years that followed may have been the toughest climb I ever had to make professionally. I had to restructure the team to fit with the new reality of shrinking market share for independents and the changing distribution model. That earned me the unfortunate moniker "Neutron Roy"—riffing on the nickname originally awarded to Jack Welch of

GE for his ruthless housecleaning—by a few of my colleagues. It meant parting ways with many of my dear friends for decades. One of them was Sean, my best friend and brother-in-arms. We had fought many business battles together. We had travelled, laughed, and partied together for years.

How was I supposed to execute on this? It was one of the hardest decisions I had to make. Many nights I couldn't sleep, thinking about this. I felt like I was about to betray my best friend. Delivering the message to him was even harder. I said nervously, "Sean, you know I think the world of you, but this is business. You have been a great ally for me, but the time has come for CI to part ways with you."

It was much harder for him to listen to the message. I could see that. Sue and Aaron were very upset by this too. Business can be heartless, but people always emerge from it fine in time. Though our friendship has now dwindled down to the occasional phone call, I'm happy that we are at least still speaking to each other. It didn't work out that way with many others.

When I was focused on making CI's Western team the best in the country, I travelled a lot more. I was hardly ever home. I only saw Sue and Aaron on the weekends. I was travelling so much that in ten years, I spent over one thousand nights in the Starwood Hotels chain, which earned me elite status for life. But on the home front, my absence left a deep emotional deficit.

Every time I packed my travel bag, it was hard to look at Aaron's sad little eyes. He missed me a lot in the same way I had missed Appā. I would spend time with Aaron on the weekends to make up for it. I enjoyed watching him play soccer and basketball and compete in track and field events. I always believed that kids should play both team and individual sports. Competing in a team environment and competing against oneself can instill values in kids that set them up for success.

I was competing against others. That was my job. But I was also always competing against myself to be better. And to be a better father, like Appā was.

Aaron had speed. He loved competing in track. His events were the one-hundred-metre sprint and hurdles. He would win gold in both pretty much at every event, or he'd at least medal. I was so proud of him. But he was starting to become complacent. I could see that. Complacency always leads to failure. His coach was having difficulty getting Aaron to focus on his starts and strides. Things came to a head at a large event at Burnaby's Swangard Stadium. Aaron was in top shape and running well that season. He qualified for the hundred-metre final with the fastest time of the eight finalists. But the final was the last event of the day, around four in the afternoon. It was only eleven in the morning.

"Aaron, I want you to stretch, stay hydrated, and stay in the shade."

"Okay, Dad," he replied like an obedient son.

But later I saw him with his buddies clowning around and acting irresponsibly. So, I went up to him and said, "Your final will be soon, and I really want you to focus on that."

"I will be fine," said confident Aaron.

I left him alone. I knew he was about to learn something important.

He looked very tired, while his competition looked ready. They had been stretching and fuelling themselves the whole time. I saw Aaron at the starting block, and I knew that he would never forget the next few moments. He was going to lose badly.

The starter gun went off. Aaron had a bad start, bad strides, bad form, and a terrible finish. He came fifth. The kid who qualified with the fastest time didn't even make it to the podium. He looked dejected.

The beauty of sports is that competition sifts out all the extraneous factors and all the excuses. There was no institutionalized racism involved in this outcome. There was no shadowy white figure who made him run slower. All the kids who were at that starting block had an equal advantage. His failure was all on him.

While I understand that this race was completely fair, not all of life's races are like this, and in some cases, admittedly, there are those who have a head start. I'm not denying that. As a society, we should all do what we can to lower the barriers to those who are underprivileged. At the same time, we can't blame every personal failure on society. Personal responsibility supersedes everything. I knew blaming others would never lead to my success; it would only guarantee dependence and failure.

Aaron's failure was of his own making. I saw Aaron hunched over with his hands on his knees, trying to catch his breath and shedding a few tears—and no parent loves to see their kid suffering. But this lesson was more important than a few moments of disappointment. His trainer was hurrying toward him. "Where are you going?" I asked.

"I'm going to console, Aaron. He looks upset." Who wouldn't want to make a nice young kid feel better? Well, me.

"Why would you rob him of this great life lesson? I want you to stay here with me. Do *not* tell him he was great. Because he wasn't. Let him reflect on it."

His coach abandoned his unnecessary self-esteem-boosting mission.

I see this as a fundamental flaw in how society has been dealing with individual failure. The self-esteem movement has destroyed a generation of people and set them up for failure. Of course, I want kids to have self-esteem. I'm not arguing against it. But they also need to learn the harsh reality of what it takes to *deserve* self-esteem. Different inputs will lead to different outputs. Trying to equalize that output by rewarding everyone in the same way only leads to reinforcement of this bad behaviour. As someone who oversees a large team with many young people, I witness the negative effects of what our schools have done. Not in all cases, but most.

On our drive home, Aaron was silent. After about ten minutes, I broke the silence. "How are you feeling?"

"Not feeling good," Aaron confessed.

"Well, how can you?"

"I'm upset I didn't medal today, Dad," Aaron lamented.

"I hope you are upset at yourself, but not at the result. Because you can't be upset by the result you didn't get with the work you didn't do."

He nodded his head in agreement.

Maybe that sounds harsh, but I know very well what it feels like when someone you love and trust refuses to make excuses for you. If you subsidize undesirable behaviour, you will get more undesirable behaviour. My father never accepted second best from me, and neither does my wife. Whenever I'm defeated or feeling sorry for myself, Sue will fire me up and motivate me by saying, "This is not the man I married. Get up and fight." I'd rather someone show confidence in me than make me feel better about my blunders. And I treat Aaron the way I want to be treated. A kick in the butt can be the highest form of respect. I have received many kicks in my butt from Bill, always well-meaning.

We are all worthy of a life we desire. But it can only happen if we exhibit the right behaviour and mindset. Be like that bird in D.H. Lawrence's poem. Have no self-pity. We are all individuals capable of shaping our own futures and building our own lives. At the same time, we are all shaped by the people around us and by their values. If you want someone to be weak, tell him nothing is ever his fault. If you want him to be brittle, tell him that what others think of him defines him. If you want to see what he is capable of, make sure there are no excuses available. Providing excuses is as dangerous as leaving sharp objects and prescription medication lying around.

Aaron has given his family a lot to be proud of, but nothing makes my heart swell more than his resilience. On one occasion, Aaron came to me at halftime in his soccer game and said, "That kid called me a darkie and made fun of me." He pointed at a white kid.

I replied, "You do have a darker skin. How did his comment make you feel?"

"My feelings were hurt."

I understood his angst. "Well, Aaron, idiots are plenty in this world, and you will meet them throughout your life. The only way you can shut them up is by showing them what you can accomplish. Now go back and show that kid what a darkie can do."

Aaron went on to score two goals in the second half. On the way home, I said, "That kid just wanted to get under your skin. Maybe he was frustrated. It doesn't matter. Don't ever let anyone know that they rattled you, and do not ever allow someone you don't know to have power over your emotional state." Sue and I have been consistent on this message. This runs deep in his veins now.

I know that for a fact. A year after we moved to Toronto, a skinny kid with long platinum-blond hair called Aaron a terrorist during a fierce semi-final soccer game. Aaron didn't miss a beat: "Easy there, Rapunzel." And he carried on like nothing had happened.

Every parent heard what that kid called our boy. The referee gave Rapunzel a red card right away. The kid and his father protested the decision even though the father heard what his son had said to Aaron. The coach came to us and asked if we wanted to take this further, but we said no. Aaron had handled the problem on his own. What would he gain from some sort of commission? Besides, Sue and I thought the kid's father was punishment enough. Whatever values were shaping this young soccer player, they wouldn't serve him well.

The world of high-stakes youth soccer, helicopter parents, and entitled young athletes was something I could never have foreseen as my friends and I rode our bicycles around the dusty streets of Point Pedro, or when government artillery and attack planes shattered the quiet of those days. It has never been easy for me to reconcile that world with this one.

But still, something in the way my parents brought me up prepared me for a world I couldn't have imagined. My father, of course, drummed into me the importance of hard work and a commitment to excellence. He took it as his job to shape me and then to send me out into the unknown.

My mother was more like Del Budd, now that I think of it. She met the world with mostly cheerful composure. And when a crisis arrived, she sacrificed for her boys without hesitation. She didn't fly an airplane, but she put the lives of her sons ahead of her own when the bullets were flying and the shells shrieked overhead. There is no greater courage than that.

I had a duty to look after her. Am'mā was living in her own condo that I bought for her. It was twenty minutes away from my new home in Toronto. I had picked our home because, among many attributes, it had a heated driveway. I'd always wanted to have one, just like Mr. McRae.

Am'mā was happy to have me back in Toronto after almost two decades of being away from her. I was also happy to be back and closer to her. She needed help. A lot of help. She was struggling to perform basic functions and had deteriorated so much mentally and physically. Her paranoia was dialled up exponentially. But she was still fighting hard to live a dignified life. Due to my workload, I only saw her on the weekends. I would take her out for meals. She hardly ever cooked. When she did, it was barely edible. A lady who was once an exceptional cook was now no longer. Her famous fish curry was no more.

She had a fall and was hospitalized for a month. Then she underwent a minor surgery on March 26, 2018. I drove her in the early morning to the surgery. Sue and Uncle Mahēs (Am'mā's brother) took turns being with her at her place during the daytime. I took the night shift and stayed with her. I walked her to bed, and she was moving very slowly. I helped her to lay down.

"Mahān, can I have some water by the bed?"

I filled her water bottle and placed it on the nightstand. "Am'mā, whatever you need, please wake me up. Do not get up on your own."

She nodded, but I knew my mom. She was very independent.

As I turned the lights off, she said, "Please come here, Mahān." I went by her side. She asked me to lean in even closer toward her. When I did, she gave me a kiss on both cheeks and said, "Thank you for everything." It made me well up. She had gone through a lot since she was forty-four and all alone without Appā. She had endured so much sorrow in her life. Many misunderstood her, including me at times. They didn't know her condition. Mental illness is a stigma in most communities, but especially in the Tamil community.

I tucked myself into a sleeping bag on the floor in the living room next to her bedroom. I had had a very long day: up at four for a workout before I drove her to surgery; downtown for our executive committee meeting; back to her place after work that night. The minute my head hit the pillow, I was gone.

When I suddenly woke up around 2:45 a.m., I saw the washroom light was on. I knew she had gotten up on her own without asking for assistance. Typical Am'mā. Or maybe she'd called for me, and I didn't hear her. I popped out of the sleeping bag and walked along the corridor that connected the living room and the washroom. I saw her hunched over, head tilted down, one knee on the ground, her body against the door frame of her bedroom. When I touched her hand, it felt cold.

Immediately, I put her on her back to try to give life to the woman who gave life to me, by performing cardiopulmonary resuscitation in a feeble and desperate attempt to save her, while calling 9-1-1. But to no avail. I stood there feeling suffocated over her lifeless body. Memories of our past shared activities and their loving and tender nature played in my mind. The emergency team arrived and did their best, but she didn't respond.

My Am'mā, Indra Ratnavēl, bid adieu unexpectedly on March 27, 2018. She was born in Point Pedro, Sri Lanka, and called Toronto, Canada, home for twenty-nine years. My Appā's death on April 21, 1988, was the defining moment of her life. Reminders of her happier days with her husband were everywhere. A deep ache always followed her and tormented her for thirty years until her last breath. My father died of a bullet and my mother died of a broken heart. How I wished to meet the soldier who fired the fatal shot at Appā. Man, how I would mangle him up so badly, I thought. But would it change the outcome?

Her eyes were still open; it reminded me of the lady I had pulled out of the rubble in Point Pedro. I gently closed her eyes. The emergency crew left. I was waiting for the body removal. I sat next to her, just as she had sat next to my father's lifeless body. I didn't call anyone. I regressed back to a life I once knew. My resentment rose. All the progress I had made in my sessions with my shrink came unbundled at that very moment, in that corridor of the condo. My corridor of emotion was flooded with stark anger. I wanted to smash the shit out of everything and everyone.

Then Del Budd's advice for a happy life came back to me: "Well, you have to look at the funny side of life or you will go around moping all the time." A funny thought emerged. My old man had thirty years of quietness without her. Now she had joined him. He would be losing his freaking mind. "Go easy on him, Am'mā, and quit bugging him about his drinking and smoking," I said quietly to her, as though she could hear me. That put a smile on my face. It was time for me to let others know of her passing.

Though I was absolutely gutted, I was also relieved that I was there with her during her last moments and that her passing was hopefully peaceful and painless. "Thank you for everything," those were her last words to me and would forever be etched in my memory. I will cherish it. I want to remember her for how she took great care of me and my brother when we were growing up in wartorn Sri Lanka, and subsequently how I took care of her when she arrived in peaceful Canada in 1989. I did all that I could to give her a life of dignity and assurance. Perhaps in time this could offer me some solace.

I was grateful for having had her in my life for forty-eight years. My mother was no longer, and she had been relieved of all her anguish.

‖‖‖‖|

THE CANADIAN

I love Canada. It isn't just that this country took me when my family
was facing death in Sri Lanka, or that a senior person at CI took me under
his wing when I needed a break. I can honestly say that throughout my
career, I have received support, respect, and fair treatment in this country. It's not one person or one thing. You can't understand a country from
one or two anecdotes any more than you can understand the market from
one or two data points or one or two stocks. That's why it makes sense
to look at the whole index. You can't make generalizations unless you
look at the big picture. I now have decades here in Canada. One person
or experience, good or bad, can never define it. But when I look at it all,
there is no question: Canada is a special place.

I am always grateful for the opportunity to express my gratitude whenever I am asked to speak publicly about my experience as an immigrant.

In June 2017, I was asked to give a Walrus Talk at the Vancouver Art
Gallery about my experience in Canada. There were a few other speakers
as well. In my speech, I briefly mentioned the very first Canadian I ever
met: the visa officer at the High Commission of Canada in Colombo,
Sri Lanka, Robert Orr. After my talk, one of the other speakers came up
to me and said that he knew Bob from his days in the diplomatic corps
and provided me with Bob's contact information. I was thrilled and sent
Bob an email right away. A few days later, he replied. We set up a lunch
meeting on September 21, 2017, in Ottawa.

Three decades later, it was nice to again meet the man who had granted me entry to Canada. I gave him my sincere thanks. I was a little surprised that he thanked me, when I felt strongly it should be the other way around.

"You have no idea how much it meant to hear from you and to know that things worked out so well," he said. "As a visa officer, you would see the 'before' picture, but rarely do you know what happened after to people you had the opportunity to accept."

Talking to Bob really brought into focus a lot of things that had been rattling around in my mind. When I first met him in his official capacity, Bob seemed like all of Canada to me. But he was only one human being. I might have been just another statistic of war to him back then, but he treated me like a human being. One glance at the scars on my back was all it took to evoke real sympathy. Those scars were evidence of a kind of pain you can't witness without imagining what it must feel like to receive them. Real empathy is the bedrock of civilization and of the world's great moral codes. They all say the same thing: treat others the way you want to be treated.

I think that was what was so rewarding about getting to see Bob again. I got to know him as a fellow human being, not just as a consular official. I was heartened to know that, all these years later, he still thought about the people to whom he had issued visas as fellow humans, and that he still cared. I was happy to make his day. But he had made my life here possible. I hope he knows that. We are still in touch.

The thing is, as much as I admire and respect Bob, my friendship with him is not unique. I have been a Canadian for a long time now, and I have met countless Canadians who have treated me with the same openheartedness. I remember once walking through the lunchtime chatter of the business crowd at Calgary's Petroleum Club during the Stampede when I heard a booming voice from several tables away.

"There goes my favourite brown guy!"

The room got a lot quieter. I peered through the crowd to identify the speaker. Then I saw this barrel-chested man in a ten-gallon hat and cowboy getup.

He walked up to me and gave me a big bearhug, "I love you, brown guy."

"I love you, too, honky," I replied loudly.

We both broke out into laughter. The business crowd went back to their chatter and negotiations once they'd witnessed two old friends' tomfoolery.

It was one of our great clients and, more importantly, an amazing friend, Brian Hein. One of the nicest people I have met in my life. So kind-hearted and generous in spirit. Our relationship was almost two decades old. It was people like him who had given me a chance when I was young and inexperienced.

I have met many people like him across Western Canada, from Winnipeg to Victoria. I have slept in their homes. I know their spouses and kids. I've gone on hunting and fishing trips with them. I've had clients bring me fresh moose meat to business appointments. I've attended the Calgary Stampede with them. Never missed one in twenty years, until the pandemic shut things down in 2020.

I suspect I got to know Canada in a way few immigrants have: by travelling through small towns, giving sales speeches to rooms full of farmers and co-op managers in Dawson Creek, Prince George, Smithers, Fort Nelson, Brooks, and Lethbridge. Often I would be the only non-white person in the room. One time, when it was my turn to address the audience, I said, "Geez, it's a good thing I'm here, otherwise this might look like a Klan convention." The room erupted in thunderous laughter. They got it.

Other times, to break the ice, I'd make jokes to help defuse the social anxiety in a room. Like if a guy was named James and I called him Jim, I'd say, "Oh, you white guys and your complicated names." They got that too.

How many times have I heard, "Oh, that's an interesting last name! Where is it from? Is it short for something? Tamil, eh? Where are you *originally* from?" Like many Tamils, I have been asked that a *lot*.

Does asking a question like this make you a racist? I imagine that depends on how you define racism. But do such questions bother me? Why should they? I am proud to be Tamil. Why would being asked about it bother me?

As for my name, well, the length of Tamil names is an objective fact. They're long. Tamil names, when translated to English, take on a vast array of letters. Mostly vowels. It can look like an optometrist's eye chart. The Tamil language does have 247 characters. We have to find a way to use them all! My last name has eight letters. That's a short name by Tamil standards. My mother's maiden name has sixteen. You can't fit that on a hockey jersey. Should I be embarrassed that the alphabet of my native language has more letters than English does? For the life of me, I can't see why. No one has ever explained to me what I have to be embarrassed about.

Of course, I do realize that such questions are considered impolite in some circles. Every culture has its own manners, and I respect that. If asking where someone is from is like using the wrong fork at dinner, I get it. It's frowned upon, and it separates the self-consciously polite people from those who may pay less attention to subtle rules. That's fine. But before we dismiss the people who ask those questions as boors or something worse, I need to be clear. I have done a lot of fundraising events with my clients and friends. Some of them might have been politically incorrect, but they were the first to donate to charities. And when the 2004 tsunami laid waste to Sri Lanka, many of my Western Canadian friends called to see if my family was okay. They wanted to donate whatever they could.

I am proud and honoured to have been able to learn about Canada the way I have. I feel as though I have had the opportunity to see the *real* Canada, not the one people talk about in op-ed pieces. The generosity and warmth of the Canadians I have met match up with the humanity of the first Canadian I met. Canadians have treated me the way I would treat them.

Of course, if you grow up in Canada, you may never notice how exceptional it is. You may not notice that in many other places—perhaps most—ancient hatreds still shape everyday life. It is not everywhere that you can walk into a room of people who look different from you and expect to be greeted warmly. What we have here is special. And I want to make sure my son never takes it for granted.

Still, I was surprised one lazy Saturday morning by a jarring question from my son. "Were you sad when you were in prison, Daddy?"

The morning's tranquility was shattered. Honesty isn't easy in a moment like that. Not when it invites the ugliness of the dark past to the sunny breakfast table. Once he had asked me what happened to his Appāppā and I lied, saying he had died in an accident to spare the kid from my nightmares.

I was shocked by the question. I had never told him that I had been in prison. He must have overheard conversations between Sue and me. But this was no time to lie.

"Yes," I said.

"Are you happy now?"

"Yes, very happy."

"Why, Daddy?"

"Well, because I feel safe to live with my family in Canada—that's why."

He gave me a peck on the cheek and said, "Why is Canada safe for Tamils?"

"Well, Aaron, in *this* country, people of minority groups do not wind up dead."

That was probably the wrong answer to give a six-year-old. At that age, injustice is something that happens on the sandbox scale, and death is something distant and abstract. Aaron probably had no idea what I was talking about. He just went on doing his own thing.

But I thought about it a lot. And I see now that the reason Canada is safe is that Canadians treat others the way they want to be treated, just like Bob Orr.

Canada has taught me some important lessons. I didn't arrive here fully formed or brimming with wisdom. Like all young people, I thought I knew more than I actually did. One important lesson was offered to me at an investors' meeting in Lethbridge, Alberta.

If you have never heard of Lethbridge, ask an urban dweller what it's like. Odds are, you will be told it's a town full of rednecks. That's what I thought too. To make things worse, when I walked into the hall where all the investors were sitting down to dinner, the only spot I could find was with an older, blue-collar couple. I assumed I was in for a dreary evening trying to make conversation with these bumpkins.

I discovered how wrong I was as soon as I sat down and made an observation about the wine. As it turned out, the husband knew more about wine than I did. When I mentioned that I was from Sri Lanka, the husband spoke knowledgeably about Northern Sri Lanka; it turned out that he had spent months there, volunteering in the effort to rebuild in the wake of the 2004 tsunami. Despite whatever I thought I could tell about this couple from their appearance, they were well read, widely travelled, and generous, decent, warm-hearted human beings. We remain friends to this day.

When I got back to my room that night after hours of great conversation, I was humbled and ashamed. What had led me to think I had been entitled to judge them? That in itself bespoke a blinding vanity. And I *was* blind. I thought I knew who they were at a glance, and I was completely wrong.

I have never forgotten that lesson. You can't tell what a person thinks from what they look like. Few people would disagree. We all learn that in school. But many of us act as though you *can* tell. Some people think I'm oppressed just because I'm not white. Some people think a white person who is not wearing fashionable clothes is a bigot.

As a youngster, I had seen Sri Lanka fall to pieces in a war rooted in a very real and deadly form of bigotry. I know what *real* hatred looks like. It is human nature to prejudge people in a group based on what we've heard or our past experiences. There is no changing that. It is what comes next that we control. We take those prejudices and compare them to the individual. If our eyes are truly open, we are often humbled.

A bigot is a person who doesn't change their mind regardless of the character of the person they meet—no matter what colour their skin may be. Trust me, there are plenty of brown bigots. The overwhelming majority of white people I've met are not. Like other characteristics, bigotry has nothing to do with skin colour.

Just to be clear—this is a source of great optimism to me. This is why Colonel Fernando saved my life. He didn't see me as a Tamil or an ethnic enemy. He saw me as a friend's son. That's humanity. And this is why I have many Sinhalese friends. Their ethnicity does not implicate them in the policies of a government that killed many innocent Tamils. I treat them the way I would want to be treated. They do the same for me.

It is amazing what you can learn over dinner. When I go to small towns, I meet people who don't even think about race. When I have dinner with well-to-do urbanites, I sometimes get the impression that race is *all* they think about.

For the members of this group, group identity is more important than individual identity. Since I'm a person of colour, I must therefore fall into the oppressed group. Nice white ladies often go out of their way to sympathize with me about all of the barricades that racism has thrown up to thwart my success here in Canada.

Oddly, I don't see things that way. I think I've done all right. I was named one of Canada's fifty best executives in 2020 by *Report on*

Business. The award was for individuals leading their companies through COVID-19 and helping build a better country in the process. I'm not saying I deserved all that. When *Report on Business* contacted me about it, I thought they had the wrong guy. My point here is not that I have done a great job. My point is that white Canada has not held me back. It's that Canadians have helped me every step of the way.

I have to admit that this testimony almost never changes people's minds. One particular well-to-do progressive made the argument that if I hadn't been oppressed by white privilege, I must therefore have *benefitted* from it. In her view, I am now part of the denigrated, despised "one percent." Since I live in a nicer part of Toronto and have moved up a few rungs on the economic ladder, in her view I'm now incapable of understanding or sympathizing with the plight of people of colour, despite my past. "You have sold out to the system," she claimed. She may have meant that as a compliment—since now I, too, would be entitled to make a spectacle of hating myself. But what boggled my mind was her assumption that by becoming successful, I had also become *white*. This sentiment is also common among some brown folks. According to them, I'm a *'coconut'*: white on the inside, brown on the outside.

Recently someone took offence when I said that I believe in lowering the barrier, not the bar. I believe in meritocracy, and I only hire talent, regardless of race, religion, or sexual orientation. To my amazement, a white lady replied, "You don't understand the struggles of people of colour." It was a virtual meeting so I thought I must have had my camera off. But no. It was on. This white woman was looking at my '*coconut*' brown face and assuming that she knew better than I did what life is like for someone like me.

That logic is simple: if you happen to be a person of colour, you are *by definition* oppressed. If you are not oppressed, you are not a person of colour.

I know many people who hold these opinions have good intentions, or claim to. Others just go along with the crowd. Still others may be closet racists, who believe that their self-accusations mark them as morally superior. It is pure moral exhibitionism. Maybe they are looking for abolition from sins they didn't commit. Guessing what is in the hearts of the woke is not something I am interested in. It is mostly irrelevant.

What is important is that we all understand that the kind of sympathy that is so often on offer feels a lot like condescension. The immigrants and people of colour I know want no part of it. In fact, most of us don't want to be seen as members of a group at all, let alone members of a group to be pitied.

Most of the people denouncing themselves are not oppressing anyone. They are giving power to themselves that they do not actually possess. Repenting for their whiteness is just a way of presenting themselves as morally superior people. It is a narcissistic ploy to make themselves look good to the world, and it has nothing to do with fighting for equality. It takes zero courage to hold such a moral stance.

It took me over thirty years to get here. As a South Asian migrant who rose from nothing to assume a leadership role on Bay Street, I don't believe that there is a shadowy white man out there trying to keep me or people of colour down in life. Like many newcomers, I achieved success through hard work and determination. Now so-called progressives want to discredit that and take it away from me? No thanks.

I know I am not the only immigrant who is bewildered that those who claim to be on our side have so little respect for what immigrants and refugees go through. Uprooting yourself from everything familiar means remaking yourself—and it is up to each of us to make sure that the person we become is a success. I wanted to take the lid off the self-made restrictions I had put on myself—and I always wanted to be focused on winning. I wanted to exhaust my potential. I didn't want to quit until I had nothing left to give. I was given a toolbox and a set of tools. I was supposed to work those tools as hard as I could—for every heartbeat that I had. I had to create my own life. I had to go from "Subēndraṉ" to "Roy." I had to put on seventy pounds of mostly muscle. I had to learn how to properly enunciate words, and I had to learn to crack jokes and endear myself to Canadian audiences. I had to outwork everyone and everything. I *never* wanted to be a victim. Don't call me that.

Progressives often express bewildered dismay when immigrants vote for political parties that espouse an ethic of responsibility and hard work. But there is no mystery there. Immigrants are pretty much *by definition* people who believe in responsibility and hard work. Just ask one.

I could have ended this book a few chapters ago. Scared boy escapes ethnic violence. Immigrant kid rises from the mailroom to the executive suite. It's a good story. I am very proud of it. When I was working in that factory on the outskirts of Toronto, I could barely dream of the way things worked out. I would have been happy for the dream to conclude with corporate success. But life is never so uncomplicated. Reality just keeps happening. And the mental habits that helped me understand my new country and succeed in it didn't just go away. I'm still curious. I still like to talk to people. But something about Canada has changed, and not for the better. It has transformed from a bulwark of a free and colour-blind society into a Social Justice utopia whose only inputs are skin colour, gender, and race and whose only outputs are grievance, division, and victimhood.

Living in a free society, like Canada, for many years, I never had to worry about speaking my mind. One of the most valuable pieces of advice my mentor Bill Holland ever gave me was to speak my mind openly, particularly when I knew I might be cutting against the grain. That confidence has helped me succeed. Could he offer that advice to a mailroom employee today? Could I?

I couldn't in good conscience wrap up my story before I got to the end. That would have invited a misleading interpretation. It would have been dishonest. It would have been a disappointment to my father, who insisted on the power of reason and clarity of expression to winnow out the truth. And it would have been a poor way to thank Mr. McRae and Del Budd, who fought in the Second World War to protect Canadian freedom and then invited me to benefit from it. Dissembling would be no way to repay my debt to Bob Orr and the country that has done so much for me. For that matter, it would be no way to repay Uncle Fernando and Aunty Swarṇā, who showed me the meaning of courage and humanity. So, this is my third act. I'm speaking up so the world can hear me.

Not that everyone wants to hear what I have to say. And that is my point. Anyone is welcome to disagree with me. That is what freedom is for. But I am finding out that a lot of people do not see things that way.

In August 2019, I spoke at an event. During the Q&A session, I was asked, "Does racism exist in Canada?" I replied something along the following lines to an audience of colour: "If you are a minority anywhere in the world, it doesn't matter, but sometimes you have to deal with idiots and bigots out there. But it doesn't fundamentally make a huge impact on your ability to make a difference and make a positive contribution. And please stop telling your children that there is a shadowy white man always trying to keep them down in life. If you keep telling them that, why would they even try? It is a poisonous chalice, and please stop doing it." Most of the audience clapped.

Those who didn't agree with me waited until later that night to confront me. They wanted me to retract my statement and repent. They were in my space, surrounding me and trying to intimidate me. I told them to take a hike. I was routinely tortured at the age of seventeen to confess to things I didn't commit. I wasn't going to be pushed around by a mob in Canada.

But the internet has given mobs new ways to swarm. A few days later, my endorsement of resilience and meritocracy became "controversial." Even some of my friends were asking me to delete any videos of my comments that were out there. The event organizers never released the video, out of fear of reprisal I imagine. But I have an amateur video of my comments still with me, and what I said is not controversial at all according to many who I have shown the video to.

But my point here is not that I was right. Not even close. Maybe I'm wrong. Maybe I am even controversial. If so, let's discuss. The problem is that we have lost the art of disagreement. What troubles me, and what has convinced me that there is a third act, is my fear that attractive euphemisms—*hate speech, incitement to violence, disinformation, harm reduction*—are nothing more than weapons used to shut down free speech. If they can be used against a Tamil immigrant, they can be used against anyone.

As someone who has seen legitimate suppression of free speech in Sri Lanka, I am more than troubled by this emerging trend in the Western world. I must speak up! I want to question these new ideas. You can't replace truth with your own version of reality. People have rights; ideas do not. Feelings really do not matter to facts. Just because someone is offended, it doesn't mean they are right. You can criticize any idea.

And yet we are drifting toward a world in which freedom of speech is seen as a right-wing cause. I have been angrily denounced by a self-identified fifth-generation Canadian as "a fascist, racist sympathizer." My crime in his eyes was defending the right of all Canadians to think and say what they believe.

These types of encounters led me to a deeper sense of concern about the future of my country. All around me now, I see these Canadian elites rejecting the same liberal, colour-blind principles that once made Canada such an attractive destination for newcomers like me.

As I have said, this immigrant has learned a lot from Canada. I feel it is my responsibility to offer something in return. Here is my warning: Canadians are repudiating what made this country so great.

I have seen what happens to a society when it embraces a radical version of identity politics. I know exactly what happens when we dehumanize someone we disagree with. I have seen the gruesome deaths, the unimaginable injustice that follows, step by step, from the refusal to acknowledge the fellow humanity in those we see as our opponents. Look, I don't want to pretend I am a saint. I am not above being seduced by my own opinions. I think I am a pretty fierce competitor too. There will always be rivalry and ambition. I am not so naive that I think that all we need to do is love each other. But we do have to respect each other. The moment we are sure we are right because of membership in this or that group, we are wrong. By definition.

This is why true freedom of speech is crucial. We need to be exposed to ideas we are not familiar with, even if we disagree with them. If we are not, we will not be able to see other people as equally human. If we don't understand their ideas, we will come to think they *have* no ideas. When I see the enthusiasm for censorship in the Western world today, I can't help thinking of an unprecedented biblioclasm in Jaffna in 1981. A mob sponsored by Sri Lankan cabinet ministers Cyril Mathew and Gāmiṇi Dissānāyake (both avowed Sinhala supremacists) burned the Jaffna public library to the ground on May 31, 1981. This library was considered one of the biggest and best in Asia at the time of the attack. It housed 97,000 precious books, palm leaf manuscripts, and culturally important, irreplaceable scrolls of historical value as well as the works of Tamil philosophers, artists, and authors. The Tamils' rich history was destroyed by this horrendous act, wiped from the face of the earth as if we did not exist. Gāmiṇi Dissānāyake was assassinated by the LTTE on October 24, 1994. Violence against ideas leads us to the brink of a bloodier kind of violence.

Dehumanizing the opponent or a group is the precursor to creating a narrative that actively seeks to disadvantage them in order to silence them. This is a strategy of revenge—the shoe on the other foot, disguised as a just cause. It can only lead to tragedy. Why would we even flirt with that?

The Canada that I came to as a teenager was a prosperous liberal democracy, a colour-blind haven for immigrants and refugees. Its governing ethos—which I have both celebrated and sought to uphold—was one of individual meritocracy, regardless of superficial markers of identity. Yet among the crowd of largely white middle-aged liberals who now make up my neighbours, friends, and fellow schoolyard parents, I detected a strange and unsettling fixation on race that, oddly, presented itself as anti-racism.

Coming from a country like Sri Lanka, I was all too familiar with racism. As a minority, I'm fully aware that sometimes I have to deal with racists and ignorant people out there. Many people around the world and in Canada are suffering today from the historical legacies of racism and facing racism and ignorance in their day-to-day lives. No doubt, there is still much work to be done to end inequality in Canada.

I appreciate the tireless, valiant efforts to bridge the racial divide and address injustice. But let's face it: we're pushing on an open door. Have you ever heard someone come out in favour of racism? To suggest there is systemic racism in Canada is not only disingenuous but very offensive to a country I call home as a man of colour.

It is my view that our society has veered dangerously into the trap of identity politics. We now classify people primarily by race and skin colour. This used to be the very definition of racism. I see more and more racial hate and rhetoric spewed by those who claim to fight for equality. That the behaviours we corrected in our children one or two generations ago now pass for acceptable behaviour is mind-boggling. Bullying, name-calling, shunning, gossiping, destroying reputations, and practising personality before principles are now accepted, applauded, and even celebrated. It is a disgusting mess that we will find it hard to walk back from.

This is the current alchemy of racism. Blaming an entire group of people for crimes they didn't commit is racism. Judging anyone by skin colour is racism. There is nothing more racist than this.

THE FUTURE

Is Canada racist?

I get into arguments with people these days who claim Canada is a racist country. Yes, I have occasionally heard insensitive comments like, "Oh, you people love curry, right?" But just because someone says something ignorant, it does not make them some kind of bigot. Moreover, the question remains: What do you wish to focus on? Where do you want to spend your energy? What is ultimately going to be productive for *you*? (Also, I do love curry.) Yes, I have met racists in Canada—barroom bigots who told dumb jokes or made insensitive remarks. But they haven't held me back from success. Nor have they stopped Canada from being a thriving hub for prosperous immigrants.

And yes, as a travelling salesman, I heard my share of politically incorrect comments. But that didn't stop my clients from buying what I had to sell. Amazingly, throughout my quarter-century-long career in the investment industry, I have never encountered what could be described as unambiguous racism. Except that one time during a group lunch at a very high-end Japanese restaurant in Toronto, one of my superiors barked, "You should go back to where you came from," when I asked for a fork to eat my sushi. Maybe he was joking. I'm still not sure after all these years.

Sure, there are annoying racist people everywhere. I remember this one incident. I pulled into a spot at the U of T Scarborough campus parking lot. I didn't realize that there was another person waiting for the same spot. I just hadn't seen him. I heard a loud honk as I got out of the car, and an irate guy with many facial piercings, as though he had tripped and fallen into a tacklebox, shouted, "Hey, Paki, you stole my spot!"

He was furious. Rightfully so. After all, I had stolen his spot, albeit unknowingly. But "Paki"?! Unlike the first time I had heard it at the condo when I was working as a security guard, I decided to correct him on the mislabelling. "I'm not a Paki; I'm from Sri Lanka," I said in an effort to help this racist man.

He snapped back, "Okay then, Sri Lankan Paki."

I busted my gut laughing, to his utter frustration. He had the same blank and stiff expression as a dog would if you tried to put him on the phone.

If you want to be successful in life, you can't go around being offended by every little thing. My dad had a saying: "You can't control what people say. You can only control how you react to it." I knew that being thin-skinned would not help me in life. By the way, soon after that comment at the Japanese restaurant, I learned to eat sushi with chopsticks. "Assimilate," Appā said!

Perhaps that sounds racist. Only a racist would suggest an immigrant assimilate, or so we are told. And yet might *not assimilating* also be racist? It's not as though only white people can be racist. I've been privy to many conversations in which Tamil people said many horrible things about other races. The prejudices and discrimination within the Tamil community based on caste and regionalism are not relegated to Sri Lanka; they are alive and well here in Canada.

It's not just white people, and it's not just Tamils. Human history has shown us, over and over again, that ever since we stopped dragging our knuckles and started walking upright, we have been on alert for the differences that divide us. You can't identify a racist by the colour of their skin, because we are all capable of this vile bigotry.

We become focused and then fixated on the differences that divide us, amplifying them, assigning all kinds of non-existent suppositions to them. The next thing you know, we start referring to others as "those people." We are starting to hear it from our politicians. And who does that more than anyone here in Canada? Not the farmers and truckers out west. It's the "woke."

I remember my first encounter with a racist very well. Back then, I was shocked and, yes, offended. But I've thought about that night many times over the years. That night, when skinny little Subēndraṉ was called a Paki by the guy in the fancy car, it was Subēndraṉ who won the confrontation. I didn't open the gate, and the guy exposed himself as an ugly bigot. I didn't like it, but what I took away from that little battle was that the rules work. Maybe that guy thought he could bully me because he was white and I wasn't. Or maybe he was just a bully who would have found some other way to insult a white security guard. Does it matter? No. Here in Canada, I had the rules on my side. I stood my ground, and the blowhard had to back off. The rules work.

The freedom and the opportunities I enjoy in Canada are precious to me. Coming from my background, I'm all too familiar with racism. Canada has been a beacon of hope for me. I came here as a teenager from a very oppressive country and managed to excel. To me, this country represents fairness and civility—especially to those who ended up on the wrong side of the racial order in the countries of their birth. This is why people still flock to Canada. The fact that they are here is a powerful message. They have taken huge risks to come here. They have given up nearly all that is precious to them to come here. That is about the biggest bet a human can make. Those bets, and the optimism behind them, are a message to us: Canada is the best country they can think to live in. We should be listening to them.

Things have changed since 1989, when I was one of the very few non-white workers at my company. Our workforce ended up having many people of colour in management positions, even before diversity and inclusion became trendy. Since the time I arrived here at the age of eighteen, I gained the gift of freedom and fairness in Canada. Like many immigrants, I was determined to overcome my tortured past and build a new life. Canadian kindness taught a young kid that there is light in a world of darkness.

The secrets to success are the same now as they were when I started out three decades ago: be likeable, learn from those who have done it, and work hard. There is dignity in hard work. There is no dignity in blaming others. Habits play an important role as you go about your life. They allow you to efficiently complete the most challenging and repetitive tasks that life presents. Being conscious of what you do that is consistent with your goals and being accountable for your daily actions are the keys to creating excellent habits that can increase your odds of success.

So, it is especially perplexing when I hear some of my fellow new-comers reflexively blame their problems on racism, despite the fact that most are successful and enjoying liberty and freedom. This is why I worry about the ignorance that is corroding Western society. Many who have lived here for generations seem to have nothing but com-plaints about the West. But from the standpoint of many of us who have lived under authoritarian regimes and travelled around quite a lot, Canada is a damn sight better than anything else on offer. People who thought Western civilization was a bad deal will bitterly regret it if they ever come under the heel of real oppression, which they are flirting with today.

It's always easy to criticize freedom, democracy, and capitalism while enjoying the associated benefits of it. You never find such fake revolutionaries living on a farm. Because they are too busy working for a living. All these revolutionaries live in urban settings. They

maintain moral narcissism about historical statues and street names—
but using smart phones made by captive labour in horrendous conditions somehow does not impact their moral virtue at all.

Though they are not without flaws, Western societies are the freest
and fairest societies ever created by humans. I and folks like me who
have lived and experienced the horrors of totalitarianism and terror
can readily attest to this.

To be clear, I am emphatically not advocating a world of dog-eat-
dog survival of the fittest. We must always speak up loudly against
injustice. It is the only position that is consistent with our own morals
and democratic ideals. There is still much work to be done to end
inequality in Canada and the world, so we should celebrate this country for building a system of laws that can defend and advocate for the
equal treatment of minorities. Collectively, we as a country must
address incidents of racism in a productive and pragmatic way, so we
can create a just society for the future.

I take my lead from men like Bill, Ray, and Mr. McRae, who inspired many—their names are now inscribed on hospital wings and
university buildings. I believe in action rather than activism. Whenever
the media presents us with a fresh injustice, we tend to follow a well-
thumbed playbook: take to social media, donate to a social justice
organization, and get a group of disaffected people together. While I
believe this is important, I also believe there is more to do.

We must work tirelessly to ensure everyone has access to education,
skills development and training, and a fair shot at opportunity. We must
create corporate cultures that are true meritocracies in hiring practices,
promotions, and compensation. There is an imperative within all
humans to make a mark. Action is what defines us. Action, not suffering. We must do everything we can to lower the barrier but not the bar.

Let's put it this way. Would you tell your own kids that playing the
role of victim is the best way to navigate life? Of course not. So, I will
let you in on a little secret: hard-working immigrants often find it

insulting that activists would advocate for immigrant and minority kids to take on roles that they would never allot their own children. We don't tell our kids they are victims, and neither should anyone else.

So, let's not start with the premise that Canada is a racist nation. Instead, as newcomers, let's acknowledge that Canada has been good to us. I became a Canadian not only as a matter of law but also in my deeply felt personal identity. I'm not looking to excoriate Canada's values; I want to urge our leaders to live up to them.

From my former corner office at 2 Queen Street East, I was able to see the Ed Mirvish Theatre awning where I collapsed three decades ago when I heard the news helicopter overhead. The St. Michael's Hospital emergency helipad was pretty much right next door. Whenever I heard the chopper, I would get the chills. I know I'm no longer in Point Pedro. I know that. But that sound will always conjure the horror of war for me.

The intolerance I hear creeping into conversation here in Canada is a lot like the whir of helicopter blades for me. It reminds me clearly of the madness that tore apart Sri Lanka. What convinces me that my third act is necessary is my sense that this country is sleepwalking into quicksand, which I can clearly see in our path. What lies in store for us here is what I have already experienced. Many Tamil families lost fathers, mothers, sons, and daughters. The result of that kind of loss is a lifetime of pain. For years, I couldn't write or speak about my pain and suffering, as I never found the right words for it. I bottled it all up and tried not to bring my feelings to life—but to build a life in the way I had imagined: prosperous, yet simple.

I could not have understood the implications of doing that then. But now, as an adult with a son of my own, I had to acknowledge my shortcomings and the scars from my experiences as a teenager. Life is suffering, said Lord Buddha. I was born in a country where the majority practised Buddhism but made Tamils like me suffer. My imprisonment and torture made happiness a phantom concept for me for many years. I was always playing the musical chairs of emotion: sadness, fear, anger, and resentment. Anxiety and even paranoia. Rage was always lurking below the surface. That is the world we are creating in the name of utopia.

You can't teach violence and hatred and also expect day-to-day life to be unaffected. You can't build a society on intolerance.

Once you allow rage and anger into the world, it seeps down into the deepest parts of you. Once we lose our sense of shared humanity, our own humanity begins to slip away. We have to fight to hold on to it. Like many refugees, I know the worst of it. People like me know what it feels like when trust in our fellow humans corrodes. I am not the only one who lashes out at the world—even at those I love the most.

I don't have a dimmer switch, but a toggle switch. I have behaved very badly. I have been verbally abusive and very loud. I have made Sue and Aaron very scared. Especially the boy. I exploded in rage. Punched walls and kicked doors! When Aaron started crying, I realized what had just happened. Though no one was in physical danger, I was immediately ashamed of myself. It was the worst self-induced shame of my life. Our home was on a large lot. I must have been very loud because the neighbours heard it too. I couldn't care less what they thought of me. But I did care what my son thought of me. Unfortunately, Aaron has seen me at my worst.

I can't blame anyone for this. Only me. My hope is that he saw his dad trying to overcome the demons of his past and, on that account, I hope he forgives me for my past infractions. When all this is over, among many things, I will be judged by this: What kind of human did I produce? It is important to me that Aaron is a well-adjusted, thoughtful, and caring person who adds value to the society that he inhabits and is constantly focused on improving himself. Clearly, I'm flawed, but I'm constantly fighting to bury my demons to become calmer and more relaxed.

But none of us who has seen such horrors can ever leave them behind—because to do so would mean turning our backs on those who were less lucky. It's hard to enjoy the Canadian dream when my nightmares leave me racked with survivor's guilt. I would not wish this curse on anyone.

Does it seem impossible that such a nightmare could descend on Canada? That kind of horror does seem foreign to many Canadians. But not to all. Not to those who have fled it. Not to those who have seen it and how it gains a toehold and turns neighbours into enemies. It starts as something no one could object to: the call for equity.

In Sri Lanka, it was a dangerous idea under the guise of fairness. Deceivingly, it went beyond diversity and equality to engineer predetermined outcomes, regardless of cost. The real intention was to curtail the number of Tamil students selected for certain faculties in the universities. It was designed to go after successful Tamils of the North—the Jaffna Tamils.

Though Tamils were the minority and the Sinhalese were the majority, Tamils had a majority complex and Sinhalese had a minority complex. When the British ruled Sri Lanka, the state language was English, which greatly benefitted English speakers in acquiring jobs in government. Tamils lived in areas where they had access to English-medium education in missionary schools like my beloved alma mater Hartley College in Point Pedro. My Appā and the generation before him greatly benefitted from an English-medium education, which resulted in higher positions in society.

The issue was compounded further by the fact that Jaffna Peninsula was mostly a dry and infertile zone, where crop yields were low. As a result, Tamil parents placed so much stock in education. They firmly believed that better education would lead to economic prosperity for their children and allow them to avoid a life of unemployment and hard labour. They pressured their children to master English, mathematics, and science as a means of securing good employment. This created a situation where a large proportion of Tamil students enrolled in universities, particularly in professional fields such as medicine and engineering.

But Tamil success became a political problem for the federal government, which did not want to see one ethnic group pull ahead of another. The result was a 1971 law that curtained the number of Tamil students admitted to certain faculties in the universities in the name of "standardization." That is, the law sought to bring about what might be called "Tamil privilege"—but which Tamil parents would call the outcome of hard work and strong family values. Such a law could not curtail the input. So it was engineered to produce a predetermined output, in favour of Sinhalese students. For example, under this law, an urban student needs to have a minimum score of 250 to enter the engineering faculty, while their rural counterpart (predominately Sinhalese) only needed to have a score of 227 to secure a spot. If you were a Tamil student from the North and scored 249, you were out of luck, which led to an economic disadvantage. But a Sinhalese student with 227 was on the path to becoming an engineer.

The same logic was applied to other faculties such as medicine, dentistry, bioscience, and physical science. Instead of lowering the barrier, this law lowered the bar for Sinhalese students. It was not meritocracy, just racially driven madness. The law, over time, succeeded in legislating the Tamils into poverty. The intended, predetermined outcome was successfully achieved at the cost of failure to the Sri Lankan nation ever since. Canada was among the many countries who benefitted from Sri Lanka's brain drain.

There is an important lesson here to those who think this is the way to achieve equality. Be careful what you wish for. A society shouldn't try to advantage one group by taking away from another. If we do that, then the population advantaged by this effort will get the idea that they do not have to work hard to achieve success because it will be guaranteed to them. And the disadvantaged group who worked hard to achieve success will get the idea that no matter what they do, they will never succeed. This kind of shift in attitude will be the beginning of the end of any civil society and proud country.

Sri Lanka is a prime example of this. More and more young Tamils became disadvantaged and unemployed without university degrees. As the saying goes, "An idle mind is a devil's workshop." This was a contributing factor to the ethnic strife. Young Tamils picked up arms to fight their oppressive government.

Sri Lanka's ingrained anti-Tamil sentiments and whipped-up nationalist hysteria were very powerful cement for the most odious system, which made it easier for the leaders to con their citizenry. Sure, mugging the blind is against the law, but it's also easy. To prevent it, civil society depends, for the most part, not on the police but on civilized people making the conscious decision not to do it.

Now, the country is an unmitigated disaster. Sri Lanka went from a thriving democracy with freedom of speech as its governing ethos to thug law. I truly believe the decline of Sri Lanka's moral fibre represents the single most serious threat to its own survival. In 1948, when Sri Lanka gained its independence, it was considered to be the postcolonial nation most likely to succeed economically and democratically. Unfortunately, since then, Sri Lanka has been governed by leaders with a penchant for racial division. Through the hatred that they sowed, they have succeeded in destroying the country.

It would break my heart to see it again here.

I have learned from my life, as a teen prisoner in Sri Lanka and as a free man in Canada, that it is a lot more productive to look for things in common with others than what divides us. It is a lack of a meaningful life that leads to hatred. I have been there. Most of my early life decisions were born out of hatred. It has taken me the better part of a lifetime to escape the clutches of the past. I focus now on what we all have in common. No matter what colour our skin is, what our race happens to be, there is a basic universal truth: we always have more in common than different across all races, religions, and political ideologies. Instead of deepening our past divisions, we need to strengthen our present bonds.

We all have the same basic desires for safety, shelter, and sustenance. And deepest of all, according to Viktor Frankl, "the greatest human need is meaning." We must create meaning, not destroy it.

I worry that we are destroying meaning. We are turning our backs on the values that have brought us to the very pinnacle of civilization and prosperity. We live in the wealthiest, healthiest, most literate, most tolerant society the world has ever seen. By far. None of our ancestors lived nearly as well as we do.

But success breeds complacency, and complacency breeds decadence.

The utter height of decadence is the luxury of self-hatred and self-flagellation. How can this be luxury? Like Greeks smashing plates at a wedding in an act of conspicuous consumption, the Western world is gleefully dashing itself to bits. Maybe this is meant to show how ethically superior the heirs of European civilization really are. Or maybe the West really is lost. But one thing is for sure. Self-loathing is possible only to those who enjoy a position of comfort, peace, and affluence. To magnanimously blame yourself for the crimes of history is to announce that you have arrived.

Of course, no one is allowed to acknowledge that. And just as the first rule of Fight Club is that you do not talk about Fight Club, the first rule of the new liberalism is that you do not acknowledge that Canada, or wherever in the West you may live, is actually a pretty great country. Canada must be denounced, along with anyone who dares to defend it.

But where does that leave someone like me? Or all of Sri Lanka's Tamils, who are desperately suffering and dreaming of being one of us? Or the millions of people around the world who would leave everything behind to come here? Are we to be denounced in the name of *tolerance*?

The existence of people like us shows how important the issue of freedom of speech has become. We cannot be expected to not say that Canada is a wonderful (if imperfect) country. We have already said it just by coming here.

But it is a mistake to frame cultural questions as though one side is right and the other is wrong. An open and honest dialogue is required to find the common ground that allows us to find meaning. We need to encourage debate and share ideas, not denounce them simply because they go against our beliefs.

People of the free world, especially the next generation: freedom of speech is a first-order issue. Wake up before it is too late. Don't oppose ideas. Expose yourself to better ideas. Don't take your freedom for granted. Fiercely protect it at any and all cost. Whichever side the freedom-hating mob is on, choose the other if you value freedom and liberty. We must protect the sanctity of the individual. Don't surrender your intelligence and independence to these online hall monitors of righteousness. Don't allow yourself to be pulled over by the woke police and virtual stone throwers for saying perfectly reasonable things. Don't subscribe to their bad faith arguments. Stand up against the tyranny of the minority!

It is far easier to denounce freedom than to attain it. While people in many parts of the world are seeking freedom and liberty, we are eroding ours. Freedom of speech is a non-negotiable Western value. We all need to die on this hill. Free speech is core to Western civilization and to our identity. I'm an accidental Sri Lankan by birth, unapologetic Tamil by heritage, and a proud Canadian by choice. A free human. This is my new identity.

With the freedom I enjoy in Canada, a few days before Father's Day, I woke up to the growl of a garbage truck and the treetop chorus chirps of carefree birds around my neighbourhood. I was still in

COVID-19 lockdown. Looking out the window of the beautiful winding boulevard, I realized that I have come a long way from Point Pedro. But my journey hasn't been one unbroken boulevard of green lights. There were plenty of hurdles on the mostly level playing field.

Some victim-mindset folks might have complained, in my shoes, that a skinny Tamil kid with a name like Subēndraṉ wouldn't get a fair shake trying to sell investment products to the rural folks in Western Canada. But was complaining about systemic racism going to give me the outcome that I wanted? Absolutely not!

If you say you are a victim, then you will get sympathy from people, that much is certain. But sympathy never solved an issue. If your habit is about you being a victim, then you will remain one. If you habituate yourself to being a victor, then you will go on being one. Societies are the same way. I have seen that right here in Canada. In just one generation, most Tamils outside of Sri Lanka have gone from misery to prosperity. From victims to victors.

The first indicator of success is individual decision making. Don't co-sign on groupthink. Hard work wins. You can't control the outcome, but you are 100 percent in charge of the effort. Before you whine about your life, go to the nearest mirror and take a look at yourself and ask, what could I have done to change the outcome?

When I was a skinny kid and trying to put on some muscle mass, my personal trainer at the time said, "To shock the nervous system, try doing deadlifts at the end of your next leg routine instead of the beginning." This advice has been very helpful for me not just in the gym but also in life. I learned that to break through my plateaus, I must get out of my comfort zone and try doing things that my body and, even more so, my mind aren't already used to.

I truly believe the best way to improve a society is through self-improvement of the individual—by each person battling with their flaws, weaknesses, and blind spots. If you can't change yourself, you can't change the world. A society doesn't need to act before you do.

Turn the moral mirror on yourself. Don't act out your virtue on others. Act out your virtue on yourself. Put your moral mouth where your self-proclaimed virtue is.

Resilience is the ability to bounce back from life's inevitable disappointments, failures, and pains. Resilience is the opposite of fragility. Being fragile is about letting everything upset you. If just about everything upsets you, then you will spend a lot of your time unhappy and unproductive, which will ultimately lead to a miserable existence.

Demand equal rights, not equal results. Results need to be earned. Despite all this, sooner or later bad things will happen to you—that's the leitmotif of life. But how you deal with the bad things in life will determine your destiny and the future. If life handed you bad cards, shuffle the pack and pick another set of cards. Humanity has no better path forward than to accept this fact with humility.

Our challenges may be different from those that faced hunter-gatherers, but our hardwiring is not. Human desires and wants always outnumber our available resources—and one must make individual choices. I can change what I do, but I can't change what I want. There is a message I want to get out to anyone who is pursuing a dream: if it sucks while doing it, that is how you know you are doing it correctly. And that person who is trying belongs to a rich history and a long lineage of people who had to jump through hoops to get where they are today.

For more than two-thirds of my life, I have lived without my father in it—a fact I still have a hard time accepting. I'm getting there. Slowly, but grudgingly. As someone who lost a parent as a teenager, I am part of a club that no one wants to belong to. Unfortunately, there are no perks to being a member. Aside from the loss potentially lighting a fire in my belly. All I hope is that he would approve of how I turned out, despite his absence.

In the past, I was always running and paranoid. My internal motor was constantly firing in high gear in order to win at life. I was always trying to do everything intensely well, and I was transparently competitive. I never wanted to rest—at the cost of family and friendships. But now I'm starting to fall in love with life. I've started to appreciate what is good and what is important. One is my relationship with others, especially my family and friends. "Zero is everything else," as Appā would say.

From a boy who was tortured to a teenager in Canada trying to find my way and now as a grown man with resources, I have learned over and over again, that regardless of the circumstances, this is true: outcomes in life aren't necessarily about intelligence, race, or talent, but about personal habits. Your habits decide your future. Attitude and behaviour have far more bearing on success than your race.

There is a part of me that died in Sri Lanka, that I will never get back. When I found myself in the accidental luxury of Canada, I had the freedom to pretend. But I had trouble sleeping for years. I was either sad or mad—never glad. I had to change hurt into hope. If I have learned anything in my time on this planet, it is the power of hope. Hope provides a positive vision for the future about what's possible, motivating us to look forward. Hope can emerge from distressing and even tragic situations.

My Appā's death made me grow up fast and become a fighter. I used that pain as coal for my furnace of ambition. "I sure would like to talk with him again," I said to myself, looking out my living room window, as the garbage collectors removed the trash. But the birds in the treetop were singing again. A metaphor for my life!

I doted upon Dad. All I am left with is his portrait on my desk and the indelible life lessons he taught me—which I live by while letting go of the horrors of my past. I was terrorized in Sri Lanka, transformed in Canada, and finally triumphant in my mid-life! In that spirit, with every passing day, no matter the rage inside me, no matter the pain in my heart, no matter the nightmares in my head, there is some moment, some beauty, some extraordinary display of life that helps me breathe, helps me smile, and helps me be grateful for all that I have, all that I am, and all that I am becoming.

After many years, I flashed a smile for Appā and me. No more tears. I'd like to think in some ways I was able to lead a life that he always wanted to have. My gratitude to him is a constant awareness that makes sense of my terrible past. His memory, however, gave me a peculiar way of finding hope. Three decades of his absence and the strong presence of his memory had given me a defensive wall, drive, and determination, which helped me to attain conviction, courage, and confidence. I either shaped myself in his image or am a disappointment. I hope it is not the latter.

I have been reckless and lucky. I avoided death twice as a boy. Knowing that, I feel blessed. Every additional day alive is a bonus. As Appā's favourite Tamil poet and lyricist Kaṇṇathāsaṉ penned in the philosophical song "Niṉaippathellām Nadanthuviṭṭāl" (*If everything you think happened*): *"If you keep thinking about what happened, there will never be peace."*

Uncle Fernando's words still echo in my ears: "Welcome home, son." I still believe that single act of kindness is why I'm alive today. I believe he gave me a second lease on life. I'm indebted to him forever. Now in my early fifties, sliding into the back nine of my life, living in my new home called Canada, as a husband and father, I realize this more than ever.

I was nobody from nowhere—prisoner #1056 with a painful past. I had been through enough torment for a few lifetimes. When the pain is here, it never goes away. Emotional wounds do not heal, but they fester. Scars never subside. They never leave. The scar on my right bicep is always there, visible when I shave in the mornings. It stands there as a reminder of my terrible past. But I had to go to war with the man in the mirror to create a whole new identity. An empty stomach and broken soul taught me many valuable lessons. The positive things in my life always came when I faced life's biggest challenges. Loss is not just something that happens. It really becomes a part of you, and I feel like I have learned so much over the past thirty years. It really has made me more conscious of life and how I want to spend mine—and to make the most of it. To pay homage to Appā's request when we parted at the airport in Colombo, "I ask that you live." No more rage!

I have worked on my own self-discipline. My survival was all on me. I didn't have an entitled mindset. I fought through a long series of failures and successes. I knew I couldn't achieve something abnormal by acting normal. I fought with my demons. I found inspiration in suffering. It was a test I couldn't cheat on. I alone had to face the challenge. In that process of building a life of dignity, I learned about grit and humility. I learned to evolve my beliefs, not to self-validate them.

The tally of my shortcomings doesn't determine my identity and destiny. What mattered was how I answered when life presented me with challenges. What counted was how I met a challenging moment when there was a lot at stake. It has been a hard-won battle. "It's a win of epic proportion," as Bill would often say. The tie my father gave me at the airport still stands as a symbol of this hard-won battle. I'm eternally grateful to him and Canada!

The larger lesson that can be learned from my transition is that the freedom to make a living and to shape one's life is a good thing—and it has been rewarding for many like me who migrated to Canada and other Western nations. The laws of hard work and risk taking, in which every person strives to move upward by working toward what they desire, are the "unseen hand" that allows everyone in the family and country to prosper.

I recognize that we are all unique with distinctive needs and varying opinions. Whatever our goal in life, freedom incurs a personal responsibility. We will be rewarded for our good choices and penalized for bad ones. That's the price of freedom. People often speak about their rights and entitlement, never about their personal responsibility. The system of freedom and choice has helped to realize the benefits of Canada, and immigrants like me are better off because of it. It is the only system we Tamils have found in which our personal freedom, progress, and prosperity can coexist. The benefits of a free society.

We must never forget that responsibility is as much a gift as freedom. I will never forget the look of anguish on my father's face when Captain Udugama led me away, possibly to my death. Love bound him to me. Responsibility bound him to me. Tearing that bond meant unimaginable pain for him. No one wants to see that expression on anyone's face, especially a friend's. I saw it one day on Bill's. He had learned that his son was in the grips of an illness that might never let him go. I am haunted by what he said that day: "I have control over things I don't care about. But things that matter, I can't control." My heart broke for both him and my own father that day.

The things that matter. No, we can't control them. But we can be responsible. We can do what we know is right. We can't control how others feel, but we can treat them the way we would want to be treated. We can't protect everyone, but we can lend our strength to those who need it. And we must never rob anyone of the gift of responsibility any more than we would the gift of freedom. Because it is the same thing.

My father and I shared a remarkable bond. Sometimes it hurts to remember this. When he suddenly died, my heart shattered into many pieces. I thought my life had ended as well. But I didn't recognize that it was just beginning. I never wanted to feel that pain again, so I hardened myself and my heart. But finally, I have grasped that without experiencing pain, it is impossible to discover or appreciate joy. The two are inextricably intertwined.

Life handed me plenty of reasons to be angry and distraught. But I just needed to focus on one reason to be grateful. Now, I have come to the realization that no matter how long this life lasts, it is always preparing us for hardship and pain. We should never hope for an easy life because life itself is suffering—as the Buddha teaches. But the determination to persevere and find meaning in life is what ultimately makes you a winner. It is not about money or power. But it is about not giving up or shying away from the fight. Because the experience you gain in suffering is what propels you forward to your desired destination. It is the fullest expression of what life is about. In prison, I saw death as freedom. Then survival became a form of torture. Today, I find a 'life well lived' to be a form of protest against the pain of my past.

I have taken my share of slings and arrows. But I embraced possibility and risked a bigger dream. That dream was never out of the realm of possibility. I wanted to write my own life's notes—not to read someone else's notes. I was never ashamed to be wanting more! A big part of me was always fighting to live. I went from life being so dark that I thought the best option was to not be here. Today, I'm the most grateful guy walking the planet.

There is still a ton of runway left for me. To paraphrase Robert Frost, I have miles to go before I sleep.

For that chance in life, I feel like I'm one of the luckiest Tamils alive.

EPILOGUE

Dear Dad,

I am unsure of where to even begin. The first thing I can say is that it is a privilege to be your son. Also, I am doing well, and life is really good in this amazing country. You made the right call by sending me to Canada.

To celebrate this, I wrote a book. I have known for years that I would one day write a book. A book about being terrorized as a young boy who experienced a brutal civil war in Sri Lanka and was then transformed in Canada in his late teens and early twenties. I wanted to tell the world my survival story. A Tamil boy's survivor story.

It's not just my story. I wanted this book to give voice to a generation of Tamil immigrants who are coming of age now in Canada and other Western nations. People who left Sri Lanka as children, or whose parents fled what you saved me from.

As I finished it, I realized how much of this book has been written by you.

Imagine. After your untimely death, people said what they always say. "We will always be here for you." Or "Let us know if you need anything." Now, here I am thirty-five years later, and those people are nowhere to be found.

What is still with me after all these years are the many indelible lessons you taught me: "Sympathy never solved an issue." "If your habit is to be a victim, then you will remain one." "Fixing your problems is your own responsibility." How could I forget them? Though you have been gone for decades, it seems you are always walking with me. You are my calm, absent advisor and a vital source of my ongoing progress.

On June 9, 2022, I addressed the University of Toronto 2022 Spring Convocation. I was deeply honoured and humbled by this invitation from my alma mater. Hopefully, I have imparted your wisdom to the new graduates in my short speech. My hope is that you are proud that I have come this far: from a struggling student to addressing the recent graduates. From an angry kid to a decent human, for the most part.

I'm also passing those lessons to your grandson, Aaron. I have told him that the world will never be perfectly fair and that through-out his life he will hit hurdles and experience hardships. Sue (your daughter-in-law, by the way) and I will always be there for him, as you and Mom have been for me. But while he is always, always loved, he is never, ever entitled. I told him as Grandpa likes to say, "The world owes you nothing, except for freedom and choice."

To that end, he now knows that he needs to concentrate his efforts on struggling with himself, not the society around him. I know it would be important to you that Aaron is a well-adjusted, thought-ful, and caring person who adds value to the society that he inhabits and is constantly focused on improving himself. He can never improve himself by doing battles with the past moral failings of society. I hope to help him meet this goal.

Conquering my personal mountain was something I struggled with in my daily life for decades, and I still do. On August 26, 2019, when I summited Mount Kilimanjaro with Sue and Aaron to honour Mom, to raise awareness and money to combat mental illness, I looked up at the morning sky painted in hues of purple and pink. The air carried a dust of snow, and I was surrounded by dove-white mountains as far as my eyes could see. I had never experienced such feelings as what I felt when the clouds vanished and revealed the whole world below the mountain I had just climbed. I had a sense that I was on the world's rooftop, at a heaven-touching height. What I felt was a relief. I felt like my struggles with the past were behind me.

Then I remembered Mandela's famous words: "There are many more hills to climb. I had taken a moment here to rest, to steal a view of the glorious vista that surrounds me, to look back at the distance I have come." Standing so far above the trials of everyday life that day, I dared to think of the fact that he and I had both spent time in prison. And though it would be sheer vanity to compare my path in life to his, I do acknowledge the same sense of responsibility: "But I can only rest for a moment, for with freedom come responsibilities, and I dare not linger, for my long walk is not ended." There are many more serrated mountaintops for me to ascend, Dad.

Finally, there is one more thing I never got to say. Thank you for sending me to Canada—despite my loud protests. That, along with your lessons, is a legacy I mean to honour.

What a country!

With love,
Your son

INDEX

RR = Roy Ratnavel